JAPANESE LABOUR LAWS

Case Studies and Comments

JAPANESE LABOUR LAWS

Case Studies and Comments

KOZO KAGAWA
Graduate School of International Cooperation Studies, Kobe University, Kobe, Japan

Foreword by

DR. JOHN ZECHARIAH
Former Professor and Dean, Graduate School of Business, Spicer Memorial College, Pune, India

DEEP & DEEP PUBLICATIONS PVT. LTD.
F-159, Rajouri Garden, New Delhi-110027

JAPANESE LABOUR LAWS

Case Studies and Comments

ISBN 978-81-8450-006-6

Typeset by ASHISH TECHNOGRAPHICS,
3190, Mohindra Park, Shakur Basti, Delhi-110034.

Printed in India at MAYUR ENTERPRISES,
WZ Plot No. 3, Gujjar Market, Tihar Village, New Delhi-110018.

Published by DEEP & DEEP PUBLICATIONS PVT. LTD.
F-159, Rajouri Garden, New Delhi-110027.
Phones: 25435369, 25440916
E-mail: ddpbooks@yahoo.co.in • deep98@del3.vsnl.net.in
Showroom:
2/13, Ansari Road, Daryaganj, New Delhi-110002 • Telefax: 23245122

Contents

PART III

SUPREME COURT JUDGEMENTS ON LABOUR RELATIONS: CASE COMMENTS

Foreword

Japan is remembered for its exceptional economic performance in Asia. Japan today, it is said, is a meeting point between the new and old, as well as the East and West. Human element has been a very important factor in Japanese economy. It is accepted that Japanese workers perform much better than their counterpart in other countries today.

The characteristics of Japanese, harmonious labour-management relations, have drawn considerable international interest today. Japan's unique system of lifetime employment, enterprise union, stable labour-management relations, seniority wage and "shunto" (spring offensive) have increased the degree of attention and interest among industrialized and developing countries. These days however, there is a rapid change, one can see in this area.

Prof. Kozo Kagawa is a Professor at Graduate School of International Cooperation Studies, Kobe University, Kobe, Japan. I know him as a professor, researcher and a great friend. I am happy that he could bring out this book on Japanese Labour Law, as a memorial event, on the occasion of his retirement from Kobe University, Kobe.

This book is intended to describe the important issues in the field of Japanese Labour Law, including case comments of Supreme Court judgements on labour problems. *The important features of this book are:*

(1) This volume attempts to clarify and interpret all important issues to understand Japanese

labour law problems and industrial relations in Japan.

(2) The case comments on Supreme Court judgements are mentioned in this book for readers to understand concretely Japanese labour law.

(3) The latest information and relevant statistics on various topics, which are normally not available, are in this book. Therefore, I am confident that this book will help all those who are interested in labour study.

(4) The comparative study between Japan and Asian countries on various labour issues is dealt with very well.

Recently, we find few books and material on Japanese industrial relations written in English, by non-Japanese writers or in collaboration with Japanese and non-Japanese. Prof. Kagawa's contribution is most timely and welcome at a time when Japan is witnessing dramatic changes in its economy and society. So it is useful to publish books in English, on Japanese labour law, by a Japanese professor. It is necessary to write factual conditions in English to foreign readers, in order to promote mutual appreciation which the author has done well.

JOHN ZECHARIAH
Former Professor and Dean,
Graduate School of Business,
Spicer Memorial College, Pune, India.

Preface

I have written some articles on Japanese labour law and case comments on the Japanese Supreme Court judgements in the field of labour for the last 20 years. My articles were written for papers to be submitted at various kinds of international conferences on Labour Law and Industrial Relations. Case comments were a part of International Labour Law Reports published by Martinus Nijhoff Publishers in the Netherlands. These case comments were written in cooperation with Prof. Hiroya Nakakubo, Kyushu University. But this book is a collection of case comments written only by myself.

In memory of my mandatory retirement from the Graduate School of International Cooperation Studies, Kobe University, I decided to publish this book in English after arranging with the above-mentioned printer by myself. This book does not cover all-important problems on Japanese labour law. Another purpose is to try to show Japanese labour law to foreigners. I want to follow the pioneers communicating Japanese labour law to the world. As global economies are spreading all over the world today, I understand it necessary to tell factual conditions of Japan to the foreigners in order to promote mutual appreciation especially when I was Minister of Japanese Embassy in Vietnam during April 2004 and September 2005.

I have written the outline of Japanese labour law at Employment Terms and Conditions in Asia/Pacific initiated by Watson Wyatt Worldwide. This was printed in 1990, 1991, 1992/93, 1994/95, 1996/97, 1998/99,

2000/01, 2002/03, 2004, 2005, 2006. (http://hrresource.watsonwyatt.com) This part is not involved in this book.

I must express my sincere gratitude to many people. Mr. Satoshi Hirata introduced me to publish this book in India. He is a leader of Kansai NGO committee and President of Asian Volunteer Center. I am the Vice-President although I can contribute little to promote volunteer activities. My sincere thanks are due to Dr. John Zechariah, Professor of Spicer Memorial College, Pune, India for his exemplary encouragement and a special Foreword to the book. Special thanks are due to Dr. P. Jegadish Gandhi, Founder-Director, Vellore Institute of Development Studies (VIDS), Vellore, India for his help in bringing out this publication. A special word of thanks is due to Prof. S. Thiagakumar, Voorhees College, Vellore for his tedious language browsing work.

And I must express my appreciation to the publishers for giving the permission to include articles and case comments in this book. This publication would not have been possible within a short span of time without the timely cooperation of Mr. G.S. Bhatia, Managing Director, Deep & Deep Publications Pvt. Ltd., New Delhi.

India is my first foreign country where I could study Indian labour law at Delhi University from December 1974 to March 1976. I am very glad to publish my book in India associated with youthful memories.

KOZO KAGAWA

Introduction

In the post-war reconstruction, Japanese are noted for the single-minded devotion in the nation-building activities with sacrificial life-styles, thriftiness, enterprising skills, exemplary work culture and nationalism.

The changes in Japanese labour laws drew much attention from other countries. While some marveled at the changes in the evaluation of Japanese systems over the last decade, others questioned whether it is really necessary for Japan to continue with this drastic reform programme.

This compilation of essays presents a vivid report and analysis of recent trends in Japanese labour laws focusing on the amendment to labour legislation and signaling the effect of recent socio-economic changes in Japan including the deline in lifetime employment, seniority-based wages, and enterprise unionism.

The Book is divided into three parts. Part-I gives an overview of labour laws in Japan and Asian countries. Part-II highlights various issues of Japanese labour law: collective bargaining, working conditions, labour unions, worker's participation in management, labour disputes, deregulation policy of labour laws, child labour, migrant foreigners, movement of corporate social responsibility and code of conduct regarding labour and employment.

Part-III presents case-wise comments on Supreme Court Judgement in the field of labour: individual-employment relationship, labour contract, political rights, sexual harassment, part-time workers, transfer, wages, employee's intervention, overtime work, annual leave, occupational accident, dismissal and work rules, collective labour relations, collective agreement, union activities, right to strike and unfair labour practices.

Most of the issues are presented from the view point of comparative study among Asian countries.

PART I

LABOUR LAWS IN JAPAN AND ASIA: AN OVERVIEW

CHAPTER

1

Collective Bargaining

Challenges in Japan and Asia

INTRODUCTION

In Japan industrial relations law may make a legal framework for promoting industrial autonomy between labour and management on equal basis. One of the best ways to attain this may be collective bargaining and joint consultation, which we consider bilateral negotiations between the parties. Especially at the big firms collective bargaining and joint consultation has matured after both parties' long experience in dealing with labour relations issues as the economic development has achieved. On the other hands, Southeast and East Asian countries have recently experienced high economic development, which is expressed as "Asian Miracle" in the World Bank report. So it is very interesting to investigate how collective bargaining and joint consultation have changed with the progress of economic development. Does industrial autonomy come in company with economic growth through collective bargaining and joint consultation?

CHAPTER

1

Collective Bargaining

Challenges in Japan and Asia

INTRODUCTION

In Japan industrial relations law mainly aims to make a legal framework for promoting industrial autonomy between labour and management on an equal basis. One of the best ways to attain the purpose is collective bargaining and joint consultation set-up to consider bilateral negotiations between the parties. Especially at the big firms collective bargaining and joint consultation has matured after both parties' long experience in dealing with labour relations issues as the economic development has achieved. On the other hands, Southeast and East Asian countries have recently experienced high economic development, which is expressed as "Asian Miracle" in the World Bank report. So it is very interesting to investigate how collective bargaining and joint consultation have changed with the progress of economic development. Does industrial autonomy come in company with economic growth through collective bargaining and joint consultation?

In this paper the following five points relating to industrial autonomy in Japan are discussed from the viewpoint of comparative study between Japan and Southeast and East Asia. The first is the basic structure of collective bargaining, namely, level of bargaining, party on labour side, bargaining procedure, bargaining among multiple labour unions. The second paper answers how the result of collective bargaining (Roudou Kyouyaku) can regulate working conditions. Collective agreement is arrived at by mutual consent attained by collective bargaining. So the paper points out the effect of collective agreement. The third point is joint consultation. The joint consultation deals with the agenda on not only management, but also on working conditions. Especially at a non-unionized enterprise, joint consultation is very available in determining working conditions. Especially at a non-unionized enterprise, joint consultation is very much available in determining working conditions.

The fourth is how are working conditions regulated at non-unionized enterprises. Japanese union density was 23.8% in 1995 and this decreased to 18.7% in 2005. So about three-fourths of enterprises have no labour unions. At non-unionized enterprises working conditions are regulated by work rules provided under the Labour Standard Act. This shows the limitation of industrial autonomy in Japan. In the fourth point we must examine the legal effect of work rules. For example, we will examine what is the effect of the unilateral change of working conditions at the economic recession. In Japan the times of high economic growth has passed and it is now the time when economic condition is stable or goes down. This topic becomes very important in present Japan.

The fifth point is the existence of labour-management agreement (Rousi Kyoutei), which is different from collective agreement in character. This labour-management agreement is between an employer at the workplace and a labour union organized by a majority of the workers at the workplace concerned where such a labour union exists or a person representing a majority of the workers where no such labour union exists. This agreement has a big role in regulating working conditions especially at non-unionized workplace. So this system has the possibility to promote industrial autonomy at the workplace.

1. BASIC STRUCTURE OF COLLECTIVE BARGAINING

(a) Level of Bargaining

About 95% of all labour unions are organized on the basis of a company or an enterprise in Japan. And they comprise 90% of all unionized workers. So in Japan it is common that collective bargaining is conducted at an enterprise, i.e. between an employer and an enterprise-wise union. Therefore, both labour federation and employers' association at the national or industrial level has a limited role in carrying out negotiation. Namely in Japan national-wise or industrial-wise labour union federation itself has independently no right to negotiate with an employer. She can negotiate only after she is authorized to negotiate by an enterprise union. So she usually serves as a coordinator and an information center as well as guidance bodies for individual enterprise union. For example, in Shunto Offensive she formulates the standards for wage increases requested by her affiliated unions to management, and draws up a schedule for union tactics or strikes to put pressure to management. Usually an influential union starts bargaining and gets more wage increase, which establishes the pattern for wage increases. Following the pattern, other unions can be successful in promoting wage increase and other working conditions. Especially in high economic growth this Shunto tactics has brought better working conditions in weaker unions and non-unionized company. But in recent economic recession these tactics are not effective in promoting working conditions. In economic recession an enterprise union usually has exercised self-restraint in requesting wage increase because union members would fear unemployment. They show a tendency to work harder to save both the company and their jobs though they give up wage increase.

In Japan, employers' federation also has usually no right to negotiate working conditions with an enterprise union except Japan Shipowners' Association because there is a few case of industry-wide bargaining. The Nikkeiren (Japan Federation of Employers' Association) has guided to make a principle of wage increase not exceeding the rate of increase on national productivity. Some research shows that wage increase is conducted inside the limit of national productivity.

We can find enterprise-wise labour unions (house union, or in-house union) in some Asian countries (South Korea, Taiwan, Hong Kong, Thailand) indicated at Table 1 where collective bargaining is conducted on the level of an enterprise. In Indonesia enterprise union is encouraged to set-up at the enterprise having more than 10 workers by the Act No. 21 concerning Trade Unions in 2000. And the same situation can be seen in Malaysia and Singapore where enterprise unions are organized under "Look East Policy" advocated by Prime Minister Mahatir and Former President Lee Kuan Yew in order to get industrial harmony and high productivity at the establishment and plant. But even when an industrial labour union is organized, collective bargaining is conducted mainly on the level of an enterprise because it has a branch at the establishment. So the role of national or industrial union is different in collective bargaining in case of enterprise unions. Leaders of national or industrial unions perform their duties well in collective bargaining.

As a result, industry-wide bargaining is found only in limited cases (for example, All Japan Seamen's Union and etc.) in South-east and East Asia, where enterprise bargaining predominates except Philippine.

TABLE 1

Labour Union Density and Union Pattern 1989-90

Country	*Union Density*	*Enterprise Union (%)*	*Number of Unions*
Thailand	6	65	713
Malaysia	14	55	411
South Korea	24	>90	7883
Taiwan	33	42	3462
Hong Kong	19	<20	452
Singapore	17	45	83
Japan	26	>90	72605

Note: Union density refers to the percentage of non-agricultural work force that is unionized. For Hong Kong, Singapore and Japan the union density figure includes agricultural employees. Apart from Japan, where 7% of employees work in agriculture, the size of this sector is very small and so does not affect international comparisons.

Source: Stephen Frenkel ed., Organized Labour in the Asia-Pacific Region, 1993 ILR Press, Ithaca, New York, p. 311.

(b) Party on Labour side of Collective Bargaining

In Japan a bonafide labour union can be a party of collective bargaining. Bonafide union is defined as a labour organization established by employees with the primary objective of maintaining better working conditions and effecting economic improvements for its members. The Labour Unions Act provides certain requirements for bonafide unions to be qualified to get a legal personality, and to file complaints of unfair labour practices and to apply for extension of collective agreement. This qualification examination is conducted at Labour Relations Commission. But it is interpreted that it need not satisfy the requirements to bargain collectively.

In Malaysia, Singapore, Thailand and Philippines labour unions shall be registered at the administrative machinery in order to be parties of collective bargaining since labour unions are controlled through compulsory registration system. If they are not registered, they are treated as illegal organization and have no right to carry out bargaining. In these countries more severe prerequisites are demanded than in Japan adopting qualification examination. This is because these countries have a policy to control labour unions in order to maintain social and political stability for socio-economic development. And in Malaysia and Singapore furthermore union recognition shall be obtained from an employer or an administrative authority to be a party of collective bargaining. In Philippines introducing exclusive bargaining representing system, registered labour organization designated or elected by the majority of the employees in an appropriate bargaining unit shall be a party of collective bargaining.

In Thailand a unique system is adopted that a group of employees can be parties of collective bargaining besides registered labour union. Labour union can demand for an agreement relating to conditions of employment when its membership includes more than 20 percent of employees involved in the demand. And instead of the labour union, a group of employees more than 15% if it includes of the total employees, can request the demand. In this case seven representatives shall be elected for negotiation. A group of employees is permitted to be a party of bargaining under the Labour Relations Act because labour unions are very weak and little in number. In the future a group of employees is expected to be a labour organization.

(c) Procedure of Collective Bargaining

In Japan the procedure of collective bargaining is not stipulated in the Labour Unions Act. It is deemed to negotiate between both the parties. But in South-East Asian countries the procedure on collective bargaining is provided in detail in the Act and is directly linked with labour dispute settlement procedure. The issues, which are not resolved under collective bargaining, shall be referred to labour dispute settlement machinery for conciliation and arbitration. As a result,. agreement during conciliation is treated as collective agreement and collective agreement is treated as award of arbitration. On the other hand, Japan has no system of collective bargaining directly connected with labour dispute procedure. Legal problems on collective bargaining are resolved under unfair systems of labour practices.

(d) Issues of Collective Bargaining

In Japan there are no provisions on the subjects of collective bargaining under the Labour Unions Act. But it is interpreted that there are three types of subjects, namely, mandatory matters, voluntary matters and illegal matters. Working conditions and other economic treatment of workers belong to mandatory bargaining matters because an employer is compelled to bargain under Article 7, Section (2) of the Labour Unions Act. Management matters are involved in voluntary bargaining matters. An employer has no duty to bargain on personnel and management matters under the Act, but he must negotiate with them when he consents to bargain on it. Because the issues which an employer can control with are interpreted as belonging to the scope of collective bargaining as long as he assents to bargain on them. This leads to obscure distinction between collective bargaining and join consultation.

In other Asian countries some matters are excluded from the issues of collective bargaining by the Act. For example, in Philippine, issues of bargaining are limited to wages, hours of work and all other terms and conditions of employment by the Labour Code which are regarded as mandatory bargaining issues in America. The same can be found Labour Ministerial Order on uniform pattern of collective agreement of Indonesia. In Malaysia and Singapore personnel matters are excluded from issues of bargaining in order to introduce foreign investment by the Act. So management prerogatives are more broadly excluded from issues of bargaining in Japan.

(e) Collective Bargaining among Multiple Labour Unions

Generally speaking, one labour union exists in one enterprise. But we can see multiple unions in one enterprise in Japan. According to the survey of the Labour Ministry in 1993, two or more unions can be found at 16.6% of unionized private plant employing more than 30 workers. The multi-union syndrome has given rise to nearly half of cases on unfair labour practices in the private sector, which is dealt with annually by the Labour Relations Commission. In Japan, all the labour unions are guaranteed the right to bargain collectively with an employer under Article 28 of the Constitution as well as Article 7, Section (2) of the Labour Union Act, which prohibits an employer from refusing to bargain collectively with a labour union without fair and appropriate reasons.

It is an employer's obligation to recognize and bargain with any number of unions that operate in the establishment. Refusal to bargain with a majority union is not legally permissible. And even where a collective agreement may include a clause requiring an employer to bargain with a single union and not with others, such a clause is held to be null and void on the ground that it deprives the other unions of their legal right to bargain collectively.

And it is legally obligatory for an employer not to discriminate against the minority union, but to treat it in the same way as the majority union. In other words, an employer has to remain neutral in his relation with each rival union in the enterprise. This neutrality gives a big burden to an employer.

In Asia we can find four kinds of treatment to resolve multiple unionisms. The first type which is found Japan allows competitive unionism. This type can be seen in India. The second type found in Philippine introduces sole representative agent system. The third type found in South Korea and Taiwan allows only single union in an enterprise or in the plant under the Labour Unions Act in order to shut its activities in the enterprise and to exclude social and political influence from outside. Both governments fear anti-establishment movements of labour unions. The fourth type found in Malaysia and Singapore allows a registered union to get recognition when it represents certain employees or class of employees from the majority. Indonesia also may be included in the fourth type. In Indonesia only one enterprise SPSI regional committee under the certification of Labour Ministerial Regional Office may recognize union.

It is now discussed whether the third type contravenes freedom of association provided in ILO Conventions No. 87 and 96. And the fourth type has a problem that the right to organize labour unions depends upon the discretionary power of a registrar and labour ministerial officer. But an employer has no trouble to judge which labour union he shall bargain with. On the other hand, in Japan there is no problem on the freedom of association, but an employer has a troublesome duty to treat multiple unions equally. So there are problems in each system except the second type.

2. LEGAL EFFECT OF COLLECTIVE AGREE MENT

(a) Factual Situation of Collective Agreement

According to the survey of Labour Ministry in 1989, labour unions made 52,247 labour agreements and union members covered by collective agreement were 8,724,749 in Japan. About 18% of all the workers were covered by collective agreements. So only one-fifth of the workers are protected by labour unions in Japan.

In other Asian countries union density is not higher than that in Japan as shown in Table 1. So the union members covered by collective agreements are less in Japan. This reveals that work rules play bigger role in determining working conditions in Asia.

(b) Normative Effect

In Japan legal effect of collective agreement comes from West German legal doctrine. Collective agreement is divided into a part having a normative effect and one having a contract-obligation effect. Under Article 16 of the Labour Unions Act a normative effect is given to "the standards concerning working conditions and other matters relating to the treatment of workers". In the normative part, any provision of a labour contract, which contravenes the terms of collective agreement, is null and void. The provisions of the collective agreement shall replace contractual provisions, which are rendered invalid.

In the world there are mainly three types of legal treatment of the collective agreement. The first comes from England where the agreement is a gentlemen's one without legal effect. The second type is West German doctrine, which gives special contractual effect to the collective agreement. In the Asian context, South Korea, Japan, Thaiwan and Indonesia adopt the second type. The third type comes from Australia which develops compulsory arbitration system. So this type can be named Oceania type. The third type can be found in India, Sri Lanka, Bangladesh, Malaysia and Singapore. In these countries collective agreement must be registered with the competent authority. At the time of registration the officers review whether the contents of agreement comply with the standards, required by the Act. If the agreement does not comply with them, it is denied. A registered agreement shall be deemed to be an award, which will be given under compulsory arbitration system to settle labour disputes. If the party of the agreement contravenes the award, the competent authority makes order to comply with the term of the award or collective agreement. If he does not obey the order, he shall be guilty of criminal penalty. The last resort to comply with the contents of collective agreement is criminal penalty under the third type.

The third type shows a high degree of intervention by administrative authority, which can control the contents of collective agreement to adjust economic conditions on the pretext of social justice.

(c) Effect of Better Working Conditions in the Labour Contract (is one of the terms of collective agreement-advantageous principle)

According to advantageous principle, normative effect of collective bargaining does not apply to the individual contract when it provides better working conditions in terms of collective agreement. In Japan it is disputed whether this principle can be legally permitted.

The majority view answers in the negative. There are two reasons. Article 16 of the Labour Unions Act provides that any stipulation of an individual labour contract contravening the standards concerning working conditions and other treatment of workers provided for in a collective agreement shall be null and void. The majority view holds that better working conditions in the individual contract contravene the standards of the collective agreement. Japanese collective agreement has a function to decide actual working conditions uniformly in each enterprise. This idea gets along with legal doctrine of enterprise union. An industrial union is interested in providing the minimum standard of working conditions in an industry under the collective agreement. So it is natural to permit better working conditions in individual establishment because the agreement provides only minimum standard of working conditions. That is one reason. Another reason is the following.

Better working conditions can be provided in the individual labour contract through individual bargaining. But if individual bargaining is permitted, it will endanger the collective bargaining, which aims to control working conditions. Individual bargaining is used in order to by-pass the process of collective bargaining. So it is interpreted that the right to individual bargaining is not guaranteed in Japanese collective bargaining system.

I think that this cannot be received in Asia where job-hopping is popular. For example, in Thailand advantageous principle is provided in Article 20 of Labour Relations Act, 1975. and in Malaysia the collective agreement shall be an implied term of the contract between the workmen and employers bound by the agreement that the rates of wages to be paid and the conditions of employment to be observed under the contract shall be in accordance with the agreement unless varied by a subsequent agreement or a decision of the Court (Industrial Relations Act Art. 17(2)). But it is interpreted that the employer has a freedom to conclude a contract whose contents are less unfavourable to the workers than the provisions of the collective agreement. Namely the employer can make a contract providing better working conditions than those of the collective agreement. This interpretation is based on the provisions of the collective agreement which makes a minimum standard of wage rates and other working conditions. The function of the collective agreement in Japan is thought to be different from Malaysia.

(d) Extensive Effect of Collective Agreement

In Japan there are two kinds of extensive effects of collective agreement.

(i) When three-fourths or more of the workers of a similar kind normally employed in a factory or other working place are covered by a single collective agreement, the remaining workers of a similar kind employed in that factory or working place must *ipso facto* be bound by the same agreement.

(ii) The agreement, which covers a large majority of employees in a special geographical region, may be extended to other employees in that region by the decision of the Labour Minister or the Governor of the prefecture. The decision is taken at the request of one or both of the parties to the collective agreement, or in accordance with the resolution of the Labour Relations Commission.

These kinds of effect come from the West German Act. But the second type is rarely utilized because many collective agreements cover only employees of one enterprise. The first type is discussed at the court dealing with labour cases and academic circle. Though in Japan exclusive bargaining representatives system is not adopted like in America, the first type produces the result that all the employees in a factory can be covered by one collective agreement. So the first type has the similar function with representative bargaining system in America.

But there are some workers to which the first type is not applied. Temporary workers including part-time workers are not regarded to be "workers of similar kind normally employed". But it is interpreted to apply to part-time workers whose period of employment are repeatedly renewed like regularly employed workers.

In Asia we can find extensive effect of collective agreement. South Korea and Thailand have similar system with Japanese general binding power at the workplace. In Thailand the collective agreement shall apply to all employees if the union membership is over two-thirds of them involved in the agreement. In practice, however, the employer always applies the agreement to all employees if the union membership is not over two-thirds of them because it is convenient to have one set of working conditions for all employees. In Philippine representative bargaining system is introduced from America. So the effect of collective bargaining is extended to all workers who take part in the election of representatives in the bargaining unit. In Singapore and Malaysia cognized agreement shall be binding to all workmen who are employed or subsequently employed in the undertaking or part of the undertaking to which the agreement relates.

In Asia where union density is not so high, extensive effect of collective agreement is an available guarantee to assure the same working conditions of non-unionized workers as union members. So this extensive effect system is especially introduced by the Act even in Malaysia and Singapore where representative bargaining system is not adopted. But extensive effect may impede the growth of union membership because the employees who are non-members but are benefited from the collective bargaining may think that there is no need for them to join the labour union. Therefore, extensive effect of collective agreement is a double-edged sword in Asia.

3. JOINT CONSULTATION SYSTEM

In Japan joint consultation committees are organized at more than 80% of unionized enterprise and more than 30% of non-unionized ones. In theory, both may be distinguished. Collective bargaining involves problems relating to the fair distribution of the pie, while joint consultation deals with those relating to the enlargement of the pie. The former represents adversary sphere of industrial relations and the latter in turn helps to promote harmonious labour-management relations.

There are three types of joint consultation committee. Under the first type, the function of joint consultation committee and collective bargaining machinery are separate. The former deals with problems outside the purview of collective bargaining. Under the second type, joint consultation committee deals with problems including preliminary discussions and negotiations on those covered in collective bargaining.

Collective bargaining operates at the final stage of negotiation. As the third type the function of joint consultation committee is incorporated into collective bargaining machinery.

In Asia a hypothesis can be built that the first type moves toward the second or third type as joint consultation and collective bargaining come to a state of maturity.

In Japan the second or third type is popular. The distinction between collective bargaining and joint consultation is not clear in unionized enterprises because the same labour union and employer carry out both bargaining and consultation, and issues of bargaining and consultation are overlapping. Both help labour unions and employers to understand each other and to share information on management issues. More than 30% of non-unionized enterprises organize only joint consultation committees which deal with not only management problem, but also working conditions. Therefore, both collective bargaining and joint consultation are thought to be elements to bring the harmonious relationship between labour and management and, as a result, lead to economic growth. As another feature the creation of joint consultation is left to the initiative of the parties without direct government guidance.

In Asia, joint consultation is advocated to attain economic development with the initiative of the governments. We can find statutory provisions on joint consultation committee in Thailand, Taiwan and South Korea. In South Korea the Labour and Management Council Act of 1980 stipulates that the council should be set-up and held quarterly in any establishment with more than 50 employees. Though the Act stipulates that the council deals with management problems, in non-unionized establishments working conditions are decided through negotiations at the council.

In Thailand employees' committee may be organized at the workplace where more than 50 workers are employed under the Labour Relations Act in 1975.

The provisions on employees' committee are stipulated since union density is so low in Thailand. This committee has a duty to consult on worker welfare, work rule, dispute settlement and grievance procedure. The number of members elected by all the workers at the workplace is 5 to 20, depending upon the size of the enterprise. Employees' committee is an important one especially at non-unionized workplace in determining work conditions.

In Taiwan, enterprises shall convene labour-management conferences to promote cooperation between management and labour as well as to increase labour efficiency under the Labour Standards Act enacted in 1984.

In Malaysia joint council committees are advocated to be set-up under "Code of Conduct for Industrial Harmony" in 1975. In Singapore joint consultation committees are organized on the result of collective bargaining at the company level. In Indonesia tripartite committee at the workplace as well as at the national and industrial level is promoted in accordance with the principle of Pancasila under the declared policy of the government.

In Singapore joint consultation generally belongs to the first type. One reason is that management problems are prohibited from the sphere of collective bargaining under the Industrial Relations Act. But it is hoped to approach to the second type to introduce the flexible wage system. In other countries joint consultation committees approach the second or third type?

4. WORKING CONDITIONS IN NON-UNIONIZED ENTERPRISE

In non-unionized enterprise working conditions are regulated under work rules. In Japan work rules are provided under the Labour Standard Act. About four-fifths of workers are covered only by work rules.

In Japan work an employer who continuously employs ten or more workers at the workplace shall make rules. In making and revising work rules, an employer shall get the opinions of either the majority labour union or are representative of a majority of the workers where no such union exists at the workplace. The work rules shall be submitted to the Labour Standards Inspection Office together with the opinions of the majority union or representative of majority employees.

Work rules shall include the following: (1) working hours, rest periods, rest days, leaves and shifts, (2) the method for determination, computation and payment of wages, the date for closing accounts for wages and for the payment of wages and increases in wages, (3) matters related to retirement. In addition the following items may be included, (4) retirement allowances, (5) extraordinary wages and minimum wages, (6) costs of food, work supplies and other such expenses, (7) safety and health, (8) vocational training, (9) accident compensation, (10) commendations and sanctions, (11) other matters applicable to all workers at the workplace.

Work rules shall not violate laws, regulations and any collective agreements applicable to the workplace. The Labour Standards Inspection Office may order to revise the work rules. And labour contracts, which stipulate working conditions inferior to the standards established by the work rules, shall be null and void and the portions shall be governed by the standards established by the work rules.

Apart from these rules, an employer can unilaterally draw up and revise work rules. So an employer can introduce the provision on working conditions inferior to the existing ones by way of revising the work rules. But the collective agreement has the more powerful effect than the work rules. If the collective agreement exists, an employer shall terminate the collective agreement by way of either expiration of the valid term or a 90 days' notice of termination before revising the work rules.

It is now discussed whether unilateral revision of the work rule giving worse working conditions than the old one is effective or not. In other words, the problem is set whether this revision has effect on the workers who usually do not accept the worse working condition. The labour Standards Act does not have a provision on this problem. The Supreme Court decision made on 25th December, 1968 in Yoshikawa VB. Shuhoku Bus Co., ruled that the revision has a binding effect as far as it is done for reasonable grounds. On the labour cases afterwards, it has been disputed how "reasonable ground" may be judged because it is very flexible standard. We can now summarize the following four factors in determining the rationality of the unilateral revision:

(a) What is the necessity to change the working conditions from the point of managerial and economic conditions?
(b) What is the degree of curtailment of working conditions?
(c) What compensation may be gained by the employees in return for disadvantages brought on them?
(d) What efforts did the employer make to get acceptance from the employees or the labour unions?

In sum, labour cases apply the brakes and cut down working conditions unilaterally by the employers.

In other Asian countries how is this problem dealt with? This problem is more important because union density in other Asian countries is less than Japan. We can find the provision on work rules under the statute in India, Indonesia, Thailand, Taiwan and South Korea. But there are no provisions in Malaysia, Singapore, Philippine and Hong Kong.

South Korea has the same provisions with Japan. Also Taiwan has partially similar provisions with Japan. In Indonesia work rules are made by the company which is employing more than 10 workers under Act No. 13 concerning Manpower, 2003. In India, work rules are named as standing orders, which are regulated under Industrial Employment (Standing Orders) Act in 1946.

In Thailand, work regulations are stipulated in the Notification of the Ministry of Interior of 1972 on Labour Protection. Work rules shall be submitted to the administrative authority and cognized by it. And when an employer will introduce working conditions inferior to the present ones by way of changing work rules, he proposes the change and will try to get consents from employees. If more than two-thirds of employees agree with the change, all the employees are deemed to consent to the change. Then an employer submits the revising work rule to the administrative authority for registration.

In other Asian countries except Thailand I cannot find the solution on this problem.

5. LABOUR-MANAGEMENT AGREEMENT *(ROSHI KYOUTEI)*

In Japan employee representative system is not formally established. But under some labour acts labour-management agreements are demanded for requisites to decide working conditions. The labour-management agreements have similar functions with that of employee representative system at the workplace.

Let us take one example. The oldest labour-management agreement is "Article 36 agreement" stipulated under Article 36 of the Labour Standards Act. And Japanese companies make the most of "Article 36 agreement" among various agreements. Every year about 0.8 million of "Article 36 agreements" are submitted to the Labour Standards Inspection Office. Overtime and holiday work are permitted when an employer concludes "Article 36 agreement" with either a trade union organized by a majority of the workers at the workplace concerned where such a labour union exists or with a person representing a majority of the workers where no such labour union exists and submits it to the Labour Standards Inspection Office. The employer can order the workers in the workplace to do overtime and holiday work without any criminal sanction. Namely conclusion of "Article 36 agreement" has effect of exempting the employer from criminal liability as long as over time and holiday work is done under the framework of "Article 36 agreement". This effect applies to all the workers at the workplace.

But a worker is not obliged to obey the order of overtime and holiday work only under "Article 36 agreement". So there is a legal problem when a worker must obey the employer's order to do overtime and holiday work. Now the Supreme Court has held that a worker must obey the order made by the employer when it is provided in the collective agreement, work rule or the labour contract that he shall do his duty to do overtime and holiday work. Therefore, "Article 36 agreement" is not enough for the employer to order overtime and holiday work to the workers. But it is requisite for overtime and holiday work.

Labour-management agreement influences working conditions, but it is not quite the same with collective agreement. Labour-management agreement may be concluded in the form of collective agreement between the employer and the majority labour union. In the case the effect of labour-management agreement applies to non-union members as well as union members at the workplace. When there is no such labour union, labour-management agreement shall be made between the employer and a person representing a majority of the workers at the workplace. There is no provision to select him. Under the administrative guidance he can be selected by vote, show of hands, marking a list of candidates or consultation with labour unions. Nomination by the employer is not allowed. So it is required to select real employee representative at the workplace.

After the amendment of the labour standards act in 1987, there increases the provisions, which require labour-management agreements as prerequisites to regulate working condition. So indirectly the opinions of non-unionized members are reflected in the labour-management agreement at the workplace.

In other Asian countries we cannot see the labour-management agreement. In Taiwan and South Korea the Labour Standards Act succeeds to Japanese one. But the provisions on labour-management agreement cannot be found in the Labour Standards Act. Agreement relating to conditions of employment made by employees' representatives is much similar in Thailand with Labour-management agreement in Japan. But it is not the same. So we can understand that the provisions on labour-management agreement are unique in Asia. In Japan, there are more channels to communicate and discuss working conditions between labour and management than in other Asian countries

{This original paper was printed at The Japan Institute of Labour ed., Industrial Relations and Labour Law in Changing Asian Economies (Proceedings of the 1996 Asian Conference on Industrial Relations, Tokyo), 1996, The Japan Institute of Labour}.

References

Kazuo Sugeno, *Japanese Labour Law,* University of Tokyo Press, 1992.

Tadashi Hanami, *Labour Law and Industrial Relations in Japan,* 2nd ed. Kluwer, 1984.

Tadashi Hanami, *Managing Japanese Workers,* The Japan Institute of Labour, 1991.

ILO ed., *A Survey of the Current Situation in ASEAN,* ILO, 1988.

ILO ed., *Labour Relations Laws in ASEAN,* ILO, 1986.

Dunston Ayadurai, *Industrial Relations in Malaysia,* Butterworths Asia, 1992.

Chew Soon Beng and Rosalind Chew, *Employment-Driven Industrial Relations Regimes, Avebury,* 1995.

Stephen Frenkel ed., *Organized Labour in the Asia-Pacific Region,* (Cornell International Industrial and Labour Relations Report No. 24) ILR Press, 1993.

Fujio Hamada, "Unilateral Change by the Employer of Working Conditions in Times of Economic Difficulties", *Kobe University Law Review*, Kobe No. 25, 1991.

Kozo Kagawa, "Legal Problems in Multi-Union Situation in Japan", *Journal of International Cooperation Studies*, Kobe University, Graduate School of International Cooperation Studies, Vol. 3, No. 1, 1995.

PART II

DYNAMICS OF LABOUR LAWS IN JAPAN

CHAPTER

2

Labour Laws with Multiple Labour Unions

INTRODUCTION

This paper examines some of the salient legal problems affecting labour-management relations in Japanese enterprises, which have more than a single union organizing their work forces. This pertains to the issue of multi-unionism, which describes situations in which workers in a company or plant are organized by one or more labour unions. In Japan multi-unionism has been on the rise, partly due to new unions splintering off from pre-existing ones during crises such a prolonged strikes, and partly because of their merger of two companies which leaves the respective enterprise unions intact and unchanged (especially if the original companies belonged to different national trade union bodies which are ideologically opposite).

It is now estimated that about 3% of the unionized plants in Japan are affected by the problems of multi-unionism in the organization of their labour force. In spite of its apparently limited scope, the multi-union syndrome has given rise to nearly half the cases on unfair labour practices in the private sector, which is dealt with annually by the Labour Relations Commission. The annual volume of cases handled by the commission since 1969 is shown in Table 1, which indicates the growing share of complaints about multi-unionism being registered in firms employing more than 500 employees. This trend suggests the rising gravity of this problem among business corporations in Japan.

It is worth identifying that some of the common legal issues arising from multi-unionism in Japanese enterprises, with reference to both the existing code of labour law as well as the authoritative rulings in court on unfair labour practices which have been brought before them. Seven of these are discussed in greater details below. They are:

(I) Collective bargaining in a multi-union situation
(II) Discrimination in personnel evaluation and wage increase
(III) Company facilities for pluralist unions in the plant
(IV) Multi-unionism and the check-off agreement
(V) Multi-unionism and the union shop security clause
(VI) Multi-unionism and overtime work agreement
(VII) Multi-unionism and extension of the effects of a collective agreement

1. COLLECTIVE BARGAINING IN A MULTI-UNION SITUATION

Among the contentious issues canvassed in this area are the scope and nature of the obligations of the employer in a multi-union situation to first, bargain with the minority union and second, remain neutral rather than discriminating among unions. This two-pronged question about collective bargaining rights and multi-unionism is briefly reviewed in the following subsections.

TABLE 1

Number of Complaints on Unfair Labour Practices

(in Multi-union situation of private companies)

Year	*Total Number of Complaints*	*Number in Multi-situation union (Percentage)*	*Number per company size (Employee number)* ≤99	10-499	≥500
1969	489	229(45)	51	87	91
1970	513	236(46)	54	96	86
1971	495	219(44)	52	69	98
1972	650	307(47)	59	125	123
1973	564	244(43)	57	86	101
1974	625	263(42)	50	99	114
1975	745	268(36)	52	92	124
1976	675	228(34)	43	82	103
1977	615	213(35)	50	82	81
1978	634	262(41)	67	98	97
1979	529	222(42)	45	84	93
1980	474	193(41)	45	71	77
1981	540	197(36)	58	72	67
1982	524	183(35)	53	66	64
1983	483	177(37)	45	51	81
1984	402	165(41)	38	55	72
1985	405	134(33)	37	57	40
1986	401	160(40)	37	62	61
1987	555	313(56)	31	65	217
1988	404	187(46)	36	41	110
1989	303	152(50)	32	41	91
1990	250	118(47)	29	28	61
1991	251	106(42)	18	27	61
1992	243	85(35)	19	20	46
1993	317	110(37)	18	37	55
1994	323	126(39)	26	55	45
1995	284	105(37)	22	40	43
1996	302	94(31)	23	30	41
1997	318	106(33)	26	26	66
1998	330	108(33)	27	34	47
1999	380	113(30)	31	39	43
2000	363	125(34)	36	35	51
2001	314	93(30)	45	16	25
2002	368	112(30)	21	43	48
2003	340	80(24)	80	23	20
2004	282	79(289)	21	27	30

Source: Annual Report of the Labour Relations Commissions, 1969-2005.

(i) Refusal to bargain with a minority union

This is not legally permissible, according to Article 28 of the Japanese Constitution, which guarantees the rights of the worker to organize, bargain and act collectively, as well as Article 7, Section (2) of the Labour Unions Act, which prohibits an employer from refusing to bargain collectively with a labour union without fair and appropriate reasons. Such refusal is deemed by law to be an act of 'unfair labour practice'. Since Japan has not introduced legislation parallel to the Wagner Act in America, which rectifies the principle of exclusive representation of the elected union in the relevant bargaining unit, it is the employer's obligation to recognize and bargain with whatever member of unions operating in the plant. Even where a collective agreement may have included a clause requiring the employer to bargain with a single union and not with others, such a provision is normally held to be null and void on the grounds that it deprives the other unions of their legitimate right to bargain collectively, as safeguarded by the Constitution (Article 28) and the Labour Unions Act (Article 7, Section 2).

(ii) Employer's neutrality in a multi-union situation

In the absence of a statutory framework governing the principle of exclusive representation of the elected union as the sole bargaining agent in the plant, as it occurs in America, rival multiple union organizations may exist within a Japanese enterprise, giving rise to competitive unionism. Under such circumstances, it is legally obligatory for the employer not to discriminate against the minority union but, instead, to treat it in the same way as the majority union. In other words, the employer has to remain neutral in his relations with each rival union in the enterprise. The principle prescribing an employer's duty to maintain his neutrality in a multi-union situation has been dubiously enforced, however, as is illustrated by the experiences reported in two cases discussed below.

The Japan Mail Order Co. Case

The first case to be discussed involves the Japan Mail Order Co. and its two labour unions, one of which was a minority union with about 20 members and the other the majority union with 120 members. Generally speaking, the former union had been more militant than the majority union, which was, on the whole, co-operative with management. During the Spring offensive of 1972, the company offered both unions, in response to their earlier demands, an additional bonus of 3100 yen a month for each worker, subject to the work-force's consent to co-operate with measures intended to improve the firm's productivity. The majority union accepted the management's proposal promptly, but the same motion was repudiated by the minority union on the grounds that the proposed measures would lead to job redundancy, accentuated intensity of work and the union's subordination to the employer and his wish. As a result of this disagreement, the new bonus payment was made to members of the majority union, but not to those belonging to the minority union, the latter of which did not conclude a productivity deal with management. The disgruntled minority union filed an unfair labour practice complaint against the employer, alleging that the latter's failure to pay its members the new bonus was a discriminatory act on the part of the employer and contradicted the employer's obligation to remain neutral.

The Supreme Court, in its decision on 29 May 1984, ruled against the company concluding that it was within reasonable expectations that the new bonus terms which it offered might not be found acceptable by the minority union, whose pay policy differed from that of its counterpart. However, in spite of being aware of this, the employer had insisted upon a uniform set of bonus conditions. In other words, the purpose of the employer's offer in negotiating with the minority union was, it was held, to elicit its refusal. Given such intent, it was, therefore, decided by the court that the employer's bargaining approach was discriminatory against the union and its members. Its negotiating tactics were found to be manipulative and lacking in the spirit of bargaining in good faith.

The Supreme Court's judgement led to a series of controversies, especially among legal academics. An influential opinion has been one arguing hat the onus of responsibility should rest with the minority union, which exercised its choice of not accepting an equal set of conditions offered to both unions. Determining whether or not the employer had behaved neutrally should be clear and not problematic, considering his proposal to both unions of uniform new terms, which was, therefore, not discriminatory. If any differentiation had been made in the employer's offer, he would have run up against even more obvious risk of having discriminated between the two unions. If one follows this line of reasoning, it would be logical to conclude that the employer's behaviour was not unfair.

There are, as has just been discussed, two conflicting legal interpretations of the issue. In order to legitimately and conclusively decide which one is correct, it would be necessary to determine whether the daggering treatment of the two unions should be attributed to: (i) the minority union's own bargaining policy or (ii) the employer's alleged anti-union bias. And in order to ascertain and establish the employer's ultimate motive, it would be necessary not only to examine the employer's action as to appeared but also to understand associated issues such as: (i) the employer's past attitude towards both unions, (ii) the circumstances which led to the employer's action in question, (iii) the mode and mood of negotiation between the employer and the two unions, and (iv) the influence of the action, both anticipated in advance and realized afterwards, upon the state of in-plant labour relations and activities of the unions. The decision on this case should be based upon a consideration of all the factors and issues listed above.

The Nissan Auto Co. Case

The second case is that of the Nissan Auto Co., which introduced a night shift system under a new work plan of scheduled overtime after consulting only with its majority union, which had over 7600 members. The new arrangements, however, had earlier been opposed by the minority union, which had about 150 members. For this reason, the company did not attempt to obtain the latter's consent to the new overtime arrangements, which included night shifts. Instead, because of its agreement with the majority union, it limited its assignment of overtime work (including night shifts) to members of the majority union, thereby denying members of the minority union overtime work. The conduct of the company soon became a subject of dispute, and their action was declared to constitute unfair labour practice. In this case, the issues involved were not limited to allegations of the employer's discrimination, but included the damages likely to be incurred by the minority union members because of curtailed earnings due to the withholding of overtime work. The complaint was heard in the Supreme Court. In its deliberations, the court identified a number of criteria upon which a judgement was to be based. The following points were deemed important:

(i) An employer should maintain a neutral attitude towards the different unions, whose equal negotiation rights should be respected.

(ii) An employer should take into consideration the differentials in membership size and bargaining power between the majority and minority unions. It would be natural; it follows, for an employer to adopt varying attitudes towards the two unions in negotiations, in order that these would be commensurate with the discrepancies in their bargaining strength. For such purposes, it was hence deemed legitimate for the employer to put pressure on the minority union so as to bring about uniformity in treatment between the members of the two unions over such work place arrangements as overtime work and the relevant work rules; and

(iii) An employer, if harboring an intention to indulge in anti-union acts, could be found guilty of unfair labour practices. In order to establish such an intention, it would be necessary for the court to investigate not only the nature and contents of the employer's proposal (in particular, the likelihood of his adherence to his proposal) but also the background and causes of the action he took during the bargaining process, as well as the anticipated impact of such an action upon labour relations inside the plant and on the behaviour of the parties involved afterwards.

With reference to these standards, the Supreme Court arrived at the judgement that the employer had not been bargaining in good faith, since there was no reasonable explanation for why he had failed to consult the minority union in advance and had subsequently excludes its members from entitlement to overtime work. Neither did the employer make any efforts to persuade the minority union to negotiate with him on the newly introduced overtime work arrangement. Instead, the evidence seemed to suggest that the employer had been manipulating, in his bargaining with the two unions, with an apparent intent to discriminate against and weaken the smaller, minority union.

A second important legal issue arising from a multi-union situation centers upon the debated application of those legal provisions which seek to prevent employers from extending, in the process of personnel evaluation, discriminatory wage and bones increases to members of its work-force because they belong to different unions.

2. DISCRIMINATION IN PERSONNEL EVALUATION AND WAGE INCREASES

Personnel evaluation is an integral aspect of the Japanese tradition of wages and bonuses. It is based upon the individual's merit and his or her contribution at work, which determine the size of the variable part of the annual increase in his/her wages and bonus payment. The part of the pay rise based upon meritocracy is an important incentive for performance, being determined principally by the outcomes of personnel evaluation or performance appraisal exercises. Performance appraisal, generally conducted by supervisors and yet normally kept confidential, without subsequent feedback to the subordinates, tends to take into account such aspects of the individual's qualities as his/her willingness to take initiative at work, job knowledge, ability to judge, creativity and innovative capabilities, leadership, attendance, ability to communicate and negotiate with others, etc.

Under the law, any discrimination against workers and staff members when determining wage and bonus increases is liable to be deemed an unfair labour practice of the employer, if these variations are found to have been introduced for reason that: (i) these employees are members of a given labour union, (ii) they have attempted to organize or join a labour union, or (iii) they have performed the proper activities of a labour union as provided under Article 7 (Section 1) of the Labour Unions Act. Moreover, the same Act, in Section 3, also proscribes any discriminatory treatment in determining wages or bonus for employees in a multi-union enterprise by declaring that such an act interferes with control of the management of a labour union.

However, in order to make an action on a complaint possible, a union must petition to the Labour Relations Commission against the employer for unfair labour practices in a multi-union enterprise to demonstrate that: (i) the employer opposes the labour union in questions, (ii) members of the union have individually received a pay rise lower than that of those belonging to other unions, and (iii) the performance of these union members is not different from those in the other unions. In all these cases, the onus of proof tends to rest upon the party lodging the complaint—that is, the union. Evidently, it is not easy for the petitioning union to advance proof of the employer's alleged intention to oppose union. The evidence can at best be circumstantial or historical, as it must be inferred from previous acts of the employer. The responding employer has a legal duty to nullify and discharge such a claim as well. Generally speaking, it will be up to the Commission to decide whether or not the evidence put forth by the petitioning union is conclusive enough to sustain and uphold the claim.

It is in any case problematic for the petitioning union to collect sufficient information on individuals' pay to verify the claim that its members are being systematically discriminated against by the employer for reason of their union membership. Over the years, the Labour Relations Commission has, in recognition of this difficulty, relaxed the stringent evidence requirements by admitting as proof the submission of information under the 'mass observation method'. Under this method, if the union was able to demonstrate that its members as a group received lower and less favourable pay increases than did workers belonging to another union as a group, this would be sufficient to establish an employer's guilt. Again, the employer may contest such an allegation by claiming that the differential in pay increases are justified for other reasons. Such a contention may be tenable, for instance, if it could be established in the company's exercise in personnel evaluation and merit pay award is conducted in a fair and reasonable manner.

Where a case of discrimination against the union has been established on the issue of personnel evaluation, it is normal for the commission to order one of the three following remedial measures: (i) the employer is ordered to discuss and negotiate in good faith with the union, with a view to correcting the discriminatory appraisal practice, (ii) the employer is required to re-evaluate its work-force under standards which the Commission prescribes, and (iii) the employer is ordered to pay the differences in the wage bill arising from a re-evaluation which is conducted instead, by the Commission itself. On the whole, the second option is generally preferred to the other one, which has been criticized for encroaching upon or even invading the managerial prerogative of the employer in assessing staff performance. The Labour Relations Commission enjoys considerable discretion in making the appropriate remedial order. It is normally considered inappropriate for the third option to be tarnished by any illegality.

Whether or not complaints on union discrimination of this nature constitute grounds for action by the Labour Relations Commissions is also subject to a time limit, which is normally one year after the commission of the alleged act of discrimination by the employer. (Article 27, Section (2) of the Labour Unions Act). The reason for this stipulation is two-fold. First, it is recognized that it would be technically difficult for the parties involved to collect and assemble evidence if the case were allowed to lapse for more than a year before it was brought to action. Second, there is the apprehension that such delayed action would inflict enduring damage on the stability of industrial relations in the enterprise. To a certain extent, the issue of a time limit is complicated by a related question on which the Supreme Court has not yet ruled. This is the debate as to whether discriminatory wage payment arising from performance appraisal is considered a continuous practice. Three interpretations have so far been offered. The first contends that it is not a continuing practice, because the personnel evaluation exercise is normally conducted just twice a year. The second theory argues that wage adjustments are basically continuous in bridging the wage level between the past and future, not to mention the additional consideration that practices such as discriminatory evaluation are often self-perpetuating and are liable to persist once they have commenced. The third approach is to establish discriminatory wage payments arising from performance appraisal as a continuous practice, yet one, which is subject to a one-year limit, inasmuch as pay in Japan is normally adjusted once every year. In spite of the absence of an authoritative ruling on this question, the author is inclined to agree with the third opinion discussed above. It follows that it may be reasonable for the Labour Relation Commission to limit any remedial action it orders against employer discrimination on wage payment to a period of one year before alleged complaint was made.

3. COMPANY FACILITIES FOR PLURALIST UNIONS IN THE PLANT

Since unions in Japan are characteristically based upon the enterprise whose employees they serve, it is almost unavoidable for the union to depend upon the employer for the provision of company facilities for its activities, including a union office, meeting room and union bulletin board. The union's use of these employer-owned facilities raises the question of boundary, *vis-à-vis* the employer's ownership and managerial right over the control of these in-plant facilities.

The Supreme Court, in a decision on 30 October 1979, ruled that labour unions are not entitled to use company facilities without the prior permission of the employer or in the absence of an agreement with the employer. It is argued that while such use would serve the union's convenience, this does not mean that it has a right to such facilities. The only exception occurs in the event of special circumstances which would render the employer's refusal to grant the union such facilities an abusive exertion of the employer's right, which would itself constitute an unfair labour practice by virtue of Article 7, Section (3) of the Labour Unions Act. Otherwise, the use of any company facilities by the union without the employer's permission or agreement is not a proper union activity.

However, the Supreme Court's decision has been criticized by legal academics who argue that the union's activities should be considered in a more objective manner with reference to all the relevant circumstances, including their purposes and the methods of attaining such a purpose, notwithstanding the employer's consent, agreement or otherwise. The question of why the employer's consent or agreement is necessary in order to make the union's activities proper has been raised.

This argument draws an analogy to the case of industrial action by noting that 'proper' industrial actions are immune from actions for criminal and civil liabilities by virtue of the provisions of the Labour Unions Act in its Articles 1 (Section 2) and 8. The propriety of industrial actions is, therefore, usually determined by judging all the relevant circumstances, including the purposes of the striking union and its means of accomplishing them. Like industrial actions, labour unions are also guaranteed the right to conduct their union activities under the parallel provisions of the Labour Unions Act in the same Articles 1 (Section 2) and 8. It is possible that the Supreme Court judgement has adopted a narrow perspective in prescribing the limit mentioned above to the propriety of union activities. It remains reasonable to argue that the prior approval of or agreement with the employer can be taken as one of the factors, and not a principal factor, for judging the propriety of union activities.

The Nissan Auto Co. Case

In a landmark case involving the Nissan Auto Co. and its unions over the latter's differing access to company facilities, heard by the Supreme Court in May 1987, it was revealed that the company furnished the majority union with a union office but no equivalent facility was available to the minority union because no prior agreement has been reached. On the question of whether the company's refusal to grant such facilities to the minority union constituted an unfair labour practice under Article 7 (Section 3) of the Labour Unions Act, the Supreme Court rule as follows:

In principle, a labour union can use the company's facilities if there has been an agreement with the employer. However, it is by no means obligatory for the employer to provide the union with an office, although he is at liberty to lend the union these premises. However, in a multi-union situation, the employer is obliged to maintain his neutrality *vis-à-vis* all the unions involved. Such a neutrality obligation also applies to lending company facilities to unions for their activities. It will be an unfair labour practice if the employer consents to lend an office to one union but declines to do the same for the other union, unless he is able to justify his discriminatory treatment on reasonable ground. In order to establish whether or not a reasonable ground exit, the court needs to look at all relevant aspects of the circumstances, including the process of office lending, the conditions for lending, as well as the process and nature of the employer's negotiation with the other union, and the likely impact of his refusal on this union.

Apparently, the crucial test, which the above guideline implies, is that of whether reasonable grounds are ascertainable or not. Indeed, the Labour Relations Commission has ruled, in addition, that where an employer has no reasonable excuse for refusing to lend his company facilities, such an act would be deemed tantamount to his control or interference with the union's organization or management, tarnished with an anti-union motive to weaken it.

The remedial measures, which are normally available to the Commission to rectify this type of discriminatory practice by the employer, are in general of two types. First, the Commission may order an employer to enter into negotiation or consultation with the union in question, with a view towards deciding whether he will lend his company facilities to the union. Alternatively, the Commission may simply order an employer to provide the union with facilities. The latter solution appears to represent a direct corrective to a previous state of anti-union discrimination, but in fact the order does not make explicit the important step of office lending. The ramification is, naturally, that the parties are expected to enter into negotiations subsequently in order to determine the conditions and other details of lending.

4. MULTI-UNIONISM AND THE CHECK-OFF AGREEMENT

In Japan, the Labour Standards Act under its Article 24 Section 1, regulates the check-off arrangement for union dues collection. This provision stipulates that any wages due must be paid in cash and in full to the workers directly; non-cash payment is permissible only where it is otherwise provided directly; non-cash payment only where is otherwise provided either by law and regulation or under a labour-management agreement, while any deduction from wages are allowed, again only where the law or regulation so provides or if a written agreement has been so concluded with the union representing a majority of the work-force in the plant (or in the absence of such a union, with a person duly authorized to represent a majority of the work-force). Therefore, a check-off arrangement, which implies in practice a partial wage deduction by the employer in order to collect the individual's membership dues on behalf of the union, cannot be instituted unless it is covered under a written agreement. Otherwise the employer may be guilty of unlawful deduction of wages.

It is clear from the above legal provisions that such a written agreement is tenable only where it has been reached with a union able to organize the majority of the work force in the work place, that is, the majority union in a multi-union plant. The implication appears to be prohibitive for a minority union, which may wish to conclude a check-off agreement with the company. Such requirements of the law, enabling the majority union to enter into an agreement on check-off yet denying the minority union a similar right, would have been deemed as discriminatory under the principle of equal treatment of multiple unions discussed earlier.

The legal answers to this dilemma can be pegged to two solutions. The first has been to argue the protective clause of Article 24, Section (1) of the Labour Standards Act does not apply to the instance of a check-off arrangement, which does not itself purport to curtail the benefits and rights of the worker. As such, the check-off activity is in fact not a form of wage deduction *per se,* so that its regulation can be detached from the purview of the Labour Standards Act in safeguarding minimum condition of employment. The second alternative is to contend that a minority union should also be allowed to enter into a check-off agreement with the employer, in spite of the requirement for a majority representation under Article 24 of the Labour Standards Act. Since such a provision assumes that the constituency of the representative union comprises all members in the work force and that they belong to the same union, it is logical in a multi-union situation to vest all the unions, both the majority as well as the minority ones, with equal ability to conclude a check-off agreement with the company.

In Japan, however, the legal position, which has been inherited from a decision in the Supreme Court, has been to uphold the application of Article 24, Section (1) to the regulation of check-off activities. This has left, by implication, the second interpretation as a viable option for dealing with the check-off issue in a multi-union enterprise.

5. MULTI-UNIONISM AND THE UNION SHOP SECURITY CLAUSE

In Japan, a union shop is legally permissible. A union shop agreement negotiated with the union will oblige an employer to discharge an employee when he loses his union membership; this is hence an arrangement to provide for union security. The Labour Union Act, in its Article 7, Section' 1, provides that an employer shall not be prevented from entering into a collective agreement with a labour union requiring, as a condition of employment, that its employees must belong to the union concerned if it is able to represent a majority of the work-force in the specified plant or work place in which these workers are employed. In other words, the law permits an employer to reach with its labour union a union security clause such as a union shop, provided that the condition that the union represents the majority of the work force in the plant is met. Otherwise, such a union shop agreement will be deemed null and void under the law.

However, since the application of the union shop clause is problematic in a number of instances, its institution is actually limited to situations in which it does not impair the individual worker's freedom of association, which is safeguarded under Article 28 of the Japanese constitution. First, the union shop clause should not be adapted as an instrument to force an individual to join a union. Second, its enforcement should not be allowed to interfere with the right of another union to organize workers in the same plant. The following five conditions should be met in order to qualify the application of a union shop clause in a multi-union enterprise:

(i) While the majority union in the plant can enter into a union shop agreement with the employer, such a union security clause shall not affect the freedom of workers in the plant to join and participate in a minority union. In other word, such an agreement should be limited in its scope and is not applicable to the minority union.

(ii) The union shop clause shall not be enforced upon a worker who withdraws from the majority union, which has a union shop agreement with the employer in order to take up membership in a minority union in the enterprise.

(iii) The union shop clause shall not prevent a new employee from obtaining his union membership in a minority union, even after a union shop agreement has already been made between the employer and the majority union.

(iv) The union shop clause shall no longer apply if the majority union so Labour Standards Act will enable the minority union in a multi-union enterprise to negotiate and conclude with the company a separate and independent collective agreement providing for overtime work arrangements for its members.

Such a ruling by the Supreme Court, which renders a minority union in a multi-union situation competent to enter a separate collective agreement with the employer to cover its members on overtime work arrangements, is consistent with the provisions of Article 16 of the Labour Union Act, which regulates union-management collective agreements. Moreover, it is widely accepted that for the workers, the terms of such a collective agreement are likely to be more favourable than the provisions of Article 92 of the Labour Standards Act governing work rules, inasmuch as the law requires that the terms as collectively agreed upon with the minority union should not be less advantageous for its members than those already provided under the overtime work agreement with the majority union.

6. MULTI-UNIONISM AND EXTENSION OF THE EFFECTS OF A COLLECTIVE AGREEMENT

In order to strengthen a labour union's control over work conditions, especially in regulating conditions of non-union members so as to safeguard the interests on the union members covered by a collective union-management agreement, the Labour Unions Act provides, by virtue of its Article 17, the conditions under which the effects of a collective agreement may be extended outside the scope of the union's membership. Therefore, where a collective agreement already covers at least three-fourths of the workers of a similar kind who are normally employed in the same plant or work place, its term will be applied *ipso facto* to the remaining workers doing similar work in the plant.

Again, in a multi-union enterprise where the majority union organizes more than three-fourths of the company's work-force, a problem may arise as to whether a collective agreement negotiated with the majority union should by extended to cover members of a minority union with less than one-fourth of the work-force in its membership. Legal opinions so far on this issue have been diverse and include those, which support as well as those, which question the applicability of Article 17 to such a situation. It appears difficult for several reasons, from a legal standpoint, to argue convincingly in support of the application of Article 17. First, its application would reduce or even deprive the minority union of its independence from the employer by enabling the latter to intervene to regulate the employment conditions of the union's members regardless of its intent and policy. Second, such an application would deprive the minority union of its chance to negotiate for conditions better than those existing in the majority agreement with the employer. Third, a reciprocal argument is also apparent, inasmuch as the application of Article 17 would extend a similar set of benefits to members of a minority union without requiring any effort on its part, while burdening the majority union with hard negotiations with the employer in order to arrive at the collective agreement, as well as with the responsibility of keeping peace in order to uphold the agreement and oversee its application for its duration.

CONCLUSION

Central to the issue of industrial relations in a multi-union enterprise in Japan is perhaps the employer's obligation to remain neutral in order to avoid discriminating against or in favour of any of the unions organizing his employees in plant. Any failure of the employer to remain neutral will constitute an unfair labour practice. Both the Supreme Court and the Labour Relations Commission have adopted important rulings on how such an obligation is to be interpreted and applied within the framework of the existing legal code which pivots around the constitution, the Labour Unions Act and the Labour Standards Act. Within such a statutory framework, it appears logical to argue that where collective agreements governing such issues as union shop, overtime work arrangements, or even pay and working conditions in general have been concluded between the company and its majority union, these agreements and their terms should not be extended automatically to a minority union in the plant. This is because of the necessity to respect the right and autonomy of the latter union to independently negotiate and enter into a collective agreement with the employer, on the basis of its own will and resources.

{This original paper was printed at Ian Nish, Gordon Redding and Ng Sekhong ed., Work and Society —Labour and Human Resources in East Asia, 1996, Hong Kong University Press,}

REFERENCES

Ysuhiko Mtsuda, 'Legal Problems in Multi-union Situation', *Journal of Labour Law Association*, Vol. 54, October 1979, p. 22.

'Tokyo Metropolitan Labour Relations Commission *v.* Japan Mail Order Co.', Supreme Court (Third Petty Bench) Judgement, May 29, 1984, *Rodo Hanrei* (Court Decision on Labour), No. 430, July 1984, p. 15. See *International Labour Law Reports*, Vol. 4, 1986, p. 278, for an outline of and comments on this case written by Kazuo Sugeno.

Koichiro Yamaguchi, *Rodo Kumiaiho Kowa* (Lectures on Labour Union Law), Tokyo: Sogorodo Kenkyuusho, 1978, pp. 62-83

'Nissan Auto Company Ltd. *v.* Central Labour Relations Commission', Supreme Court (Third Petty Bench) Judgement, April 23, 1985, *Rodo Hanrei*, No. 450, June 1985, p. 23. See *International Labour Law Reports*, Vol. 5, 1987, p. 329, for an outline and comment on this case written by Kazuo Sugeno and Yasuhiko Matsuda. Also see Kazuo Sugeno, 'Collective Bargaining With Rival Unions', *Japan Labour Bulletin*, Vol. 24, No. 10, October 1, 1985, p. 6.

'Beniya Commercial Co. *v.* Central Labour Relations Commission', Supreme Court (Second Petty Bench) Judgement, January 24, 1986, *Rodo Hanrei*, No. 467, April 1986, p. 6. See International Labour Law Reports, Vol. 6, 1988, p. 241, for an outline and comment on this case written by Kazuo Sugeno and Kozo Kagawa. 'Hokushin Electric Co. Ltd. *v.* Tokyo Labour Relations Commission', Tokyo District Court Judgement, October 22, 1981, *Rodo Hanrei*, No. 374, January 1982, p. 55.

The representative case on this problem is 'Dainihato Taxi Co. *v.* Tokyo Labour Relations Commission', Supreme Court (Grand Bench), Vol. 31, 1977, p. 93. It is hence judged that the Labour Relations Commission has broad discretionary powers to issue the proper corrective orders. But this does not mean that they are not limited. The limits shall be determined by the purposes of the unfair labour practice system, which are to restore and maintain the normal order of industrial relations. In this connection, the Commission can issue appropriate orders for achieving such purposes. Otherwise, these powers become abused if the Commission's exercise of direction could exceed such limits.

Shigyori Tsukamoto, Rodoiinkai- *Seido to Tetsuzuki*, (The Labour Relations Commission System and Procedure), Tokyo: The Japan Institute of Labour, 1978, p. 117.

Sadao Kishii, *Danketsu Katsudou to Futouroudokooi* (Union Activities and Unfair Labour Practices), Tokyo: Sogorodokenkyuusho, 1978, p. 289.

Joju Akita, 'Continuance of Wages Difference As Unfair Labour Practices', *Rodo Hanrei*, No. 294, June 1978, p. 5.

Kozo Kagawa, 'Discrimination of Wages and Job Qualification Grading and Unfair Labour Practices', *Journal of Labour Law Association*, Vol. 54, October 1979, p. 55.

'Japan National Railway Corporation *v.* Minoru Ikeoka et al.', Supreme Court (Third Petty Bench) Judgement, October 30, 1979, Rodo Hanrei, No. 329, December 1979, p. 12. 'Central Labour Relation Commission *v.* Japan Ciba-Gigy Co.' Supreme Court (First Petty Bench) Judgement, January 19, 1989, Rodo Hanrei, No. 533, 1990, p. 7. See *International Labour Law Reports*, Vol. 9, 1991, p. 464, for an outline and comments on this case written by Kozo Kagawa.

Koichiro Yamaguchi, *op. cit.*, p. 263. Also see 'Union's Affixing Posters at Company Facilities and Employer's Right to Manage Them', *Hozo Joho*, Vol. 32, No. , 7, pp. 063-83.

'Nissan Motor Co. *v.* Tokyo District Labour Relations Commission', Supreme Court (Second Petty Bench) Judgement, May 8, 1987, *Rodo Hanrei*, No. 496, July 1987, p. 6. See *International Labour Law Reports*, Vol. 7, 1989, p. 462, for an outline and comments on this case written by Fujio Hamada.

Kazuhisa Nakayama, 'Check-off', Rodoho Taikei (Collected Works of Labour Law), Vol. 1, January 1963, p. 170.

Koichiro Yamaguchi, *op. cit.*, p. 275

'Saiseikai Social Welfare Corporate *v.* Central Labour Relations Commission', Supreme Court (Second Petty Bench), December 11, 1989, *Rodo Hanrei*, No. 552, February 1990, p. 10. See International Labour Law Reports, Vol. 10, 1992, p. 360, for an outline and comments on this case written by Kozo Kagawa.

Koichiro Yamaguchi, *op. cit.*, pp. 160-1

'Mitsui Warehouses and Harbour Works Ltd. *v.* Hiromi Miura and Masami Fikui', Supreme Court (first Petty Bench) Judgement, December 4, 1989, *Rodo Hanrei*, No. 552, February 1990, p. 6. See International Labour Law Reports, Vol. 10, 1992, p. 357, for an outline and comments on this case written by Kozo Kagawa. In this case, expulsion from one union is treated on an equal basis as the case of withdrawal from it.

'Hideyuki Tanak *v.* Hitachi Manufacturing Co.', Supreme Court (First Petty Bench) Judgement, December 28, 1991 *Rodo Hanrei*, No. 594, January 1992, p. 7.

The Labour Unions Act provides, in its Article 16, that, 'Any stipulation of an individual labour contract contravening the standards concerning the standards conditions of work and other treatment of workers provided for in a labour agreement shall be null and void In this case, the invalidated part of the individual contract shall be replaced by the stipulations of the standards. The samu rule shall apply to the part which is not laid down in the individual labour contract'.

The Labour Standards Act prescribes, in its Article 92, that:

(i) The Rule of Employment must not infringe against any

law and ordinance or labour agreement applicable to the work place; and

(ii) The administrative officer is authorized to order changes in the Rule of Employment, if it is not in accordance with the laws and ordinances or labour agreement

A Collective agreement can be concluded between the employer and the labour union where there is a union composed of a majority of the workers at the work place, or with persons representing a majority of the workers when there is no such a union. Therefore, it is permissible for the labour union whose membership covers a majority of the workers in the plant to negotiate and reach a collective agreement with the employer.

On the former, see 'All Japan Federation of shipbuilding and Machine Unions, Sanoyasu Branch *v.* Sanoyasu Dock Co.', Osaka District Court, May 17, 1979, *Rominshu* (Private Law Cases On Labour), Vol. 30, 1979, p. 661; also the same case, Osaka High Court, April 24, 1980, Rominshu, Vol. 31, 1980, p. 525. On the latter, see Koichiro Yamaguchi, *op. cit.*, p. 172.

CHAPTER 3

Worker's Participation in Management

INTRODUCTION

Worker's participation in management is a word with many meanings. In general the definition made in I.L.O. is adopted in Japan. But there is a discussion on the systems that are involved in worker's participation in management even under the definition of I.L.O.

In this paper we will consider the theme at the enterprise and workshop level. So the problems at the industry or national level will be removed. In Japan, joint consultation system at the industrial level has been made between industrial federations and labour unions and employers' organizations. And also at the national level consultation system national center lf labour unions can influence the policies of the government. These systems will not be discussed here.

Four kinds of systems will be discussed in this paper. The first is Joint Consultation System where labour union or representative of employees can influence on decision-making of the enterprise. The second is Small Group Activities including QC circle activities and Suggestion System in which workers can participate in management at the workshop level through performing jobs. The third is Worker's Director System where workers can directly participate in decision-making. The fourth is Employee Stock Ownership plan where workers can participate in management as stockowners.

In Japan there is no special law on worker's participation in management except Safety and Health Committee provided by Industrial Safety and Health Law. Almost four kinds of systems are conducted on a voluntary basis. Namely they are often made by collective agreements or individual consent of both employer and employees. Therefore, the success of these systems depends mostly on employers' and labour unions' willingness.

I. JOINT CONSULTATION COMMITTEE

(1) Historical Background

"Pioneer" joint consultation system was introduced after the First World War by the employers' association named 'Kyochokai'. In 1929 the number of companies establishing this committee was 112 which spread to about 300 by 1936. The purpose of this association was to protect firms from invasion of leftist labour movement. And the labour unions had misgivings that this committee was a tool for compelling them to cooperate with the employer. Therefore, this committee could not successful.

Just after the Second World War Japan faced with the destruction of the economic base worsened by inflation. Japanese workers were encouraged to organize labour unions by the Supreme Commander of the Allied Powers (SCAP). At that time the Communist Party of Japan mostly guided the labour unions. Under SCAP pressure, employers showed little resistance to such unionization. But the Central Labour Relations

Commission made a policy to establish Joint Management Committee in order to prevent labour disputes and to promote productions. In the Committee labour unions impeached employers for their management and intervened employers' authority and prerogative. So employers disliked this committee. When radical labour movement burnt it out, this committee was abolished or lost its authority to discuss on management problem.

At the third stage Japan Productivity Center has advocated joint consultation committee on a voluntary basis between labour unions and managements since the latter half of 1950's. After Japan Productivity Center was established in 1955, Japanese economy continued to grow with an average annual growth rate of about 10 or more percent. Economic development was achieved by a large-scale investment in key industries by the introduction of advanced technologies and equipments from America and European countries and by high productivity of workers. Joint consultation committee has performed certain role in Japanese economic growth.

Japan Productivity Center put forward joint consultation committee as distinguished from collective bargaining. It said that collective bargaining aimed to deal with the problem how profits were divided between workers and managements, but that the problem how profits themselves could be increased should be discussed at joint consultation committee. Namely, it thought that the theme of this committee was a matter of common interests between workers and managements.

The fourth stage started from 1973/74 oil price crisis and continued for a few years. The operation of joint consultation committee was extremely widespread during this stage. To overcome the recession and adjust to the change of industrial structure, the companies tried to conduct the rationalization of management or introduced technological innovation through a process of consultation with the labour unions. On the other hand, the social responsibility of companies was seriously discussed during this stage. The origin of this discussion was the occurrence of pollution problems. There were companies, which bought up the goods to increase their prices. So it was widely asserted that the companies should aim to attain social justice. To get the purpose the national centers of labour unions except Sohyo (General Council of Trade Unions) proposed to promote worker's participation in management, being influenced from the discussions in European countries.

After the fourth stage there was little discussion on worker's participation in management. But joint consultation system got firmly fixed in Japanese enterprises.

(2) Statistical Analysis

Joint consultation committee is founded on enterprise, establishment and workshop levels. The statistics of joint consultation committee are collected on the level of establishment.

According to the Survey of the Labour Ministry in 1989, 58.1 percent of the surveyed establishments had joint consultation committees. 73.3 percent of establishments employing more than 5000 employees and 50.5 percent of establishments employing less than 99 and more than 50 employees had such committees. 77.8 percent of the organized establishments had such committees, but only 38.7 percent of unorganized enterprises had them. 47 percent of establishments with such committees had only one committee, while 5.1 percent of them had more than one committee, and 44.1 percent of them had subordinate specialized organizations under the joint consultation committees such as production committee, labour welfare committee, working hour's committee and safety and health committee. An average number of subordinate organizations were 3.3 in each enterprise.

Joint consultation committees are composed of an

equal number of management and labour representative. In the organized establishments 88.1 percent of the labour members of the committees were representatives of the labour unions. This means that the members of the committees for labour side mostly overlap the representatives of collective bargaining because representatives of labour unions usually attend collective bargaining, which are generally held on the level of the enterprise establishment or the workshop.

On the other hand, employers in the unorganized establishments appointed employees elected 75.2 percent of them and 26.6 percent. Appointment by employers shall be avoided because there is a possibility that only those who represent the interests of them would be appointed.

The average number of meeting per establishment was 14.2 for one year. The number of them was 21.3 per establishment employing more than 5000 employees, while it was 7.1 per establishment employing less than 99 and more than employees. There is no law on joint consultation committees. The committees were based on the collective agreements in 77.2 percent of the organized establishments, while they were founded on rules of employment in 45.7 percent of the unorganized establishments.

(3) Level of Participation and Agenda of the Committee

The level of participation conducted by joint consultation committees is following. There are four levels of participation.

The first level is that an employer makes a report and explains the agenda of the committee after or before decision-making. The second level is that an employer shall hear opinions of representatives of employees on his reports and explanations. The third level is that an employer shall consult with representatives of employers on the agenda under materials and information, which he represents, and that labour representatives can propose to amend or to refuse the decision-making. The employer may proceed even if no agreement is reached, but he will respect the veto of the labour side and modify the ideas. The fourth level is that an employer shall get consent from labour representatives to prosecute decision-making. The fourth level is very similar with collective bargaining. Table 1 shows the ratio of establishments according to the agenda to be covered by the committees and level of participation. High figures on the ratio of establishments can be seen at safety and health, working hours and holiday, labour welfare and change of working mode. In case of safety and hygiene, the employer shall establish a safety committee, a health committee or a safety and health committee for each workplace in establishments employing more than 50 employees under Industrial Safety and Health Law. So it is natural that the agenda of safety and health shows high percentage.

Generally speaking, we can find from Table 1 that the committees more often cover the agendas concerning working conditions than the agendas concerning management. Furthermore working conditions are mostly consulted at level 3, where management and labour representatives actually negotiate on working conditions. Though working conditions are thought to negotiate mainly in collective bargaining, they also are dealt with in join consultation committee. This means that there are matters dealt with in both collective bargaining and joint consultation. As a result the difference between them tends to be vague.

The next point is that agendas concerning management are discussed in most of the surveyed establishments. But the level of participation almost gets no further than level 1. The figure of level 3 is high only in case of rationalization of production. So it can be thought that information on management is very well exchanged between management and labour side.

TABLE 1

Ratio of Enterprises according to the Agendas

(to be covered by the committees per level of participation)

Sl. No.	Kind of the agenda	Ratio of Enterprise	Level 1	Level 2	Level 3	Level 4
(1)	Agenda concerning management					
	Fundamental principle of management	56.5	77.6	8.5	11.7	2.2
	Fundamental principle of production or sales	59.5	66.3	12.5	18.6	2.5
	Establishment or reorganization of company machinery	59.6	61.3	13	19.4	6.3
	Rationalization of production or office work	55.8	39.3	18.5	37.5	4.6
(2)	Agenda concerning human resources management					
	Standard of recruitment and placement	50.9	42.2	21.1	29.3	7.4
	Transfer or detachment	58.3	29	17.6	37	16.4
	Temporary layoff, redundancy and dismissal	61.9	10.6	8.4	55.7	25.2
(3)	Agenda concerning working conditions					
	Change of working mode	79.2	11.1	11.7	57.9	19.4
	Working hour and holiday	85.8	9.1	9.6	56.3	25.1
	Safety and hygiene	85.6	11.5	17.8	61.9	8.8
	Compulsory retirement	69.9	13.1	6.9	48.4	31.6
	Wages and bonus	69.9	16.2	4.4	52.7	26.6
	Retirement allowance and pension	65.7	16.6	5.5	49.7	28.3
(4)	Other matters					
	Plan of education and training	63.3	40.9	18.8	32.8	7.5
	Labour welfare	81.5	14.8	20.4	56.5	8.3
	Cultural and physical activity	72.8	16.5	22	53.1	8.4

(4) Joint Consultation and Collective Bargaining

In theory there are some points of difference between joint consultation and collective bargaining. The first point is that labour side can resort to strike when collective bargaining is at a deadlock, while he can not go on strike after the failure of joint consultation. As the second point the employer is even refused to bargain collectively without good reasons under Art. 7, Sec. 2 of the Labour Unions Act. But this article does not apply to joint consultation. The third point is that collective agreement shall be concluded when consent can be gained at collective bargaining. Both parties of agreement have legal responsibility to conduct the terms of consents under the collective agreement. But in case of joint consultation, management is not legally bound by the result of joint consultation. Management is not legally bound by the result of joint consultation and retains the discretion to carry it out, though actually management abides by it.

Three Types

There are three types regarding the relationship between joint consultation and collective bargaining.

The first type is named "separation type". In this type joint consultation committee does not deal with the agendas discussed at a collective bargaining. So the subjects to be discussed are apportioned between two machineries. Matters concerning working conditions are handled only by collective bargaining, while joint consultation discusses matters on production and management problem. This type is consistent with the recommendation of the Japan Productivity Center advocating clear-cut demarcation between them.

The second is named "preliminary negotiation type". In this type management and labour union has joint consultation meeting at the preliminary stage of collective bargaining. If an agreement is reached during joint consultation, it may become final and bind both parties. If the subjects remain unsolved at joint consultation committee, they are referred to collective bargaining and negotiated at the bargaining table.

The third type is "mixture type". In this type there are two kinds of subjects to be discussed in joint consultation committee. One type (for example, production and management problems) is discussed only on a consultative basis and is not referred to collective bargaining. The other type (for example, working conditions) is at first discussed in a joint consultation committee and is referred to collective bargaining when an agreement cannot be reached on a consultative procedure. So this type is a mixture of the first and the second type. The second and the third type are prevalent in Japan. This means that the distinction between collective bargaining and joint consultation is not clear. One reason is that the parties to collective bargaining and joint consultation are usually the same. Another reason is that collective bargaining and joint consultation is conducted on the same level, namely, at the enterprise and the workshop level.

We can find the second feature in the second and third type. It is thought that as joint consultation becomes more extensive, labour unions become weaker because they cannot resort to industrial actions on the subject discussed in consultation procedure. This is the reason why in principle labour unions contend against joint consultation. But in Japan joint consultation serves often as preliminary steps to collective bargaining. So this system does not deprive the labour unions of the right to strike.

This leads to the third feature. Both parties can discuss matters on management and production, and working conditions at joint consultation committee in an amicable atmosphere free from the tensions caused by collective bargaining with a view to maintain mutual understanding, but without weakening the function of collective bargaining. Through mixture of joint consultation and collective bargaining labour side can secure much deeper discussion with management and promote a wide understanding of management policy and can influence management's decision-making.

II. WORKER'S PARTICIPATION AT WORKSHOP LEVEL THROUGH PERFORMING JOBS

As worker's participation at the workshop floor level, we will discuss on Small Group Activities involving QC Circle Activities and the Suggestion System. It is thought in Japan that these two systems produce high level of productivity and quality through employees' participation at the shop floor level.

(1) Small Group Activities

Small Group Activities mean that a group of activity made by small members at the work shop level voluntarily to make and execute a plan or target concerning the business in order to promote productivity and quality.

According to the survey of the Labour Ministry held in 1989, 52.1 percent of 10,087 establishments conducted some kinds of small group activities. The percentage was higher in major establishments employing more than 5000 employees (76%) and in electricity, gas, power and water supply industry (94.8%). The percentage was 65.2 in manufacturing industry.

As for the purposes of activities, the highest rate was 62.1 percent for improving productivity. The next was 47.2 percent for improving quality. Fostering group consciousness accounted for 32.9 percent. 21.4 percent aimed at development of employees' ability and 21 percent were for improving safety.

In the case of 82.8 percent of establishments all employees working there participated in such case of activities. This sets up a question whether small group activities are conducted voluntarily. In 61.6 percent of establishments the activities were carried out during working hours. But in 33 percent they were done outside of working hours. In 53.8 percent of the latter cases wages or allowances were paid to such activities. But they were not paid in 41.8 percent among the latter cases.

Why were they not paid to such activities? Management answered that they were conducted voluntarily and without employer's indications. But there are some cases where all employees are actually compelled to participate in such activities by the employer. On this case it is very questionable that wages or allowances are not paid to such activities outside of working hours.

How are the results of small group activities dealt with? According to the above-mentioned survey, 77.6 percent of establishments give the chance to express them at the conference of small group activities. In 63.1 percent of establishments good groups win official commendation. 51.1 percent of establishments request small groups to represent reports.

One of the small group activities is QC circle. QC circle which is the subject of discussion meet is the most important activity.

(2) QC Circle

Till about 30 years ago Japanese goods and products had been said to be of low level of quality. Management found that the improvement of the quality of products was the most important strategy to overcome the hardships, which Japanese economy faced after the Second World War. For that purpose the Union of Japanese Scientists and Engineers was founded in January 1949 and began to publish a journal named Quality Control (Hinshitsu Kanri) in 1950. This quality control technique came from the U.S.A., Dr. W.E. Deming visited Japan in 1950 to spread the techniques. This visit brought great influence on Japanese management. But it was after 1960s that QC circles were established at the workshop level. Especially QC circles were popular after the latter half of 1960s because QC techniques were improved in Japanese style. The Union of Japanese Scientists and Engineers founded its QC circles. In 1962 only 23 circles were registered, but in 1967, 11651 circles were registered with 142955 persons as participants. In 1980, 115254 circles were registered involving 1062759 participants. At the end of February in 1992, the number of registered circles was 343009, and the number of participants was 2653490. But it is said that unregistered circles are three to five times more than the registered circles in number.

Next we will consider how QC circle activities are related with worker's participation in management at the workshop level. A QC circle is a group of 5 to 10 employees. The leader is a foreman or assistant foreman. The leader must be trained in problem-solving techniques as well as in handling groups. Their most important role is to establish mutual trust between them and QC circle members and to enable the members to work as a team.

At first circle members learn to use the so-called "seven tools" (1. Pareto charts, 2. Cause and effects diagrams, 3. Stratification, 4. Check graph) by utilizing statistical quality control techniques. Then the circle members determine a target for improving quality or productivity. It is important to successful operation that they are free to select the target though the leader who would give advise on the selection of the theme. Next Pareto analysis is carried out to confirm that the target has a practical value. After that they make a cause-and-effect diagram. They set out diagrammatically all possible causes of the effect. Then they examine the causes among their routine works. The result of the examination is presented at the meeting held once or twice in a month. Considering the result, the members put forward the various ideas to form the solutions. And they select one possible solution after discussions on the ideas. To select it they may consult concerned specialists. After the solution proves excellent on trial, the members present the solution to the company. At the final stage it is important for the company to give the members of QC circle rewards or chances to make it public because the recognition made by the company is a powerful motivator.

To find the solution the members must understand their roles fulfilled in the production system of the company especially in the manufacturing industry. So it is not permitted that they know only the sphere of their own jobs. They must know other employees' jobs as well as their own jobs. Namely they must know several kinds of jobs as multiple skilled workers. This brings job enlargement of job enrichment. The members can get job satisfaction through QC circle activities.

There is another aspect of QC circle activities. It is the engineers' task to design and operate manufacturing equipments, handle materials and to make work procedures. But the employees themselves also can know and understand the task through daily works at the workshop level because they are not parts of machines. There are some areas, which the employees at workshop floor know better than the engineers. Through the works, they can find and feel how to improve production methods. This becomes the target that QC circle selects. Therefore, QC circle activities intervene engineers' tasks. This means indeed the worker's participation in management, especially in production management.

How are the conditions to realize the worker's participation in management through QC circles activities?

One is educational career of employees. Almost employees working at the workshop level are graduates from high schools. Employees are highly educated beyond the compulsory education level. So they have talents to improve the working procedures by themselves and show tendency to feel happy at their participation in QC circle.

Another is long-time employment practice. In this practice, employees receive training within the enterprise after being hired and experience various kinds of jobs through rotations, transfers and promotions. They usually complete their occupational career at the same enterprise till 60 or more age. As a result they are strongly concerned with the development of their enterprise. They recognize that their QC circle activities are connected with the development of the enterprise.

The third is the attitude of enterprise-based labour unions. The labour unions do not positively oppose QC circle activities. They know that QC circle activities promote high productivity and quality, which leads to the prosperity of the enterprise. The labour unions may be opposed to the enterprise about the division of profits, but they cooperate with the enterprise in order to enlarge its whole profits. Namely they realize the substantial benefits of QC circle activities, which employees can get.

But there is a big problem in QC circle activities. They may bring about redundancy as a result of rationalization caused by improved high productivity. Are Japanese labour unions not opposed to QC circle leading to redundancy? As a principle Japanese management tries not to dismiss workers concerned against their will even if there are redundancies. Japanese management makes a supreme effort to maintain employment through reductions of overtime works, stop of new recruitment, relocations, temporary rest with pay and training. A personnel cut is held as a last resort to recover the enterprise. Therefore, the labour unions do not actively oppose to QC circle activities because of the policy of employment security.

(3) Suggestion System

In the suggestion system, an individual or a group proposes to improve work procedure, manufacturing equipments and so on. So it partially overlaps QC circle activities. A group's suggestion is conducted in QC circle activities. But an individual's suggestion is in distinction from QC circle activities.

The suggestion system originated in "suggestion box" in U.S.A. but it was popular during the decades after 1955. In 1959, Japan Research Association for Suggestion System (Nihon Teian Seido Kenkyukai) was established, which became national center for promoting suggestion system.

The Ministry of Labour made a survey of the suggestion system conducted only by an individual employee. According to its survey held in 1989, 54.9 percent of the surveyed enterprises have the suggestion system. The percent is 75.9 in case of the establishments employing more than 5000 workers. But the average percent is gradually declining. We can find 68.8 percent at the survey of 1972, 74.1 percent in 1977 and 66.4 percent in 1984.

The average number of suggestions per an enterprise in a year is 9259.3 in 1989, out of which 51.2 percent is adopted according to the survey of the Labour Ministry. The contents of suggestions are, in turn, improvement of efficiency and productivity (81.1 percent), safety and health (53.3 percent), labour welfare (38.5 percent), development and sales of new products (34.8 percent), education and training (20.7 percent) and improvement of work organizations (16.7 percent). These are concerned mainly with production and management problem.

The suggestion system is usually operated in the following. The printed forms of suggestions are regularly collected once a month from suggestion boxes or foreman to whom employees submit them. They are reviewed by the board of examiners whose members are representatives of each section in the enterprise. Adopted suggestions are provided certificates of commendation on prize money. And it is the most important to execute the suggestions. This enhances worker's autonomy, self-development and willingness to work harder. So QC circle activities and the suggestion system have similar effects on workers at the workshop level.

III. EMPLOYEE MEMBER AT THE BOARD OF DIRECTORS OR STATUTORY AUDITORS

When an employee will be a member of the board of directors or statutory auditors, he can directly participate in the decision-making of the company. In general, a general meeting of shareholders is an top decision-making machinery and a board of directors is an executive organ. But a board of directors substantially decide principles of management and they are approved at the meeting of shareholders. Especially when substantial discussions are not done at the meeting of shareholders like in Japan, procedure to get approval is nominal. Therefore, we can understand a board of directors as top decision-making organ.

In Japan an employee cannot be a member of the board of directors or statutory auditors. Under Art. 335 Sec. 2 of the Companies Act (Art. 276 of the old Commercial Code), an auditor shall not at the same time be a director, manager or any other employee of a stock company or its subsidiary. So an employee cannot be an auditor. On the other hand there is no provision in Companies Act to prohibit to hold both positions of a director and an employee. But under Art. 2, Sec. 1 of the Trade Unions Law, persons who represent the interests of the employer can not be members of the trade union. Namely members of the board of directors cannot be members of the trade union. In other words only non-union members can be members of the board of directors.

In Japan former trade union leaders often become members of the board of directors. According to the survey of Japan Federation of Employers' Association held in 1981, 74.1 percent of 313 big companies have formerly executive members of the trade unions at the board of directors. And 16.1 percent of 6121 directors had experience as union officers.

Japanese trade unions are almost enterprise-based unions and usually blue-collar and white-collar workers belong to the same union. When a union member will hold a managerial position, he must withdraw from the union. After that he may have a chance to be a member of the board of directors. Directors are generally selected among employees of the company. They can be directors from the ranks of middle management through internal promotion. Therefore, former trade union leaders have high possibility to be directors because they also have leadership to manage the business. But this is not named as worker's director representing worker's interests.

If a non-union member would be a director as a representative of employees, what problems can be found? The biggest problem is how the status as a director and a representative of employees can be harmonized in one single person's mind. Under Art. 355 of the Companies Act (Art. 254, Sec. 3 of the old Commercial Code), a director has a duty to abide by the provisions of the laws, ordinances and articles of the company and by the resolutions of the general meetings of shareholders and to execute faithfully the business of the company. This involves a duty to keep information secret, which are provided at the meeting of the board of directors. Therefore, even worker's director cannot notify them to the trade union or union members. A majority at the meeting of the board of directors carries a resolution. If it would be disadvantageous to workers, worker's director must obey the resolution. In this case he cannot act as a representative of workers once after the resolution has been passed. As mentioned above, even worker's director must act only as a member of the board of directors under the Companies Act. This reveals that it is so difficult for a worker's director to act at the board of directors as a representative of workers.

IV. EMPLOYEE STOCK OWNERSHIP PLAN

Employees can get stocks of their companies on their own initiatives. This is not called as employee stock ownership plan. In this plan a company promotes the employees to possess stocks of their own company. Namely the company initiates this plan.

In Japan this plan has become popular since 1970. According to the survey of National Stock Exchanges Committee, 65 percent of listed companies adopted this plan in 1974, 85 percent in 1982 and 94 percent in 1991. Employees holding stocks under this plan are 1649000 in number in 1974. And in 1991 the number increased to 2388000.

Japan Institute of Securities examined purposes of this plan in 1985. The result was shown at Table 2. We can know that the largest purpose is to form employees' estates. The next is to increase awareness for participation in management. The third is to form stable shareholders.

Next we must look at the present conditions to operate the plan in order to understand the second purpose. In Japan there is no special law to control the plan. Usually association for employees' shareholders (Mochikabukai) is organized to operate the plan.

This is a voluntary association. Members of this association are limited to permanent employees. A stock company or a trust bank is entrusted to manage stocks. There are two types of getting stocks. One type is that stocks can be bought under the name of the member from the fund accumulated at the association. Some amount of money is deducted from wages or salaries by this employer every month and is sent to the fund set-up at the association. The stocks are managed at a trust bank. Another type is that stocks are bought under the name of the president of the association. A stock company manages the stocks. The members own them jointly. But they have their quota under their shares of the funds. Certain amount of money deducted from wages is accumulated at the funds of the association. Usually a subsidy is given to the funds by the employer in order to promote this plan. A dividend on shares is put in the funds in order to promote this plan. A dividend on shares is put into the funds in order to get more stocks. When they will retire from the

TABLE 2

Number of Companies Classified by Purposes to Introduce the Employee Stock Ownership Plan

Purpose	*Number of Listed Companies*	*Number of Unlisted Companies*	*Total*
Formation of estate for employees	888 (41.9%)	216 (33.5%)	1100 (39.9%)
Division of profits	5 (0.2%)	0 (0%)	5 (0.2%)
Formation of stable shareholders	347 (16.5%)	91 (13.9%)	438 (15.9%)
Increase of awareness for participation in management	468 (22.3%)	197 (30.4%)	665 (24.1%)
Increase of productivity	10 (0.5%)	4 (0.6%)	14 (0.5%)
Fixing of employees	82 (3.9%)	45 (7.0%)	127 (4.6%)
Promoting to value companies	153 (7.3%)	45 (7.0%)	198 (7.2%)
Promoting to take interest in companies	146 (6.9%)	45 (7.0%)	191 (6.9%)
Others	10 (0.5%)	4 (0.6%)	14 (0.5%)
Total	1303 (100%)	647 (100%)	2752 (100%)

company, they can actually get their quotas and dividends.

Under both types of this plan employees can get more of profits if the company will conduct profitable management. Therefore, employees are so much interested in management as shareholders. For example, the association takes the initiative to precede a general meeting of stockholders smoothly. The members of the association have competence to attend a general meeting. At the meeting they will protect their own company from outside criticism and intervention in management under the direction of the association.

CONCLUSION

It is understand that the joint consultation committee and small group activities including QC circle and suggestion system are popular as means of workers' participation in management in Japan. There is no law on workers' participation in management except safety and health committee. These systems are not compelled to establish by law. They are made in various forms on a voluntary basis and often by collective agreement. So they can be operated flexibly.

Generally speaking, it may be judged that these systems produce fruitful results to Japanese industrial relations and production system. Joint consultation committee functions as an effective channel of communication between management and labour. Employer has the willingness to provide information on management policies, financial situations and production problems to union officials and representatives of employees. Union Officials and representatives of employees have strong interests in management and production problems. They feel strongly that their lives depend on their companies' prosperity because they want to be employed till their mandatory retirement age. For this purpose they want to participate in the management at various levels on the ground of cooperative industrial relation.

{This article was written for New Delhi Conference of International Association of Labour Law and Social Security, which was to be held in April 1993. But this conference was cancelled because of some reasons. This original paper was printed at Review of Social Sciences (Doshisha University, Department of Social Sciences), Vol 47, 1992}.

References

Japan Institute of Labour, *Labour Unions and Labour-Management Relations* (Japan Industrial Relations Series No.2), Japan Institute of Labour, Tokyo, 1986, pp. 30-31.

Ishikaw, A., Workers' Participation Systems in Japan in *Workers Participation in Management in Four Asian Countries*, edited by Ishikawa, A., Asian and Oceanic Studies in Industrial Democracy, Series No. 1 (1981).

Japan Productivity Center, *Labour-Management Consultation System*, Japan Productivity Center, Tokyo, 1983.

Mitsufuji, T., Joint Consultation Committee and Participation in Management (in Japanese), Japan Institute of Labour, Tokyo, 1960.

Japan Productivity Center, *Advancement of Japanese Style Participation in Management* (in Japanese), Japan Productivity Center, Tokyo, 1975.

Domei, *To Attain Participative Economic System* (Interim Report of Committee on Participation in Management), Domei, Tokyo, 1974.

Ministry of Labour ed., *Present Situation of Communication between Labour and Management* (in Japanese), Ministry of Labour, Tokyo, 1990, p. 13. This is analyzed in Hanami, T. Worker's Participation in Japan in Industrial Relations in Japan and the European Community ed. by Ministry of Labour, Japan I.L.O Association and Japan Institute of Labour, Tokyo, 1992.

Mitsujuji, T. and Hagisawa, K., Recent Trends in Collective Bargaining in Japan, International Labour Review, Vol. 105, No. 2, p. 140.

In European countries collective bargaining is mainly conducted at the industry level. Therefore, works council is necessary to deal with problems in the enterprise level. They have different functions. This point is distinct between Japan and European countries.

The result of field work on joint management committee in Japanese steel company can be seen at Nitta, *M. Workers' Participation in Management* (in Japanese), Tokyo University Press, Tokyo, 1988 and Nitta, M., Conflict Resolution in the Steel Industry—Collective Bargaining and Workers' Consultation in a Steel Plant, ed. by T. Hayami and R. Blanpain, Industrial Conflict Resolution in Market Economies, 2nd Edition, Kluwer, Deventer, 1989, pp. 237-54.

Ministry of Labour ed., *op. cit.*, Ministry of Labour, Tokyo, 1990, p. 21.

Karatsu, H., Small Group activities and Working Hours Law (in Japanese), *Journal of Labour Law*, No. 59, pp. 121-28. In this article some cases were reported that Labour Standards Inspection Bureau recommended the employers to pay overtime allowances to the employees conducting small group activities because their activities were done as overtime works.

Inagami, T., *Labour-Management Communication at the Workshop Level* (Japanese Industrial Relations Series No. 11), Japan Institute of Labour, Tokyo, 1983, p. 31.

Sugimoto, T., Foreword to Celebrate 30th Anniversary of QC circle Journal, *QC circle Journal*, No. 362, p. 4.

Ishikawa, K., Quality Control in Japan in *The Japanese Approach to Product Quality*, ed. by Sasaki, N. and Hutchins, D., Pergamon Press, Oxford, 1984, pp. 1-5.

Koike, K., *Understanding Industrial Relations in Modern Japan*, Macmillan Press, Hampshire, 1988, pp. 151-58.

Ministry of Labour ed., *op. cit.*, Ministry of Labour, Tokyo, 1990, p. 23.

According to the survey of Japan Human Relations Association, the average number of suggestions per enterprise was 23357.8 in 1973, 55109.9 in 1980, 81898.6 in 1985 and 90933.4 in 1991. The figure in 1989 is ten times as much as that of the survey of Labour Ministry. This came from the difference of the surveyed companies. The average number per employee was 4.71 in 1973, 12.82 in 1980, and 29.6 in 1991. From this survey we can find quantity growth in suggestion system. But now quality of suggestions is demanded.

Sankei Newspaper Company included the union president on its Board of Directors in 1974 though it was illegal. Two years later, the union president was elected to the Board of Auditors by the shareholders with the approval of the union.

Romujiho (Journal of Labour Administration) No. 2718, p. 61, No. 2905, p. 72, and No. 3051, p. 73.

Law for the Promotion of Workers' Property Accumulation was made in 1972. If the price of shares would fall, it does not help to accumulate prosperity.

It was disputed in Kumagaya-Gumi case whether the subsidy came under Article 294-2 of the Commercial Code prohibiting offering property interests to any person with respect to the exercise of rights of shareholders. In this case it was judged that the subsidy was not against Article 294-2 because it was paid for promoting labour welfare. (Fukui District Court Judgement in 29 March, 1985 reported in Hanrei Times nol. 559, p. 275).

CHAPTER

4

Labour Disputes

INTRODUCTION

This is a paper sketch of the history of labour disputes in Japan. Labour disputes can be analyzed from many points of view, but here two following points will be focused on: characteristics of labour disputes and their settlement under the Japanese industrial relations systems.

Labour disputes are defined to mean either the conditions when disputes occur or the conditions when there is a danger that they might occur due to a disagreement of claims in connection with the labour relations system arising between the parties concerned under the Labour Relations Adjustment Act of 1946. This definition is used in this paper, and, therefore, individual and collective disputes and disputes over rights and interests are involved in the definition of labour disputes.

Historical research is useful to developing countries. Although the Japanese experience has shown a typical pattern of labour disputes as a latecomer among industrialized societies, it is not certain whether that experience can serve as a model for other Asian countries. This problem should be considered based on the labour circumstances of each country.

Harmonious relations have now been established between employers and employees in Japan. But the past was not free from conflicts. Cooperative relations are not automatically established, but have been achieved through mutual endeavors during more than 100 years of industrialization. It is also clear that the government played a major role in shaping harmonious industrial relations. Japanese labour relations are generally divided into four historical periods:

(1) Gradual economic growth and oppression of the labour movement in the prewar period (1868-1945);
(2) Restoration of the economy to the prewar level and turbulent industrial relation (1945-1955);
(3) High economic growth and establishment of the collective bargaining system (1955-1975);
(4) Stable economic growth and harmonious industrial relations (1975-present).

1. THE FIRST PERIOD

After the Meiji Restoration in 1868, industrialization began under the strong leadership of the Meiji government, which had to achieve industrialization as rapidly as possible because of the threat of colonization by Western countries. Japan had suffered from unequal treaties with the USA, France, the UK and others. Therefore, the government policy focused on acquiring the status of a civilized nation by attaining economic and military development. This policy was encapsulated in the slogan "*fukoku kyohei*" (rich county and strong military force). The Meiji government established modern industries, for example, shipbuilding, steel, textiles, arms, etc., for which the technologies were transferred from European countries.

At the time of the Meiji Restoration, the Japanese economy was non-industrial, with as much as 80% of the work force engaged in farming and fishing. It was not until the end of World War I that a majority of the labour force was employed outside the agricultural sector. Many remained close to their agrarian origins, moving back and forth between farm and factory. Until the early 1930s, the majority of wage earners were female. Young girls from rural areas mainly worked in textile mills or other light manufacturing industries. They were forced to work as cheap labour under miserable conditions at the beginning of industrialization. Their lives and work have been described in well-known nonfiction books by Gennosuke Yokoyama (*The Lower Ranks of Japanese Society*, 1897) and by Wakizo Hosoi (*The Tragic of Women Factory Workers*, 1925)

Japan had experienced workers protests against employer exploitation as early as the 1870s. These protests were generally conducted spontaneously because workers could no longer endure low wages and long working hours. At coalmines or public works, workers resorted to violence because they were forced to work hard within *takobaye* and *naya* (labour-boss houses).

From the latter half of the 1890s, labour unions were gradually organized among skilled workers such as printers, steel workers, and streetcar operators. In one famous example, Fusataro Yakano and Katayama Sen organized a moderate type of craft union (Labour Union Organization Committee) modeled on the American Federation of Labour in 1897. But this committee disappeared after the oppressive Public Peace Order and Police Act was enacted in 1899. Some union leaders at that time who had almost no job experience were inclined to become involved in socialism or anarchism.

The government had authoritarian power to maintain the political-social system in order to achieve national goals. The organized labour movement was repressed under criminal law. In 1899 the Public Peace Order and Police Act was enacted, prohibiting citizens from joining groups, committing violent acts, making threats or public defamations, or agitating to engage in strikes under heavy penalties. It was forbidden under the expansive interpretation of this act to propose to improve working conditions and induce workers to engage in a concerted work stoppage. Labour unions were deemed to disrupt public order and peace by the government, which tended to treat labour unions as the nucleus of the socialist movement. Therefore, the government used the police to prohibit or control labour disputes because they were thought to interfere with productivity promotion and the social order. This oppressive policy was maintained until the end of World War II.

The Public Peace Order and Police Act were repealed in 1925. But in the same year the Public Peace Maintenance Act was enacted to prohibit the socialists and communist movement because the Japanese Communist Party was founded in 1922 and subject to Profintern (Red International Labour Unions). This act was not specifically directed against labour, but effectively checked union activities through government control. Members of the Communist Party led the leftist groups of labour unions, and consequently oppression of the party naturally controlled labour union activities.

In spite of oppressive circumstances, it was difficult to stop the organization of labour unions with the progress of industrialization through booms associated with the Sino-Japanese War (1894-1895), Russo-Japanese War (1904-1905), and World War I (1914-1918). The Yaikai (Fraternity Association) was founded in 1912 as the first national labour federation under the leadership of Suzuki Bunji, a Christian graduate of Tokyo Imperial University. This federation took a moderate stance in order to obtain recognition by employers, emphasizing the bargaining function of unions and aiming at self-help activities. This enjoyed increased membership under "Taisho democracy" with its slight liberalism during the Taisho era (1912-1926). In 1919 the Yuaikai succeeded in changing its name to Sodomei (Japan Federation of Labour). But after World

War I, Sodomei was split owing to sharp ideological competition among socialists, anarchists, communists, and nonpolitical business unionists throughout the 1920s and 1930s. Police following the devastating Great Kanto Earthquake of 1923 destroyed anarchists with the assassination of their leader Osugi Sakae. Communists were driven underground or jailed. Only the moderate wing of Sodomei was permitted to continue its activities.

Before World War II no legislation granted legal recognition to labour unions. But there were attempts to pass the Labour Union Act from 1919 through 1931. These attempts failed in the upper of lower house of the Diet because employer organizations strongly opposed the act. In spite of oppressive conditions, labour unions were gradually organized, as shown in Table 1, during the period from the end of World War I to the mid-1930s. This led to an increase in labour disputes, as shown in Table 2. The Labour Disputes Conciliation Act was enacted in 1926 to settle strikes and other conflicts through a tripartite commission composed of government, employer, an employee members, although the right to organize labour unions was not granted. Most of the disputes resulted in union defeats.

Another development was seen during this period in the field of industrial relations. In large companies top managers began to realize the need to stabilize their work force. Until that time, the patron-client relationship (*oyabun-kobun*) served to match supplies of and demand for workers in the new industries of Japan. Many *oyakata* not only provided workers to employers, but also managed and supervised their followers (*kobun*) in the workplace. Therefore, companies took indirect responsibility for recruiting, selecting, and training workers, even assigning them to jobs or tasks. But in the circumstances the worker turnover rate became high because *oyabun* often ordered their followers to transfer from one workplace to another for higher wages. In order to take direct control over workers, firms established the lifetime employment and seniority-based wage system. This system aimed to secure worker loyalty to companies and resulted in unions based on the enterprise rather than on an industrial or occupational basis.

After the Manchurian Marco Polo Bridge Incident, Japan strengthened armament development to control colonial areas. For this purpose labour unions were changed into "Industrial Patriotic Labour Fronts (SANPO)" whose function included allocating workers on a priority basis to the industries deemed essential for military purposes in the latter half of the 1930s. Labour unions were thus dissolved, but each company set-up own its own SANPO devoted to improving productivity for the war effort. This SANPO movement strengthened the internal employment system by closely identifying workers with firms and by reducing status distinctions between white- and blue-collar employees. This provided an important basis for enterprise unionism after World War II.

TABLE 1

Number of Unions, Union Members, and Unionization Rate, 1907-1994

Year	*No. of Unions*	*Employees Member*	*Rate (%)*
1	*2*	*3*	*4*
1907	40		
1918	107		
1919	187		
1920	273		
1921	300	103,412	
1922	387	137,381	
1923	432	125,551	
1924	469	228,272	5.3
1925	457	254,262	5.6
1926	488	284,739	6.1

(Contd.)

1	*2*	*3*	*4*
1927	505	309,493	6.5
1928	501	308,900	5.3
1929	630	330,985	6.8
1930	712	354,312	7.5
1931	818	368,975	7.9
1932	932	377,625	7.8
1933	942	384,613	7.5
1934	965	387,964	6.7
1935	993	408,662	6.9
1936	973	420,589	6.9
1937	837	395,290	6.2
1938	731	375,191	5.5
1939	517	365,804	5.3
1940	49	9,455	0.1
1941	11	895	0
1942	3	111	0
1943	3	155	0
1944	3	155	0
1945	707	378,481	4.1
1946	13,622	3,936,815	46.8
1947	23,323	5,692,179	45.3
1948	33,926	6,677,427	53.0
1949	34,688	6,655,483	55.8
1950	29,144	5,773,908	46.2
1951	27,644	5,686,774	42.6
1952	27,851	5,719,560	40.3
1953	30,129	5,842,678	40.2
1954	31,456	5,968,186	38.8
1955	32,012	6,166,348	38.8
1956	34,073	6,350,357	36.2
1957	36,084	6,602,275	36.1
1958	37,823	6,881,571	32.2
1959	39,303	7,077,510	31.5
1960	41,561	7,561,316	31.6
1961	45,096	8,154,174	33.7
1962	47,812	8,783,691	34
1963	49,796	9,269,776	34.4
1964	51,457	9,652,350	34.4
1965	52,879	10,069,761	34.6
1966	53,985	10,308,120	33.9

(Contd.)

1	*2*	*3*	*4*
1967	55,321	10,475,869	33.8
1968	56,535	10,774,814	34.1
1969	58,812	11,143,482	34.9
1970	60,954	11,481,206	35.0
1971	62,428	11,684,263	34.5
1972	63,718	11,772,008	34.1
1973	65,448	11,967,333	32.9
1974	67,829	12,325,147	33.8
1975	69,333	12,472,974	34.4
1976	70,039	12,374,288	33.7
1977	70,625	12,293,052	33.2
1978	70,868	12,232,614	32.6
1979	71,780	12,173,913	31.6
1980	72,693	12,240,652	30.8
1981	73,694	12,355,372	30.8
1982	74,091	12,418,347	30.5
1983	74,486	12,410,988	29.7
1984	74,579	12,358,075	29.1
1985	74,499	12,417,527	28.9
1986	74,813	12,342,853	28.2
1987	73,138	12,271,909	27.6
1988	72,792	12,227,223	26.8
1989	72,605	12,227,073	25.9
1990	72,202	12,264,509	25.2
1991	71,685	12,396,592	24.5
1992	71,881	12,540,691	24.4
1993	71,501	12,663,484	24.2
1994	71,674	12,698,847	24.1
1995	70,839	12,613,582	23.8
1996	70,699	12,451,149	23.2
1997	70,821	12,284,721	22.6
1998	70,084	12,092,879	22.4
1999	69,387	11,824,593	22.2
2000	68,737	11.538,557	21.5
2001	67,706	11,212,108	20.7
2002	65,642	10,800,608	20.2
2003	63,955	10,531,329	19.6
2004	62,805	10,309,413	19.2
2005	61,178	10,138,150	18.7

Source: Fujita, W. Nihon no Rodo Kumiai (Japanese labour Unions) Tokyo: Japan Institute of Labour; 1972; and Ministry of Labour, Annual Report of Labour Statistics, various years.

TABLE 2

Disputes and Number of Employees involved before World War II

Year	*Number of Disputes*	*Employees Involved*
1	*2*	*3*
1897	32	3,517
1898	43	6,293
1899	15	4,284
1900	11	2,316
1901	18	1,948
1902	8	1,849
1903	9	1,356
1904	6	879
1905	19	5,013
1906	13	2,037
1907	57	9,855
1908	13	822
1909	11	310
1910	10	2,937
1911	22	2,100
1912	49	5,736
1913	47	5,242
1914	50	7,904
1915	64	7,852
1916	108	8,413
1917	398	57,309
1918	417	66,457
1919	497	63,157
1920	282	36,371
1921	246	58,225
1922	250	41,503
1923	270	36,371
1924	333	54,526
1925	293	40,742
1926	495	67,234
1927	383	46,672
1928	397	46,252

(Contd.)

1	*2*	*3*
1929	576	77,444
1930	906	81,329
1931	998	64,356
1932	893	54,783
1933	610	49,423
1934	626	49,536
1935	590	37,734
1936	547	30,900
1937	628	123,730
1938	262	18,341
1939	358	72,835
1940	271	32,949
1941	159	10,867
1942	173	9,625
1943	279	9,418
1944	216	6,627
1945	94	38,931

Source: Fujita, W. Nihon no Rodo Kumiai (Japanese labour Unions) Tokyo: Japan Institute of Labour; 1972; and Ministry of Labour, Annual Report of Labour Statistics, various years.

2. THE SECOND PERIOD

Japan faced the destruction of its economic base immediately after World War II. Most cities had been devastated by air attacks destroying a quarter of living accommodations. There was almost complete destruction of industrial facilities and the food supply. But the Occupation Forces had a policy to liberalize the union movement for the democratization of the Japanese economic, political, and social structure. Under the decree of the Supreme Commander of the allied Powers (SCAP), the Trade Union Act was enacted in 1945, the Labour Relations Adjustment Act in 1946, and the Labour Standards Act in 1947. These acts were reaffirmed within the context of the new Constitution promulgated in 1947, which guaranteed the right to organize unions, bargain, and act collectively.

This change of policy can be explained by the following. Before World War II, labour unions in Japan were suppressed because they were regarded as barriers to productivity or effective production activities, and in 1944 they disappeared completely. Under the "New Deal" policy, the USA demonstrated that unions were partners in the democratization process, and through collective bargaining they could achieve higher wages, which would increase the purchasing power of workers, and, in turn, there would be more consumption and the economy would revive. So after World War II, it was believed that the Japanese way of looking at unions was wrong and that the US system should be introduced. By losing the war, Japan was forced to go through a value change, shifting toward New Deal thinking.

Japanese workers responded dramatically to SCAP's initial strong encouragement to organize labour unions. The number of union members rose from zero to over 6 million, representing about 50% of workers in a few years from the end of World War II. Labour unions were almost all organized on an enterprise basis and included both blue- and white-collar workers, although SCAP did not offer guidance on what type of unions should be organized. Enterprise unions were spontaneous attempts by workers to exercise their newly vested rights and to protect their employment and income within the enterprise system in the context of a highly unstable and chaotic economy. As a national center of labour unions Sanbetsu-kaigi (Congress of Industrial Unions of Japan) was organized under the leadership of communists, and Sodomei (Japanese Federation of Trade Unions) was revived with experienced prewar unionist leader.

With high unemployment and starvation wages, the number of labour disputes and workers' involvement increased remarkably (Table 3). For example, labour unions took direct control of plants and factories. This tactic was called the *saisan kanri* (production control) strategy. This occurred most frequently in April and May 1946, comprising more than

TABLE 3

Labour Disputes, Number of Employees involved, and Working days lost in terms of Strikes for more than half a day and Lockouts

Year	*Strikes for more than half a day and lockout*		
	Disputes	*Workers Involved (1,000 persons)*	*Working Days Lost (1,000 days)*
1	*2*	*3*	*4*
1946	702	517	6266
1947	464	219	5036
1948	744	2,304	6995
1949	554	1,122	4321
1950	584	763	5468
1951	576	1,163	6015
1952	590	1,624	5075
1953	611	1,341	4279
1954	647	928	3836
1955	659	1,033	3467
1956	646	1,098	4562
1957	830	1,557	5652
1958	903	1,279	6052
1959	887	1,216	6020
1960	1,063	918	4912
1961	1,401	1,680	6150
1962	1,299	1,518	5400
1963	1,079	1,183	2770
1964	1,234	1,050	3165
1965	1,542	1,682	5669
1966	1,252	1,132	2742
1967	1,214	733	1830
1968	1,546	1,163	2841
1969	1,783	1,412	3634
1970	2,260	1,720	3915
1971	2,527	1,896	6029
1972	2,498	1,544	5147
1973	3,326	2,235	4604

(Contd.)

1	*2*	*3*	*4*
1974	5,211	3,621	9663
1975	3,391	2,732	8016
1976	2,720	1,356	3254
1977	1,712	692	1518
1978	1,517	660	1358
1979	1,153	450	930
1980	1,133	563	1001
1981	950	247	554
1982	944	216	538
1983	893	224	507
1984	596	155	354
1985	627	123	264
1986	620	118	253
1987	474	101	256
1988	498	75	174
1989	362	86	220
1990	284	84	145
1991	310	53	96
1992	263	109	231
1993	252	64	116
1994	230	49	81
1995	209	37	72
1996	193	23	38
1997	178	47	106
1998	145	26	98
1999	154	25	84
2000	118	15	32
2001	90	12	29
2002	74	7	12
2003	47	4	6
2004	51	6	9

Note: Including disputes beginning during the period as well as brought forward from the previous period.

Source: Ministry of Labour, *Labour Disputes Statistics*.

40% of disputes accompanied by tactics. This action was first permitted by SCAP as a way of supplying needed goods because some employers made little effort to restore even the essential level of production. But later it was declared to be an illegal invasion of management rights by the Supreme Court.

In collective bargaining labour unions were not accustomed to negotiating rationally with employers. Kangaroo courts were often held at the bargaining table. Union officers continued to confine employers in negotiating rooms illegally for long hours until they agreed to union proposals.

Labour unions in both the public and private sector engaged in an increasing numbers of strikes and other actions to demand wage increase throughout 1945 to 1946 (Table 6). This spreading unrest culminated in a joint call by the national center Sanbetsu-kaigi for a general strike to be conducted on February 1, 1947. Its aim was not only to achieve wage increases, but also to overthrow the conservative government. General MacArthur prohibited the general strike on the evening before it was scheduled to occur, believing that such action would be a challenge to the authority of SCAP.

After the general strike was prohibited, SCAP changed its occupation and labour policy. SCAP adopted the policy of dealing with the public sector under separate laws in order to ensure provision of national and local government services. The National Civil Service Act enacted in 1947 denied national government employees the right to strike. As a parallel law, the Local Civil Service Act was enacted in 1950. The second major change was the enactment of the Public Corporations and Government Enterprise Labour Relations Act in 1948 to regulate employment relations in government-owned corporations such as the national railways, telephone and telegraph, tobacco and alcohol monopoly, postal service, forestry agency, and printing and minting bureau. In 1952 a similar act was enacted for labour relations in local government-owned corporations. These acts not only limited rights to organize labour unions and engage in collective bargaining, but also denied the right to strike or carry on other forms of industrial action. As the third change, the "Red Purge" was conducted by SCAP in 1950 after the outbreak of the Korean War, and more than 10,000 communists and other leftist union activists were ousted from industries and government. It is thus clear that SCAP did not encourage unionism as a way of democratization from 1947.

SCAP began to base its policy on rebuilding the Japanese economy in order to make Japan an ally in the Cold War era. Large enterprises began to take firm measures for achieving economic stabilization through the "Dodge Line" in 1949, and SCAP allowed the formation of Nikkeiren (Japan Federation of Employers' Associations). As a result of the execution of the Dodge Line policy, radical economic deflation occurred in Japan. As a result, massive dismissals were conducted in even large companies. Labour unions carried out bitter "anti-sacking" strikes. Major strikes in this period included a 63-day strike by the Japan Coal Miners' Union in the fall of 1952, a strike at Nissan Automobile Company in 1953, a 113-day strike by the Mitsui Coal Miners' Union in 1953, strikes at Amagasaki Steel Company an Muroran Plant of Nippon Steel Company in 1954, and a strike at Omi Silk Company in 1954.

Those strikes had the following features. The labour union demanded a wage increase, but the company gave dismissal notices to some workers due to rationalization. Workers ignored the notices and continued to report to work. Then the company locked out all the workers in the plant. During the dispute there was a split among union members and a creation of a "second union". Thereupon the company cancelled the lockout for members of the second union and called them back to start production. Violence occurred between members of the first and second unions and the police intervened to protect the members of the second union. In the end, members of the second union broke through the picket line formed by the members of the first union and production resumed. After that the first union became a minority, losing many members as they returned to work in the plant.

There were ideological and political conflicts behind union splits. Japanese labour unions had a strong commitment to the political power struggle.

Sanbetsu-kaigi declined rapidly after the cancellation of the general strike in February 1947. Anti-communist leaders organized Mindo (Union Democratization Alliance) and succeeded in winning the power struggle with the communist group. Mindo developed into Sohyo (general Council of Trade Unions), including many former members of Sanbetsu-kaigi and members of the leftist group of Sodomei. The rightist group of Sodomei formed Domei (Japanese Confederation of Labour) as the second largest national center in 1954. Sohyo supported the Japanese Socialist Party and Domei supported the Democratic Socialist party. The leftist group of Japanese labour unions representing Sohyo supported the first labour unions, and the right wing representing Domei supported the second labour unions. Disunity at the national level tended to affect the solidarity of union members; resulting union splits during prolonged labour disputes.

During the second period labour disputes occurred based upon political issues. For example, general strikes were called to protest passage of the Subversive Activity Prevention Act in April 1952 and US military bases at Uchinada, Asama, Sunagawa, Daitakane, Kita-Fuji, etc. and to express opposition to a separate US-Japan Peace Treaty and US-Japan Mutual Security Agreement. It was discussed in the courts whether these political actions were legal under the Trade Unions Act. There was serious disunity because of conflicts over these political issues among national labour unions. Labour unions supporting opposition parties were countervailing powers against the conservative Liberal-Democratic Party.

3. THE THIRD PERIOD

Japanese efforts and a relatively favourable international situation enabled the Japanese economy to reach its prewar level in less than 10 years after the end of World War II. The economy continued to grow with an average annual growth rate of 9% in the latter half of the 1950s and of 11.2% in the 1960s. Economic development was achieved by large-scale investment in key industries such as shipbuilding, automobiles, iron and steel, electronics, etc. with the introduction of advanced technology and equipment from the USA and European countries and due to the high productivity of workers. In 1955 the Japanese Productivity Center was established to promote productivity. The QC circle movement and kanban system were advocated in order to reduce waste and increase the quality of products.

In this period the labour movement and labour disputes became different in nature from those of the revolutionary period. After 1955 labour movement and labour disputes began to acquire the characteristics of "Japanese trade unionism" advocated by the main group of Sohyo. In Japanese trade unionism it is important to determine working conditions through collective bargaining, and to separate labour unions from political parties. In the field of industrial relations, the Shunto (Spring Labour Offensive) was introduced in 1955 for annual or regular wage increases. After that the number of unions and members participating in the Shunto increased rapidly and Shunto became the most important wage-fixing institution. In 1975, 9.8 million members participated in Shunto, representing 77% of all union members. Shunto takes place in the spring, when the Japanese fiscal year starts and students graduate from high schools and universities. A new agreement on wages takes effect from April and in Japan it is the custom to give the annual wage increase in April.

In 1955, eight unions at the industrial level in the private sector formed a join wage struggle council. A joint committee from the public sector called Kokyokigyoutai Rodokumiai Kyougika (Public Corporation Workers' Committee) also joined this wage struggle council. Major unions in the public sector, although legally deprived of the right to strike, engaged in strikes to express dissatisfaction with the failure to implement arbitration awards. As a result, union leaders were discharged by their employers, but were re-elected to their posts and demanded collective bargaining rights. The employers rejected this demand on the grounds that the Public Corporation and National Enterprise Labour Relations Act stipulated that only employees of corporations were eligible to be union officers. Thus many strikes and protests took place against the discharge of union officers. This developed into the struggle for ratification of ILO Convention No. 87.

In Japan almost all collective bargaining has been conducted at the enterprise level and it is rare for union officers at the national or industrial level to be present at the collective bargaining table within the enterprise. But in the Shunto, national or industrial federations, especially the IMF-JC group, have played a leading role in setting targets for annual wage increases and raising the wage every year, although they do not directly or formally sit at the bargaining table. For example, they formulated the standard for increases and union tactics for putting pressure on companies. They have also called for a key industrial federation to set a strike date and for other unions to consult to determine their own strike schedules.

Shunto has another purpose. Individual companies decide wages. Therefore, differences in wages and other working conditions gradually increased between large and medium and small enterprises even in the same industry. Shunto acted to standardize wage increases and small enterprises even in the same industry. Shunto acted to standardize wage increases and to reduce wage differences under the leadership of national industrial federation. In Shunto labour unions accepted the system of an average wage increase. In this system labour unions had no power to decide the wage rate for individual workers. Employers had the authority to decide the wage rate for individual workers. Employers had the authority to decide how the average wage increase should be divided among workers. There were reasons for this system. One was that the basic wage was not based on job content or on uniform criteria among companies in the same industry. Another was that it was convenient to calculate the total amount paid to workers by multiplying average wage increase by the number of workers.

This system for determining the average wage increase created a major change in the wage system to promote productivity in the form of the personnel appraisal system advocated by Nikkeiren. Under the seniority-based wage system the basic wage was determined by looking at education level, age, and length of service. This system did not reflect productivity per worker. Therefore, Nikkeiren proposed to divide wage increase amounts by evaluating worker performance. This aimed to reflect productivity of individual workers in determining the basic wage. This is one of the reasons why Japan has achieved high economic growth. But the personnel appraisal system carried with it serious legal problem and engendered disputes.

During Shunto the collective bargaining system was established to determine working conditions. A joint-management committee was advocated to communicate management affairs between labour and capital by the Japan Productivity Center. In this period when Japan had undergone a major change in industrial structure due to a switch of energy resources, staffing plan, new production plans, and transfer of workers became important problems to be solved by labour and management. A joint consultation committee dealt with these management affairs because they were related to the problem of how profits could be increased. Collective bargaining aimed to deal with the problem of how profits should be divided between labour and management. Therefore, the Japan Productivity Center proposed a joint consultation committee as distinguished from collective bargaining.

In theory there are some points of difference between join consultation and collective bargaining. The first point is that labour can resort to a strike when collective bargaining is at a deadlock, while a strike cannot be resorted to after the failure of joint consultation. The second point is that an employer cannot refuse to bargain collectively without good reason under Article 7, Section 2 of the Trade Unions Act. But this article does not apply to joint consultation. The third point is that a collective agreement is concluded when consent is gained, and both parties have a legal responsibility to carry out the terms of consent. But management is not legally bound by the results of joint consultation and maintains discretionary power over whether to carry them out or not.

In Japan, however, the distinction between collective bargaining and join consultation is not clear. One reason is that the parties to bargaining and consultation are usually the same because labour unions are organized at the enterprise level and bargaining and consultation are also conducted at the enterprise or workshop level. Another is that both parties use joint consultation as the preliminary stage of bargaining if consent is reached during joint consultation, it may be final. But if the problem remains unsolved after joint consultation, it may be final. But if the problem remains unsolved after joint consultation, it is referred to collective bargaining and negotiated at the bargaining table. This system allows for thorough discussion between labour and capital and promotes broad understanding of management policy among workers. It also reduces labour conflicts caused by lack of communication and helps to foster amicable relations between labour and management.

Although cooperative relations were established, the two biggest strikes since the end of World War II occurred during this period. One was the Miike coalmine strike against rationalization including a partial closure of the mines. Rationalization was needed due to the energy revolution from oil to oil. The other was a one-week strike by national railway workers in 1975 that wanted to recover the right to strike. This strike highlighted the issue of privatization of the national railways. After a long debate the problem on privatization was resolved in 1985. But it was accompanied by severe labour disputes related to mass dismissals of members of the National Railway Labour Union, the leftist union in the Japan Railway Company.

4. THE FOURTH PERIOD

After the oil crisis in 1973, the Japanese economy was characterized by a soft landing in a period of stable growth. Labour and management adapted smoothly to the economic changes after the oil crisis. To overcome economic recession, manufacturing industries executed large-scale employment adjustment. It should be noted that dismissal is a method that employers usually take only as a last resort after all other methods have been tried. For example, the following methods are used in response to economic fluctuation: abolition of overtime work; increase or decrease in the number of part-time employees; transfer of regular employees within the enterprise; and dispatch of regular employees to other related firms. Japanese companies increase flexibility by minimizing the number of permanent employees; the lay-off system has not been established since it is believed that it would destroy the gold relations between labour and management.

Management and labour unions try to avoid confrontation. For example, labour union exercise restraint in requesting wage rate increases during Shunto, with the aim of ensuring stable employment and maintaining the standard of living. This is because Japanese unions are based on the enterprise and they could not continue if the enterprise failed. Therefore, enterprise unions tend to base policy on survival of the company, with the belief that the union and the company share a common fate. Enterprise unions generally have cooperative attitudes toward management in the case of economic recession.

The number of work stoppages can illustrate this tendency. The highest number of stoppages after World War II was recorded in 1974. Until that year the number of stoppages in general had increased, but there was a substantial reduction after 1975. It must be noted that the number of work stoppages decreased in times of economic recession. This shows a cooperative relationship between labour unions and management.

The parties concerned through collective bargaining or informal communication usually settle labour disputes. But sometimes they are resolved by a third party (members of the Labour Relations Commission) under the Labour Relations Adjustment Act of 1946. This act provides for four types of settlement: conciliation; mediation; arbitration; and emergency adjustment, which are carried out by the Labour Relations Commission. In Japan the parties concerned in labour disputes prefer the conciliation procedure to mediation and arbitration procedures, as shown in Table 4. Conciliation is a method of settlement whereby a conciliator or board of conciliators is appointed by the Labour Relations Commission upon the petition of one or both of the parties or on the initiative of the chairman of the commission. The conciliator endeavors to confirm labour and management claims and assists them in arriving at a

TABLE 4

Labour Dispute Settlement by the Labour Relations Commission

Year	*Conciliation*	*Meditation*	*Arbitration*	*Total number*
1	*2*	*3*	*4*	*5*
1946	144	44	0	188
1947	591	301	2	894
1948	1,066	342	6	1414
1949	1,111	185	4	1300
1950	887	227	0	1114
1951	831	202	1	1034
1952	889	162	1	1052
1953	937	131	3	1071

(Contd.)

1	*2*	*3*	*4*	*5*
1954	931	90	2	1023
1955	1,036	87	1	1124
1956	984	43	3	1030
1957	1,236	103	2	1341
1958	1,108	66	3	1177
1959	1,237	60	3	1300
1960	1,157	37	7	1201
1961	1,719	98	12	1829
1962	1,545	74	6	1625
1963	1,377	63	3	1443
1964	1,392	89	2	1483
1965	1,580	113	5	1698
1966	1,542	76	3	1621
1967	1,389	81	3	1482
1968	1,357	100	1	1458
1969	1,593	53	2	1648
1970	1,466	87	1	1554
1971	1692	74	2	1,768
1972	1622	92	4	1,718
1973	1560	56	16	1,632
1974	2108	138	3	2,249
1975	1793	66	18	1,877
1976	1468	52	8	1,528
1977	1241	26	3	1,270
1978	1126	10	1	1,137
1979	847	7	0	854
1980	975	23	1	999
1981	929	11	3	943
1982	1104	52	8	1,164
1983	930	38	7	975
1984	708	25	3	736
1985	669	17	3	689
1986	655	17	1	673
1987	762	21	4	787
1988	520	11	0	531
1989	407	19	11	437
1990	348	16	10	374
1991	330	13	9	352
1992	331	19	9	359
1993	513	30	9	552
1994	474	35	9	518

TABLE 5

Number of Civil labour cases including injunctions resolved by District Courts according to type of solution

Year	*Litigation*	*Compromise*	*Withdrawal, etc.*	*Total*
1962	128	40	199	367
1963	159	66	156	381
1964	189	45	178	412
1965	193	88	167	448
1966	296	121	685	1,102
1967	474	133	242	849
1968	418	185	378	981
1969	394	196	328	918
1970	711	249	365	1,325
1971	470	212	341	1,023
1972	505	452	397	1,354
1973	522	498	464	1,484
1974	471	485	377	1,333
1975	646	444	336	1,426
1976	440	479	420	1,339
1977	558	331	395	1,284
1978	547	277	568	1,392
1979	642	272	358	1,272
1980	668	333	405	1,406
1981	695	385	431	1,511
1982	493	452	397	1,342
1983	522	498	349	1,369
1984	471	485	377	1,333
1985	646	444	336	1,426
1986	440	479	420	1,339
1987	588	402	420	1,410
1988	571	503	398	1,472
1989	485	471	370	1,326
1990	364	511	261	1,136
1991	373	462	211	1,046
1992	429	520	275	1,224
1993	499	696	313	1,508
1994	713	857	406	1,976

settlement. A settlement cannot be reached unless both parties agree with the proposal. Settlement by compromise rather than by clear-cut decision is more acceptable to both parties. Consequently, there are few cases solved through mediation and arbitration procedures. This has led to a reduction in the number of labour cases filed in courts and at the Labour Relations Commission.

In Japan there is no system of labour courts. Ordinary courts handle labour cases. In general the Japanese tend to avoid litigation because the society frowns upon those who express their dissatisfaction openly. But when two parties cannot reach a compromise a lawsuit will be filed, as shown in Table 5. Even in this case, the courts tend to settle cases by compromise through conciliation rather than by issuing judgements. There is another reason for lack of litigation. The Japanese government has intentionally advocated compromise and administrative guidance to avoid bitter struggle. Informal dispute settlement mechanisms in the workplace are effectively used to avoid formal litigation.

Grievance procedures were imported from the USA after World War II. About 40% of the unions surveyed by the Labour Ministry had formal grievance procedures. But such procedures have rarely been used in Japan. One reason is that Japanese workers dislike referring individual disputes to formal procedures. They prefer to solve them informally through managerial staff. For example, after work employees often discuss individual complaints with managers over a drink. Then managers tend to settle disputes personally for employees. Another reason is that the joint consultation system has become more popular than grievance procedures. Labour disputes are reduced in joint consultation where labour unions and managers exchange information and opinions in advance.

But there have been some problems in the past 20 years. The first is the decline in union enrollment. The highest unionization rate was 56% in 1949, and peak membership of 12.6 millinon was recorded in 1965, a rate of 36%. After that both membership and unionization rate gradually declined. The rate fell to 29% in 1984, 24.1% in 1994 and 18% in 2005. It is estimated to be less than 20% at the beginning of the 21st century. One major reason for this decline is the change of industrial structure from secondary to tertiary industry. After the oil crisis there was rationalization in the manufacturing industry, which is highly unionized. But in the service sector it is difficult to organize unions because the size of firms is relatively small in terms of number of employees. This decline in unionization rate has led to a decreasing number of labour disputes and strikes. But there is the problem of how to settle labour disputes in non-unionized companies. It is usual in non union zed companies for employers unilaterally to set labour conditions. Trouble may occur when employers reduce the labour conditions during economic recession. If a harmonious solution cannot be found, disputes tend to take a violent turn, especially in small- and medium-sized companies.

The second reason is the existence of peripheral workers: part-time workers; temporary workers; dispatched workers and female workers. Permanent workers in Japan organize most unions. Part-time and temporary workers are excluded from labour unions. Therefore, labour disputes involving peripheral workers are not settled by labour unions. For example, there is discriminatory treatment between female workers and permanent male workers. They are protected by administrative guidance under special labour acts, but they must be considered how to settle the increasing number of labour disputes involving peripheral workers in the future.

The third reason is the multi-union situation in enterprises. According to a survey of labour unions with more than 30 members by the Labour Ministry in 2003, two or more unions can be found in 16.6% of unionized private companies. If two or more unions exist in an enterprise, the employer must bargain with all of them.

Therefore, multiple labour unions can each engage in collective bargaining for their members. The employer cannot refuse to bargain with a minority union and in Japan there is no exclusive bargaining agent system like that in the USA. Under the recognized competitive unionism, the employer must treat a majority union and a minority union equally under Article 7 (Prohibition of Unfair Labour Practices) of the Labour Unions Act. But there are on average 200 cases filed every year with the Labour Relations Commission (Table 1). The focus now is on how to resolve this problem.

The fourth reason for the decline in unionization is that although Japan has attained remarkable economic development and the standard of living has improved, Japanese workers do not feel rich as individuals. One reason for this is high price levels compared with European levels. Another is the long working hours. Total working hours have been reduced by about 200 in the past 20 years but are still 60-400 hours longer than in European countries. Therefore, there are labour disputes dealing with the problem of how working hours should be shortened. These disputes call for serious reflection on why the Japanese have devoted such extraordinary amounts of time to work and production. It is important to ensure a stable employment system that allows each worker to enjoy an affluent life, while establishing an industrial structure to stimulate the vitality of industry and business in order to overcome the appreciation of the yen.

CONCLUSION

More than 100 years have passed from the beginning of Japan's industrialization after the Meiji Restoration. In the early years the authoritarian government strictly controlled labour unions because they were deemed to obstruct production activities. Therefore, labour disputes were often treated as public order problems under the Public Peace Order and Police Act of 1899 and Public Peace Maintenance Act of 1925.

After World War II, labour unions were formally recognized under the Labour Unions Act as the result of a policy change directed by SCAP. This policy positioned employers and labour unions as partners in the democratization process. But in a volatile economic situation, there were many violent labour disputes in which labour unions took control of plants and factories during the five years after World War II.

In the 1960s and 1970s Japan achieved high economic growth. Through the *Shunto* collective bargaining system established for determining labour conditions and the joint consultation system advocated by the Japan Productivity Center were adopted. However, the number of labour disputes increased until the oil crisis period. In that period employers and labour unions tried to foster cooperative relations. This cooperative relationship was strengthened during the economic recession after the oil crisis. The reasons for cooperative industrial relations include the feeling that labour unions and enterprises share a common fate because Japanese labour unions are enterprise-based, and that Japanese prefer to settle disputes by compromise rather than by clear-cut decisions.

Recently individual labour disputes have increased because Japanese companies have changed personnel management policy to win hard competition of business in the process of globalization: for example, diversification of labour contract, introduction of personnel appraisal system. Individual Labour Disputes Settlement Promotion Act, 2001 was made to combat with increasing individual labour disputes through administrative agency intervention. And the number of civil labour cases mainly related to individual labour disputes are increasing to more than 2000 per a year. Till now it takes a long time and high cost to resolve labour cases in the courts. Labour Tribunal System was introduced from April 1, 2006 to resolve them under simplified and rapid procedure. Labour Tribunal is composed of three members, one professional judge, one member from worker side and one member from employer side at the District Court. This is tripartism in the court system. Hearing may be held at most three times to clarify issues and fact-findings. During the hearing three members may try to make mediation. If both parties would agree with the content of mediation, the content shall have the same effect as a compromise at the court. But if not, three members shall issue the proposal of resolution. This resolution cannot be final without the consent of both parties. If the proposal of resolution would not be agreed, the case is deemed to be sued to the District Court, which will judge under the Civil Procedure Code. It is hoped that Labour Tribunal System will give fruitful results to resolve labour disputes.

{This original paper was printed at Asian Productivity Organization ed., Labour-Management Cooperation—From Labour Disputes to Cooperation, 1996, Asian Productivity Organization}.

References

Fujita, W., Labour disputes. In Okochi, K., Karsh, B., and Levine, S.B., eds. *Workers and Employers in Japan.* Tokyo: University of Tokyo Press; 1974

Hanami, T., *Labour Relations in Japan Today.* Tokyo: Kodansha International Ltd., 1979.

Japan Institute of Labour, ed. *Labour Unions and Labour-Management Relations.* Tokyo: Japan Institute of Labour; 1986.

Nakamura, T., ed., *Labour in Japan Q&A.* Tokyo: Nihon Romu Kenkyukai 1988.

Shirai, T., ed., Contemporary Industrial Relations in Japan. Madison, WI: University of Wisconsin Press; 1983.

Shirai, T. and Shimada, H. Japan. In Dunlop, J.T. and Galenson, W. eds., *Labour in the Twentieth Century.* New York: Academic Press; 1978.

Sugeno, K. (translated by Kanowitz L.), *Japanese Labour Law.* Seattle: University of Washington Press, 1992.

CHAPTER

5

Deregulation Policy of Labour Laws

INTRODUCTION

Japan has achieved economic growth under the strong administrative guidance. It actually has controlled economic activities of enterprises, which have made the domestic market closed. So foreign companies found difficulties to enter into Japan because the administrative guidance built non-tariff barrier. And from 1980's Japan was criticized against export-oriented industrial policy, which also maintained its closed domestic market. Namely Japan has a problem of how to confront with international competition arising from globalization of economy. These problems began to get into an argument with deregulation of industrial policy. Especially after the burst of the bubble economy in 1990's, deregulation of industrial policy is thought to be one of the best ways to achieve structural adjustment and to recover economic recession.

What is the role of labour laws to respond to these economic problems? In order to tackle these problems labour laws on labour market are being amended to make rigid regulations soft and flexible. But meanwhile, the other parts of labour laws are rather amended to make the regulations harder from the viewpoint of protection of the weak. Namely all acts in the field of labour laws are not deregulated. The sphere of deregulation is selective. So we will examine recent amendment on labour laws in the following sections.

1. AMENDMENTS IN THE FIELD OF LABOUR MARKET

(a) Deregulation of Workers' Recruitment

There are some regulations under the Employment Security Act in 1947 concerning methods of recruitment. In principle, employers can use public employment placement service free of charge to recruit workers. Schools and qualified labour union may also provide free employment placement by notification to or permission of the Labour Minister.

Private placement was possible by the permission of the Labour Minister for only 29 occupations such as nurses, housekeepers, cooks, models, designers, artists, doctors, interpreters and so forth because labour supply agencies were strictly prohibited. In the past private employment agencies were often reported to press forced labour and intermediate exploitation to poor and weak workers. This rose to a need for regulation on employment exchange service when the Employment Security Bill was introduced to the Assembly after the Second World War.

But the situation of labour market has undergone big changes after the rapid economic growth period. About 20 percent of job seekers only can find works through the Public Employment Services. It helps to find employment mainly for manual or un- or semi-skilled workers. It does not satisfactorily function for professional or managerial or technical labourers. Some of them began to change their jobs in order to promote their careers as specialists. Especially younger generations have the tendency to change their jobs though they can enjoy long-time employment system. And middle or old workers occupying managerial posts are rationalized just after the burst of the bubble economy. They have troubles to find employment at the Public Employment Services. They rather want to find employment with charges at private employment agencies. But under the strict control of the Act, private employment agencies have only limited competency to answer their demands.

The amendment of Employment Security Act was put into effect from 1 April 1997. There are two amended measures to allow private companies to participate employment placement services. One is the shift from "positive list" system to "negative list" system, which abolished general prohibition and lists prohibited work. So from April 1, 1997 the Labour Minister except for the following six types of works permits private placement.

- ❑ office work within one year after starting employment for new graduates,
- ❑ sale work within one year after starting employment for new graduates,
- ❑ service industry work, security work, agriculture, forestry and fishery, communications and transportation,
- ❑ skilled work in the manufacturing sector,
- ❑ work in the building and mining industry, and
- ❑ work in labour management.

Under the amendment office or sales workers can be recruited through the private placement agencies except those within one year after new graduates.

Another is the deregulation of the maximum charges paid from the client company to the private placement agency. As a registration fee 540 yen was paid to the placement agency respectively by the worker and the client company. And when the placement was successful, the charge could be fixed at maximum as 10.1 percent of the placed worker's wages paid for six months. But this rate was low for the placement of professional. So the extra fees permitted by the Labour Minister can be added to 10.1 percent of wages are those for consulting, counseling and seeking proper works based on individual request.

The amendment of the Employment Security Act is trying to make external labour market flexible and new businesses on extensive scales. The new amendment is now discussed to liberalize, in principle, to make private employment exchange services. The reason behind these is to give many chances to find employment through both public and private employment services in conformity with the stipulations in ILO Convention No. 181.

(b) Deregulation of Worker Dispatching Businesses

The Manpower Dispatching Business Act came into force on July 1, 1986 under the policy that the manpower supply business should be legalized and subject to certain conditions and regulations to protect dispatched workers. The dispatched workers are defined as those employed by the dispatching agency, which is the contractual employer, but works in the client company under the direction of the client company. Therefore, the dispatching agency is different from the labour supply prohibited under the Employment Security Act. There are two types of dispatching agency. One is the specific manpower-dispatching agency, and another is the general manpower-dispatching agency. In the former type, the dispatching agency must report its commencement of business to the Labour Minister and the dispatched workers are composed of solely regularly employed workers at the agency. In the latter type, the agency must get an operating license from the Labour Minister, and the workers must be registered as dispatched employees at the agency in advance, and then be dispatched to a client company in compliance with the request of the client company. Therefore, the labour contract is usually temporary in the latter type of business.

At first 16 types of works only were allowed by the Cabinet Order because under the consent of the Diet this Act did not generally legalize this type of business but allowed it as an exception limited to special businesses. These businesses were allowed under the principle that they required professional knowledge, skill and experience such as computer programming, or a special kind of labour management such as cleaning of buildings. But the number of registered workers increased from 140,000 in 1986 to 860,000 in 1998.

From the business point of view, the sphere of businesses should be extended in order to make Japanese employment practice more flexible. 10 new types of businesses were allowed on December 10, 1996. In total, 26 types of businesses are permitted under the present regulation.

Another point of deregulation was introduced to this Act. Dispatched workers are allowed to replace workers on maternity leave or on leave to care for children or elderly relatives in every type of business apart from port transport services, construction work and security guard work. The period of work is limited to one year or the maximum length of time for those on care leave for children or elder relatives. And workers older than 60 and less than 65 years can be dispatched in every type of businesses except port transport services, construction work and security guard work. The period is restricted to one year and the dispatch contract cannot be renewed. The purpose of this deregulation is to secure employment to elder persons above 60 and under 65 years because the eligible age for the pension is to be raised gradually from 60 to 65 years.

Under the amendment of Act in 1999 drastic change was made to adopt negative list system, which legalized generally worker-dispatching business, and lists prohibited businesses exceptionally. This exceptional case is port transport services, construction work, security guard work, manufacturing, medical services, business of practising lawyer, chartered accountants, judicial scriveners, etc. that is regulated by each special Acts.

Under 2003 amendment, the next drastic change was made to allow dispatched workers engaging in manufacturing industry and medical services in social welfare facilities provided by medical doctors, dentists and nurses. This work dispatch for the same work was limited for one year during 2003-2006 although the period shall be extended up to three years in 26 specialized types of works. But this one-year period shall be extended to three years from March 1, 2007. From April 1, 2006, medical services can be possible to hospitals at outlying regions and islands.

(3) Deregulation of the Labour Standards Act

Important provisions of the Labour Standards Act were proposed to be amended under the deregulation policy of the Labour Ministry. These proposals were enacted on 25 September 1998.

(a) Period of Labour Contract

A labour contract may be concluded for a definite or an indefinite term. Article 14 prohibited fixing a term of more than one year, except where the labour contract shall terminate upon completion of a specific project, such as construction of a dam. This provision has a policy to prevent negative effects caused by binding a worker for a long year. But recently only a little negative effects can be found. Rather longer period of labour contract is needed to complete some works such as research projects. So under the amendment provisions effective from January 1, 2004, the maximum period will be extended to three years except labour contract terminated upon completion of a specific project, but a worker can terminate labour contract at any time just after the end of one year. In exceptional cases, the period will be limited to 5 years only for the employment of workers with highly professional knowledge, skill or experience stipulated by the Minister of Labour and elder workers above 60 years. Deregulation of the labour contract is widened to the job requiring highly specialized knowledge and skills (for example, attorney, attorney for patent, chartered accountant, doctor, dentist) and elder workers more than 60 years old to secure employment opportunities for experts and elder workers.

(b) Working Hour Regulation on Discretionary Work

The Labour Standards Act has adopted a discretionary work system since April 1, 1988 to give discretionary power to decide how to offer services to some kinds of workers. This amendment has a purpose to expand the sphere of discretionary work system. This is one of deregulation policies in the field of labour.

Under this system, employees engaging in highly specialized and discretionary work such as research and development are deemed to have worked for a certain number of hours as set forth in the collective agreement in spite of their actual working hours. Due to the nature of such employee's duties, it is difficult for an employer to indicate the means of accomplishment and to allocate working hours. Thus the employees have a wide discretionary power to decide the method of accomplishment and the allocation of working hours.

At present, the discretionary work system covers employees involved in research and development of new products and techniques, analysis and planning on information-management systems, gathering of materials and editing, designing, and the occupation of producer and director. Ministerial Order stipulates the sphere of discretionary work system. From April 1997, the following six types of workers are included in the category of discretionary work; high level architect, patent attorney, real estate appraiser, lawyer, chartered accountant and copywriter. Totally 11 occupations are eligible for the discretionary work system

Under the amendment provisions in 1998 and 2003, new categories of works are extended for the discretionary work scheme, the new one is the occupation of planning, researching and analyzing operations which shall be decided as the discretionary work by the consent of all members at a labour-management committee to be established within the company. This aims to extend discretionary work into a part of occupations in the administration division. National center of labour unions (Rengo) objects the bill because the discretionary work system shall prolong the actual working hours spent in company and cut the time the workers will spend with their families. So Rengo contends that this system should be limited to workers who have real decision-making powers, and that the attempt to expand its sphere of application to new occupation is dangerous, as it may increase the number of occupation immune to working hour regulation. On the other hand, Nikkeiren (Japanese Employers' Association) maintains that this system should be extended to jobs such as planner of business strategy, sales, finance and so forth because the employers can save labour cost.

(c) Flexibility of Working Hour Regulation

There are four types of flexible work hour system, which allow an unequal distribution of normal working hours per day or per week under the amendment of the Labour Standards Act in 1987 and 1998.

In the first type of flexible working hour system, an employee can work for more than 8 hours on a special day, or 40 hours in a special week, if the average number of working hours for one month does not exceed 40 hours in a week. In this case an employer must stipulate in the rules of employment or the equivalent that the average working hours per week for a fixed period of no more than one month will not exceed maximum working hours. The amendment of this Act in 1998 provides that a labour-management agreement can introduce flexible working hours for one month in addition to the rules of employment.

The second type applies over a period not exceeding one year and more than one month. This system is effective in industries with frequent shifts between busy and slack seasons. The labour-management agreement must stipulate the workers covered and fix daily working hours and holidays. The weekly working hours cannot exceed an average of 40 hours under the labour-management agreement stipulated in advance between the majority union or the representative of majority employees and the employer. The daily maximum limit shall be set at 10 hours per day and 52 hours per week and rest day shall be set every 6 working days.

As the third, in certain categories (e.g. retail sales, hotels and restaurants), small enterprises employing less than 30 employees may extend the daily maximum up to ten hours within a 40 hour work upon the conclusion of a labour-management agreement.

The fourth flextime system allows workers to decide the commencement and termination of working hours within the rules of employment and a labour-management agreement to stipulate the framework of the system. The agreement must stipulate the scope of employees involved, the period of average work hour in less than one month, and the total hours of work during the period.

(d) Rest Periods

Employees who have worked more than 6 hours are entitled to rest periods totaling 45 minutes. At least one hour must be granted to those who have worked more than 8 hours. The rest periods must be given to all employees at the same time. The reasons are to ensure effective rest periods to the workers and to supervise rest periods easily exercised by the Labour Standards Inspector.

Permission to grant rest periods on an alternating basis may be obtained from the Chief of the Prefectural Labour Standard Office under Article 34 of the Labour Standards Act. This permission can be got in the following cases.

- where the workers are working at shift work system,
- where there is necessity to prevent dangers,
- where the operation requires different rest periods even at the same workplace, and
- where alternating rest periods are necessary if the workers are divided into two groups.

The amendment in 1998 stipulates that rest periods on an alternating basis can be introduced under a labour-management agreement. It shall delete the permission from the Chief of the Prefectural Labour Standards Office.

(e) Overtime Work and Work on Holidays

Overtime work or work on holidays is allowed fewer than two conditions. One is the conclusion of an agreement with the majority union or with the representative of the majority of the employees in the absence of the majority union; the other is submission on the agreement to the Labour Standards Office. The agreement should specify matters such as the business reasons for which it will be necessary to require overtime work and work on holidays, the type of overtime work permitted and the hours of overtime work permitted. There is no limit to the hours of overtime work and work on holidays except a maximum of two hours per day in the case of underground labour or jobs injurious to health. But the Labour Ministry has issued administrative guidelines on the maximum hours of overtime work in order to reduce working hours.

The Labour Ministry guideline on maximum overtime work is as follows; 15 hour per week, 27 hours per two weeks, 43 hours per four weeks, 45 hours per one month, 81 hours per two months, 120 hours per three months and 360 hours per year. This guideline has no legal force. An employer should not be punished even if he would violate the guideline. But the amendment in 1998 provides that the upper limit standard should be given legal standing under a ministerial notification for the Chief Labour Standards Office to five advices and instruction to those violating it. This fives stronger power to the Labour Standards Office to enforce the limit of overtime work than before. Regulation policy, in the contrary, is adopted in this field because the Labour Ministry thinks it important to reduce annual working hours in order to harmonize family and work life. And as another reason behind this Japan is demanded to keep fair trade by reducing working hours by other countries, especially USA.

4. LEGAL DEVELOPMENT OF EQUAL EMPLOYMENT

Since International Women's Year in 1975 and the ratification of the Convention concerning the Elimination of All Forms of Discrimination against Women in 1979, many steps have been taken by the Labour Ministry to promote equality in employment between both sexes. The important action was the enactment of Equal Employment Opportunities Act (hereinafter referred as EEOA) in 1985. About ten years have passed after this Act was effective. So recently the Labour Ministry has showed important legislative developments. Namely the amendment of EEOA and other related provision of the Labour Standards Act were enacted in June 1997 and were effective from April 1, 1999. And Child Care and Family Care Leave Act (hereinafter referred as CCFCA) was enacted in 1995 and was effective from April 1, 1999. These Acts have two purposes; one is to prohibit sexual discrimination, the other to harmonize work and family life. For these purposes, regulation on these Acts was rather strengthened. But we can also find some deregulations of overtime, holiday and night work by women under the amendment of the Labour Standards Act in 1997.

Under EEOA of 1985, the employer has a duty to endeavour to give equal opportunities to women when recruiting and hiring workers, and with regard to job assignment and promotion. "Duty to endeavour" has brought only moral duty to the employer without legal sanction against the violation of the Act. At the most this has provided the basis for administrative guidance. But the amendment of EEOA stipulates that the employer shall be prohibited to discriminate against women with regard to recruitment, hiring, job assignment and promotion. This provision nullifies the labour contract, which violates it, and the employer who violates it may be claimed damages in tort suits. But it does not carry criminal punishments.

The employer shall not discriminate between both sexes as regards vocational training, fringe benefits such as loans for building or purchasing a house or children education, and mandatory retirement or dismissal. These provisions have not been changed under the amendment to EEOA.

The Act provides for administrative guidance and mediation procedure as the machinery for enforcing the employer's duty. Employers are obliged to endeavour voluntarily to resolve complaints by referring them to the grievance machinery in their own `companies composed of representatives of labour and management. The Director of Prefectural Women's and Young Workers' Office (local agency of the labour Ministry) is empowered to give assistance in the resolution of disputes on sex discrimination. The Director shall refer disputes to mediation by the Equal Opportunity Mediation Commission composed of three members appointed by the Labour Ministry from among "people of learning and experience", if both parties agree to the referral. But this mediation procedure is not almost utilized because it is difficult to obtain both parties' consent for the referral and the settlement proposal by the Commission has no binding effect to both parties. Therefore, the amendment of EEOA provides that the Commission shall be involved on the request of one party concerned. And it introduces a new sanction of publicizing the name of a non-complying company.

There are no provisions to prohibit sexual harassment under EEOA before. Therefore, women suffering from sexual harassment must claim damages in torts suits on Article 709 or 715 of the Civil Code or under the infringement of employer's duties to provide comfortable conditions to women under Article 415 of the Civil Code. We can find above 60 labour cases on sexual harassment, which almost ended in favour of women. The courts found the employer's liability in torts on the ground that the employer infringed human dignity and sexual freedom of female employees. The amendment of EEOA introduces a new provision that the employers shall endeavour to prevent sexual harassment in the workplace. The administrative guidance is laid down for the employer to take care of employment management in order to prevent sexual harassment.

As above-mentioned, employment equality between both sexes is being fairly promoted through the recent legislative development. But there are advantageous provisions on female workers in the Labour Standards Act. These provisions must be abolished in order to attain equality in working conditions. So regulations on overtime, night and holiday work for female workers were abolished from April 1, 1999 in exchange for the strengthening of EEOA. Female workers are eligible for the same provisions on overtime, night and holiday work with male workers. This is a deregulation of the Labour Standards Act on female workers. As a result, the employer will apply the same work systems, which are used for men to women. So women workers are afraid of longtime works which will deprive them of job opportunities because they continue to do house work including child care and nursing care.

EEOA was amended in 2006 to prohibit indirect discrimination. Under Art. 6, employers shall not discriminate against employees by reason of sex in case of allocation of work, promotion, demotion, training, and fringe benefit, change of job and employment type, retirement and dismissal. Under Art. 7, measures associated with recruit, employment and etc. shall not be taken by employers except on the reasonable ground (for example, the measure is specially necessary to implement the occupation or to promote labour management) when it would have possibility to impede substantially the securing of equal opportunity under the provisions of Ministerial Order. This provision is made to prohibit indirect discrimination. For the time being, Ministerial Order limits indirect discrimination to three cases: considering length and weight at the time of recruitment and hiring, hiring on condition that she can move from workplace any where in Japan, and promotion on condition that she has experiences to move from workplaces. This shall arrest sex discrimination stronger than before.

CCFCA prohibits night work to men and women workers responsible for childcare or family care under their requests from April 1, 1999. Some of the conditions to apply night work exemption are: a child must not be in a primary school. Family member (it means spouse of the worker, parents, child, parents of spouse, grand parents, siblings and grandchild dependent of the worker) must have the necessity to be cared for more than two weeks. Only female workers requesting a night work exemption can designate the period of the exemption before one month. The request can be allowed multiple times. This exemption comes from the policy to harmonize work and family life. Three years later it will be amended that not only female workers but also male workers responsible for child and family care can request to exempt night work.

CONCLUSION

Deregulation of labour laws is mainly targeting in the field of individual labour contract and labour market in Japan. Collective labour relations are not discussed in regard to the deregulation. Because there are few direct regulations that are not discussed with regard to the deregulation. Because there are few direct regulations of the government on collective labour relation. Though Trade Unions Act was enacted, it has had only the basic framework for collective labour relations. So it has the flexible structure to keep freedom of association, collective bargaining, and the right to strike. Enterprise-wise unions and joint consultation have been voluntarily based, not depending upon statutory regulations. "Industrial autonomy" has been established through collective bargaining and joint consultation between labour and management. Therefore, the government has had a little interventional role in establishing industrial relations. Now in Japan there is no discussion on the deregulation of collective labour relations. But union density is declining from 30.8% in 1990 to 22.4% in 1998 and 18% in 2005. This is the sign that the sphere of industrial autonomy is becoming smaller and the function of collective bargaining is weakened. On the contrary, individual labour contract is of importance to regulate working conditions.

How does the deregulation of individual labour law and labour market have influenced employment practices? Are these influences useful to structural adjustment for recovering economic recession? Do new businesses increase in number? Long-time employment has been a big feature, which maintains stable employment in Japan. Even in economic recession employment security has been kept through flexible deployment of employees or flexible working conditions in an enterprise. Dismissal including economic dismissal is thought to be the last resort. Employment security can be possible under the flexibility in internal labour market such as flexible working hours and abolishment of female workers regulations.

The fluidification of employment may come from either voluntary choice of worker or convenience of the company. Recently young workers want to have freedom to change jobs for grade-up of their careers. Middle-aged or old workers are sometimes retrenched or laid off owing to bankruptcy. And unemployment rate stood at 4.8 percent in March 1999. The unemployment rate for those aged 15 to 24 was 9.1 percent and for those 60 and 64 was 12.1 percent. This is the highest figure since 1953, which suggests that the employment situation is rapidly worse.

As a result, long-time employment practice will be weaker than before, but will not disappear because only core regular workers will enjoy long-time employment based on seniority-*cum*-merit management system. There will increase atypical workers such as part-time and dispatched workers especially in banking, insurance, wholesale, retail and catering businesses who need an employment fluidication policy to be able to find new employments easily at external labour market. Private employment agencies and dispatching businesses are necessary for this purpose. The workers holding high technology and special knowledge can enjoy better working conditions under individualized labour contract. But in general atypical workers have received worse working conditions than core regular workers. So we must give utmost protection to the atypical workers concerned who will be treated with discrimination.

As the last point we must make a mention of international pressure which requests with Japan of fair trade. Japan shall avoid criticism that it exports cheap goods in large quantities made by low labour costs. For the purpose Japan must show labour policy to keep fair and international labour standards, especially ILO Conventions. ILO Convention No. 181 urges to make labour market flexible. On the other hand, UN Convention to eliminate discrimination against women presses to strengthen the regulations of EEOA.

It is now clear that all the labour acts are not deregulated in Japan. There shall be fair balance between regulation and deregulation of labour acts. Regulation is necessary to protect weak workers who need direct state intervention. On the other hand, there are some workers demanding deregulation of labour law acts who have bargaining powers individually to decide working conditions. There shall be labour acts treating two kinds of worker parties differently.

{This original paper was printed in a Journal of International Cooperation Studies (Kobe University, Graduate School of International Cooperation Studies), Vol. 6, No. 1, and 1999}.

References

This original paper was submitted to the International Symposium on Labour Law and Social Security in Asia-Pacific Area held at Peking University in October 1998.

New bill will be discussed in the Diet held in Spring of 1999.

The amendment of the Labour Standards Act in 1998 is the most comprehensive one since its enactment. In addition to the topics in this paper the following are amended; specification of working conditions, notice of reasons for termination of labour contract, annual paid holiday, level up of minimum age for labour, labour dispute resolution system where the Labour Standards Office can give advice or instruction to the concerned parties.

In the case of flexible work hour system for one year the upper limit of overtime work is as follows: 14 hours per one week, 25 hours per two weeks, 40 hours per three weeks, 42 hours per one month, 75 hours per two months, 110 hours per three months, 320 hours per one year.

Art 709 of the Civil Code: A person who intentionally or negligently violates the rights of another is obliged to compensate for damages arising there from.

Art.715 of the Civil Code: Section 1. A person who employs another person for a certain undertaking is liable for damages caused by such employees to third person in the selection of the employees and in the supervision over the undertaking, or unless the damages would have arisen even if due care had been exercised.

Section 2. A person who supervises the undertaking on behalf of the employer is also subjected to the responsibility of the preceding paragraph.

Section 3. The provision of the preceding two paragraphs shall not prevent an employer or supervisor from exercising his right to reimbursement from the employees.

Art. 415 of the Civil Code: If an obligor fails to perform in accordance with the main sense of the obligation-duty, the oblige may demand compensation for damages; the same shall apply in the cases where performance becomes impossible for any reason imputable to the obligor.

In the case of female workers overtime works were limited in the following; 6 hours per one week and 150 hours per one year for female workers engaged in manufacturing, mining, construction, transport and freight traffic industry, 12 hours per one year for those engaged in forestry, commerce, banking and insurance, cinema and drama, communication, education and research, cleaning and slaughter industry.

Takashi Araki, "Deregulation of Japanese Reforms of Labour Market System", in *The Change of Labour Market Regulation and the Theme of Labour Law System*, Japan Institute of Labour, March 1997.

Takashi Araki, "Recent Legislative Developments in Equal Employment and Harmonization of Work and Family Life in Japan", *Japan Laboiur Bulletin*, Vol. 37, No. 4, April 1998.

Hisaaki Fujikawa, " Changing Japanese Labour Legislation in the 1990's", *Proceedings of New Trends of Labour Law in Asia-Pacific Region*, Aoyama Gakuin University, March 1998 (unpublished).

Kozo Kagawa, "Japan" in *Employment Terms and Conditions in Asia-Pascific 1998/991*

Watson Wyatt (Hong Kong), January 1998.

Ryuichi Yamakawa, "Overhaul After 50 Years: The Amendment of the Labour Standards Law", *Japan Labour Bulletin* Vol. 37, No. 11, November 1998.

CHAPTER

6

Child Labour in Japan

INTRODUCTION

Recently little concern has been shown for the problem of child labour in Japan. The main reason for this is that there exists no serious problem in the field of child labour. Since Japan has achieved a rapid growth of the economy, it becomes less necessary for a child to get his livelihood. Even nowadays we can surely find some children working as deliverers of newspapers, child actors or part-timers during the vacations. And it is reported that there are some cases of violations of the Labour Standards Act on child labour, which will be explained later. But the ratio of working children is quite low. Japanese children are very busy in studying and they are often compelled to study at home after school or at weekend classes, which are different from the formal school system, for examination preparation. So in the sphere of child education we really have a lot of problems. In the field of labour, however, children are losing their place. According to this change in workforce the child labour is no longer the main subject in the formulation of national labour policy. For example, the administrative agency dealing with child labour is reduced in size and personnel through the administrative reform held in July 1984.

However, even in Japan there had been many problems on child labour until thirty years ago. So in this paper I would like to delineate some important historical facts and social policy associated with such problems. Japanese industrialization had been accomplished by introducing advanced Western technology. Manpower for it was mainly composed of three groups. The first was traditional craftsmen who were retrained to be skilled workers. The second was children of former samurais, craftsmen and peasants who had migrated to the cities. The third was female workers. As in all other capitalistic countries, women and children in Japan had worked as cheap labourers under miserable working conditions at the beginning of industrialization.

It was reported that there existed the phenomenon of tormenting sweat work for children since 1880. According to the Imperial Statistics Yearbook of 1882, children younger than 15 of age formed 16.5 percent of the whole private industrial workers. Taking a closer look according to the division of industry, 18.1 percent of the workforce in the textile industry, 14.1 percent in the chemical industry, 8.1 percent in the metal and machine industry consisted of children. In 1902 child employees under the age of 14 amounted to 65,433 and formed 13.1 percent of all industrial workers. Since then the ratio of employed children declined. (See Table 1, 2)

As the result of the industrial development in the 1900's, the demand for factory labour exceeded the local manpower supplied by the voluntary migration to industrial towns. Especially, in the textile industry it became necessary to recruit from the rural districts. Recruiting agents visited villages and described the conditions of work in exaggerated terms, over-emphasizing advantages and concealing disadvantages to satisfy the demand on the part of entrepreneur for child workforce. Children were employed for two or three years' duration on contracts between the employer and the children's parents who were in desperate need of money. Children whose employment was initiated as guarantee for the loans, which their parents had been given, were deprived of freedom. Wages were fixed in advance for the whole period of the contract. The amount of money corresponding to these advance was deducted out of the children's earnings. Children who came from rural areas had to be accommodated in factory dormitories, always to be watched lest they should escape from their miserable conditions of work in the factories.

In 1886 the compulsory education system was introduced in Japan by the Ordinance on Primary School. But the Ordinance prescribed that children whose guardians were economically poor were excused from attending schools. This system continued until 1941. The amendment of the Ordinance in 1900 prohibited an employer from employing children who had not completed the course of primary school. As a measure to facilitate the continued schooling for these children evening class was attached to the primary school.

Child labour was one of the first fields in which labour standards had been adopted. These standards centered mainly on the minimum age for admission to employment. In Japan the first statute for the protection of children was the Factory Act in 1911. This act did not come into force until 1916 because of the serious employers' opposition. Main features of the act are as follows:

(1) It applied to factories regularly employing more than fifteen workers or to those engaged in dangerous or hazardous work.

(2) The minimum age for admission to employment was fixed at twelve years of age. But a worker who was more than ten years old when this act came into effect could be employed. And light work had to be allocated for a child above ten years of age with the permission of the Factory Inspector.

(3) The working hour for a worker less than 15 years of age restricted within 12 hours, provided that until 15 years after the act had come into operation, it could be extended by two more hours. As a general rule night work from 10 p.m. to 5 a.m. was prohibited for young workers less than sixteen years of age and women. However, such workers were permitted to work until 11 p.m. with the sanction of the Factory Inspector. Moreover, there were some special cases in which the prohibition of night work was not applied depending on the industry.

As is clear from the above, this act had some serious problems. Young workers who did not apply were absolutely unprotected. This act covered only 30 percent of all the industrial workers because of the limited sphere of application. Moreover, there were cases where an employer purposely split the factories or reduce the size of them only to avoid the act's application. When the Factory Inspector came to the factory, the employers ordered children to hide themselves or to go home. It also happened that when this act came into effect, many child workers were discharged. Eventually they were employed in the factories, which were excluded from its application or became loafers or prostitutes.

According to the first national census held in 1920, it was estimated that the number of workers less than 14 years of age was about 1,150,000 (about 7 percent of all the workers). Workers in agriculture amounted to about 487,000, those in manufacturing 415,000, and those in commerce 112,000. It also should be noted that the number of domestic servants was close to 658,000. The Factory Act did not protect them. Among children above 10 and under 12 years of age only 3,321 were engaged in light work with the permission of the Factory Inspector. They were employed mainly in packing in match factories and preparation work in textile factories. This figure revealed that so many children worked without permission.

The amended Factory Act of 1923 applied to the factories (1) where ten or more workers were employed regularly or (2) where the work was of a dangerous or injurious to health regardless of the number of the workers employed. It also provided that the daily hours of work for women and young workers under 16 years of age should not exceed eleven hours, including a break of one hour. But during the first two years of the operation of the amendment, the limitation was extended to twelve hours a day.

The prohibition of night work came in to force from July 1, 1929. In 1922, 2,35,870 protected workers (child and woman workers) were employed in twenty hour operations. In general, the measure to prohibit night work did not reduce the working hours as a whole, because the workers protected were compelled to work on holidays.

The second census in 1930 revealed that the ratio of workers to whom the amendment of Factory Act applied was 39.1 percent of all the industrial workers employed. As can be seen from this figure the extent of its application was widened little by little.

In 1923 the Act concerning Minimum Age of Industrial Workers was enacted. This Act was enforced from July 1, 1926. And the I.L.O. Convention No. 5 was ratified. It lifted minimum age from 12 to 14. But children more than 12 years of age could be employed if they completed primary school curriculum. Therefore, the clause that light work was allowed for a child less than 123 years of age was repealed.

The government intervened to regulate recruiting by issuing the Regulation for the control of the recruiting of workers by private persons with fees in 1924. And also in 1925 the Regulation for the control of profit-making employment agencies was promulgated, placing such agencies under the strict control of administrative authorities.

The Ordinance for the administration of the Factory Act stated that wages should be paid at least once a month in cash. The Ordinance allowed that part of wages to be deduced from cash payment as savings. It only required that the employer should establish a scheme for the administration of savings fund. And it was considered illegal to make a contract of employment, which fixed in advance either the sum payable to the employer for breach of contract or the amount of indemnity for damages. But these clauses did so little to protect child labour. In fact savings was compulsory and in practice it served as a means to prevent turnover of a child worker from sweating labour. And also the contract of indemnity restrained child workers to resign from jobs. (See Table 3)

The Factory Act prohibited employment of workers less than 16 years of age to do work injurious to health, such as handling of harmful or poisonous materials and labour industry surroundings. But in reality particularly in spinning factories cotton mill girls suffered from tuberculosis due to long working hours and night work and the bad environment of work.

The Social Bureau was established in the Home Affairs Ministry in 1920 to deal with labour problems and those of social welfare. So problems on child labour fell under the jurisdiction of the Social Bureau. In 1938 the Social Bureau became a part of the Ministry of Health and Welfare. On September 1, 1947 the Ministry of Labour was separated from the Ministry of Health and Welfare under the direction of the Labour section of the ESCAP.

Following the gold panic of April 1927 and the world unrest of 1929, Japan experienced the so-called Showa Era panic of 1930. This upheaval produced serious effect on the livelihood of the nation. Especially in the rural areas the well-being of farmers become worse than before because of this panic and the low level production of agriculture. So their children were compelled to work to make additional house income and in some cases became prostitutes to pay their parents' debts.

In 1911 Korea was amalgamated into Japan and Korean workers were given free access to Japan. They often worked in coalmines, textile industry and chemical factories as cheap labourers. Also their children were employed in small enterprises. They were treated discriminatorily in wages and working conditions. After the Manchurian Incident in 1939, a considerable number of Korean labourers were forced to immigrate to Japan.

Japan developed war economies after the Manchurian Incident. However, since young workers were conscripted to the military, labour forces were short in supply for producing war materials. In March 1938 the National General Mobilization Act was enacted to give Premier the broad discretional power over the conducts of domestic affairs. Under this act the government began to take wartime procedures for the control of the national economy, systematically allocating labourers and materials to meet the planned national needs. So manpower control was strengthened, and it brought forth the intensification of labour. So working hours of children became longer and longer. Students of middle and high schools were drafted into the ammunition industry.

In 1940 Restriction of Young Workers' Employment Regulation prohibited male workers more than 12 and under 30 years of age, and female workers more than 12 and under 20 years of age to change their working places without the permission of the Minister of Health and Welfare. Still more Martial Exception Regulation ceased the effectiveness of protective provisions of the Factory Act in 1943.

After World War II, Japan was faced with the destruction of the economic base. Most of the cities had been devastated by air attack with about a quarter of the housing accommodation of the country destroyed. A crisis of inflation was in progress. War-stricken families and war orphans were short of food and other necessaries of living. According to the investigation of the Ministry of Health and Welfare in 1947, there were 28,245 war orphans and 11,351 orphans who were repatriated with problems of women and minors.

Let us examine legal situation on child labour after the war. Section 3 of Article 27 of the Constitution of 1946 prohibits the exploitation of children. This provision has been the base for the legislative protection of child labour. The Children's Charter based on the spirit of the Constitution was proclaimed on May 5, (Children's Day) 1952 as official guidelines for nation's policy for children.

The Labour Standards Act, which is the most basic statute in the field of contract of employment law, was enacted and carried into force on September 1, 1947 in place of the former Factory Act. This Act does not apply to any enterprises or offices that employ only relatives living with the employer as family members, nor to domestic employees in the home. The scope of application becomes much wider than the Factory Act. The protective provisions of the Act are as follows:

(1) Minors under full 15 years old shall not be employed as workers. Under the 6-3-3-4-education system introduced under the guidance of the Allied Occupation of Japan, compulsory education is provided for age 6 to 15. As a result, the minimum age of work becomes 15. (Under the amendment in 1998, a minor until the end of the first March 31 after a minor has reached 15 years of age shall not be employed) But children above full 12 years old may be employed in light labour on the condition that it is not injurious to the health and welfare of the children and that work-hours are outside of school hours, with the permission of the Chief of the Labour Standards Inspection Office.

The Chief of the Labour Standards Inspection Office shall not give the permission to the jobs mentioned below.

(a) Job performing circus or acrobatic feats for public amusement;

(b) Job of singing, playing and making other performances from house to house or on the streets and other similar places;
(c) Job in hotels, restaurants, snack bars and recreation halls;
(d) Job of operating elevators; and
(e) In addition to those mentioned in each of the preceding items jobs specified by the Minster of Labour.

Children under full 12 years old may be employed in motion-picture production dramatic performance enterprises with the permission of the Labour Standards Office.

(2) The employer shall keep a certificate at the working place issued by schoolmaster to make sure that the employer does not hinder the schooling of the children, together with the document to show the consent of the parents of guardians. Also the employer shall keep a copy of the census register, which proves the age of the minors under full 13 years old at the working place.

(3) Under the civil law minors under 20 years of age cannot conclude any kind of contract without the permission of their parents or guardians, except in the case of the contracts by which they solely receive rights or are exempted from obligations. But the parents or guardians shall not make a labour contract in place of the minors by Article 58 of the Labour Standards Act. Therefore, the parents or guardians and the administrative office authorized to cancel the contract for the future if they consider it unfair to the minors.

(4) The minor has the right to receive wages as a person independent from his parents or guardians. The parents or guardians shall not receive as proxy the wages earned by the minor.

(5) For children under 15 years old maximum working hour is 7 hours a day, 42 hours a week including school hours. They are prohibited to work from 8 p.m. to 5 a.m. Overtime work, holiday work and underground work are prohibited for minors under 18 years old Night work is prohibited except those over 16 years old who are working on shift. Also minors under 18 years old are prohibited from working in the dangerous and harmful jobs.

(6) The employer shall bear the necessary fare when minors under full-18 years old wish to return home within 14 days after dismissal. However, this does not apply if minors under full 18 years old were dismissed by reasons for which they are responsible and if the employer receives authorization from the administrative office after explaining the grounds for dismissal.

Now let us report the factual situation on child labour after the World War II. According to the census in 1950, number of children employed of 10-13 years of age was about 293,000. Of them 90 percent was engaged in agriculture, 4 percent in wholesale and 3 percent in manufacturing. They formed 0.8 percent of the total labour force.

According to the employment situation of children based on employment certificate by occupation from April 1950 to March 1951, the total number of permissions was 5586. The number of news deliverers was 3938 and it took up 70 percent of the children permitted to work. The next number was 487 who were engaged in putting paper bags on apples. The third number was 235 child actors.

During the immediate post-war period, there was a serious problem of children working on the streets. Children in town worked in selling newspapers, flowers, peanuts and fermented soybeans and shoe shining. They could not easily get employment opportunity and they earned much more than the hired children whose substantial income was decreasing because of high speed of inflation. Children engaged in the street-works were labouring till midnight at amusement quarters. They often missed schools for a long time and eventually became juvenile delinquents.

Until the 1950s we could find cases of so-called human traffic in which children were compelled to work against their will and in violation of child welfare. And from 1955 approximately to 1960 it became a serious problem to reduce the number. The Ministry of Education 1954 showed that long-term absentees for more than 50 days reached 289,435 in number. It occupied 1.8 percent of the total students of the primary and middle schools. (See Table 4)

From the latter half of 1950s, Japan has changed into an industrialized country from an agricultural country with the rapid expansion of economy. Labour force engaged in agriculture was reduced. The percentage of the labour force employed in primary industry declined from 48.3 percent in 1945 to 32.9 percent in 1960, 24.7 percent in 1963 and 19.3 percent in 1970. The ratio of the labour force engages in

TABLE 1

Labour Force of Children (less than 13 years old)

Year	*Total*	*Male*	*Female*	*Ratio of the Total Population*	*Ratio of the Total Labour Force*
1920	770594	332213	438381	1.39%	2.86%
1930	465984	172881	293103	0.73%	1.59%
1940	284851	95333	189518	0.40%	0.88%
1950	307000	169000	138000	0.37%	0.84%

Source: Report of National Census, 1950.

TABLE 2

Number of Employees by Age and Industry

Year		Spinning and Weaving		Machinery		Chemistry		Food Products		Miscellaneous		Special Industry		Total	
		(A)	(B)	(A)	(B)	(A)	(B)	(A)	(B)	(A)	(B)	(A)	(B)	(A)	(B)
1902	Total	269165	26454	34962	901	82298	30714	30153	1481	32308	4237	50614	1686	498891	65433
	Male	32699	1985	33379	692	38615	9745	16837	429	20729	1927	43363	1018	185622	15806
	Female	236457	24468	938	209	43683	20969	13316	1052	11579	2310	7251	618	313269	49627
1911	Total	475385	44389	71088	2118	69573	6719	47124	1156	57954	5875	72761	756	793885	61013
	Male	67218	2609	67271	1980	47157	3584	34202	489	37831	3646	63797	487	317378	12192
	Female	408275	41780	3817	138	22414	3135	12922	670	20123	2829	8964	267	476497	48821
1913	Total	540073	50989	93239	2226	80170	6908	43130	953	73208	7051	86432	830	916252	68957
	Male	71144	3094	88245	2079	54930	3568	35856	541	47634	3810	77787	536	375596	13628
	Female	468929	47895	4994	147	25240	3340	7274	412	25574	3241	8645	294	540656	55329

Notes: (A) = Number of Total Employees
(B) = Number of Employees under 14 years old

Source: Ministry of Agriculture and Industry Statistics, 1902, 1911, and 1913.

TABLE 3

Indices of Wage differentials by Age for Production Workers in Manufacturing Industries, 1927-1973(a)

(Age 20-24 = 100)

Age	*1927*	*1933*	*1936*	*1938*	*1948*	*1958*	*1960*	*1965*	*1970*	*1973*
Males										
12-13	30	27	29	34	—	—	—	—	—	—
14-15	37	36	37	41	57	52	52	58	59	60
16-17	52	65	65	66						
18-19	72				71	74	75	76	81	80
20-24	100	100	100	100	100	100	100	100	100	100
25-29	125	128	124	118	126	137	133	124	127	121
30-34	142	149	145	131	148	170	167	144	144	142
35-39	154	164	161	142	163	191	189	158	151	146
40-44	159	175	174	149	166	207	208	169	160	155
45-49	157	182	181	151						158
50-54	151	182	181	143	145	172	170	159	149	164
55-59	129	131	138	111						118
60+	109	109	109	93	106	—	—	106	100	92

Female										
12-13	46	50	58	62	—	—	—	—	—	—
14-15	61	63	69	75						
16-17	79	83	86	91	75	69	73	80	79	85
18-19	92				89	85	88	91	91	94
20-24	100	100	100	100	100	100	100	100	100	100
25-29	102	108	110	103	109	116	111	101	100	100
30-34	104	114	115	102	117	109	105	96	90	86
35-39	104	117	117	98	127	105		94	90	85
40-44	103	119	118	98	121	106	101	94	92	92
45-49	99	121	121	94						90
50-54	94	113	113	86	111	98		94	91	98
55-59	86	92	94	77						98

Notes: (a) Wages include various allowance payments. The data up to 1938 are daily wages and the data for 1948 and thereafter are monthly wages.

(b) The age bracket 14-17 in the post-World War II period corresponds to all ages younger than 17.

(c) The data for females 60 and older deleted from this table

Source: The data from 1927 to 1938 were obtained from Office of the Prime Minister, Bureau of Statistics, Rodolokei Jitchi Chosa [Survey of Labour Statistics] (Selected years), and 1948 to 1973 are from the Ministry of Labour, Chinginkozo Kihontokei Chosa [Basic Survey of Wage Structures] (selected years). Quoted from unpublished data compiled by Ryohei Magota, prepared for the Japan Wage Research Center, Comprehensive Seminar on Wages, 1975.

TABLE 4

Number of Arrests for Offences: (so-called human trafficking)

Year	*Number Suspects*	*Number of Victims*	
		Total	*Under 18 years*
1953	5549	7249	2095
1954	5511	8635	1802
1955	10269	14291	2912
1956	11044	15595	2690
1957	11705	16682	2427

Source: Criminal Division, Police Agency "Report of Crime Statistics".

TABLE 5

Per-capita National Income: 1934-1959

Year	*Nominal Income*		*Real Income*	
	sum (yen)	*index*	*sum (yen)*	*index*
1934-36	210	1.0	210	100
1937	266	1.3	231	110
1938	284	1.4	225	107.1
1939	359	1.7	237	112.8
1940	434	2.1	225	107.1
1941	500	2.4	233	110.9
1942	582	2.8	223	106.2
1943	660	3.1	220	104.7
1944	771	3.7	209	99.5
1946	4791	22.8	109	51.9
1947	12431	59.1	112	53.3
1948	24543	116.9	128	60.9
1949	33501	159.5	144	68.6
1950	40659	193.6	168	80
1951	53569	255.1	182	86.7
1952	59299	282.4	197	93.8
1953	66078	314.7	206	98.1
1954	68281	325.1	209	99.5
1955	75234	358.3	230	109.5

1956	83975	399.8	247	117.6
1957	90276	429.9	262	124.8
1958	92472	440.3	275	131
1959	107515	512	314	149.5

Source: Economic Planning Agency, Survey of Economic Statistics, 1961.

TABLE 6

Number of Child Workers Granted Permission by the Labour Standard Office

Year	*Number of Application*	*Number of Permission*
1	*2*	*3*
1948		4911
1949		4504
1950		5438
1951		4847
1952		5068
1953		9440
1954	8921	8344
1955	9937	9855
1956	10639	10047
1957	27689	26369
1958	14145	13397
1959	12610	12071
1960	19940	19461
1961	16218	15796
1962	17229	16925
1963	39556	38287
1964	25527	24966
1965	22695	22199
1966	16981	17318
1967	17106	16792
1968	12047	11867
1969	11322	11133

(Contd.)

1	*2*	*3*
1970	9697	9521
1971	10520	10377
1972	12166	11961
1973	11385	11122
1974	11447	11280
1975	12201	12101
1976	11022	10904
1977	11397	11292
1978	14445	14248
1979	12929	12808
1980	11585	11478
1981	12651	12518
1982	12209	11906
1983	12114	11980
1984	12171	12081
1985	10875	10771
1986		
1987	8924	8827
1988	9130	9073
1989	9188	9126
1990	7948	7902
1991	7169	7131
1992	6706	6636
1993	6044	6017
1994	5285	5262
1995	4561	4525
1996	3886	3784
1997	3580	3536
1998	4002	3936
1999	2372	2320
2000	1814	1782
2001	1539	1520
2002	1276	1254
2003	985	935
2004	986	965

Source: Yearbook of Labour Standards Inspection Office, 1948-2004.

TABLE 7

Number of Workers under 15 years old in Enterprises, (which submitted the applicable enterprise report under the Labour Standards Act)

Year	*Male*	*Female*	*Total*
August 1948	27421	31572	58993
December 1948	24996	28508	53504
September 1949	14329	7696	22025
June 1950	8057	1260	9317
December 1950	8288	979	9267
December 1951	8491	916	9407
December 1952	8957	681	9638
December 1953			17640
December 1954	19188	976	20164
December 1955			22562

Source: Women's and Minor's Bureau, Ministry of Labour, Labour Statistics on Minor Workers, 1950, 1951, 1952, 1954, 1955.

TABLE 8

Number of Newspaper Shops' Employees (under 18 years old)

Year	*Student of Junior High School*		*Student of Senior High School*	
	Male	*Female*	*Male*	*Female*
1963	201224	9748	21875	2165
1968	150540	8775	44616	2655
1973	117551	9136	56259	3231
1974	118030	9063	54770	3492
1975	114855	9003	56266	350
1976	106816	8874	61662	3629
1977	103323	8280	65252	3770
1978	101209	8463	64293	4678

Source: Yoshio Sotita, Nippon no Shinbun keiei (Management of the Japanese Newspapers Companies) Keizai Oraisha, Tokyo, 1979.

TABLE 9

Situation of Violation of Labour Standards Act on Minors

Year	*Minimum Age (56)**	*Labour Contract of Minors (57)**	*Wages (59)**	*Working Hours of Minors (60)**	*Midnight Work (62)**	*Restriction of employment for dangerous and harmful job (63)**	*Ban on underground labour (64)**	*Fare for returning home (68)**
1948	2786	510	171	5778	9617	1408	1356	108
1949	2721	1152	382	10078	22791	2934	1751	154
1950	1458	442	263	11220	22926	3667	1388	125
1951	925	232	169	6721	16686	2849	997	89
1952	798	218	92	6126	15805	2799	759	132
1953	1475	194	146	10307	22882	3781	664	148
1954	1017	86	50	7919	18191	2533	496	74
1955	739	36	60	8583	14815	2978	496	62
1956	274	12	11	4658	5657	1389	202	45

Notes: In 1956 the term of survey is Jan.-June.
Cases of violation under the item marked with an asterisk include those of adult females.

Source: Labour Standards Bureau, Ministry of Labour, and "Annual Labour Standards Inspection Report, 1957."

secondary and territory industry increased owing to the change of industrial structure. In 1955 per-capita real national income exceeded the average income in the prewar period (1934-1936). At that time the post-war disorder and turmoil ended. After that Japan has experienced high rapid expansion and social policy. The main theme on young workers is the problem of those after their completion of the middle and high schools and colleges. (See Table 5)

Judging from the number of permission to work, a little more than 10,000 children are now working. But we do not know the employment situation of children in industry and in other occupation because statistics are not available on this subject. It is estimated that children are mainly working as newspaper deliverers and child actors. In their cases there are some problems how to promote labour conditions and labour welfare in small or medium factories. (See Tables 6, 7, 8, 9)

{This original paper was printed at International Labour Law and Social Security ed., The Third Asian Regional Congress of Labour Law and Social Security, Bangkok, 1987}.

References

International Labour Office, *Industrial Labour in Japan*, I.L.O., Geneva, 1933.

Taki Fujita ed., *Nenshosha to Rodo* (The Minors and Labour) Ishizaki Shoten, Tokyo, 1951.

Ministry of Labour ed., *Japan Labour Law*, The Institute of Labour Policy, Tokyo, 1968.

Kazuo. Okochi, B. Karsh, and S.B. Levine ed., *Workers and Employers in Japan*, Univesity of Tokyo Press, 1973.

Taishirou. Shirai and Haruo, Shimada, Japan (in J.T. Dunlop and W. Galenson ed., *Labour in the Twentieth Century*, Academic Press, 1978).

Tadashi Hanami, *Labour Law and Industrial Relations in Japan*, Kluwer, 1979.

S. Umetani and B.G. Reuvens, Youth Employment in Japan (in B.G. Reubens ed., *Youth at Work*, Rowman and Allanheld Publishers, 1983).

Y. Tamura, *Nippon Rodo Hoshi* (History of Japanese Labour Law) Ochanomizu Shobo, Tokyo, 1984.

CHAPTER

7

Migrant Foreigners in Japan

Legal Aspects of Social Integration

INTRODUCTION

At the end of 1998, registered foreigners numbered just over 1,500,000, accounting for 1.2% of the Japanese population (see Table 1). The number has been increasing steadily in spite of the recent economic recession. Slightly less than three quarters come from Asian countries and almost 20% from Latin American countries (see Table 2). People from Korea and Chinese Taipei were compelled to come to Japan in the colonial period before the Second World War. They are referred to as "old comers". They and their descendants are permitted to stay as special permanent residents on the basis of their respective Treaties of Peace with Japan. People from Latin American of Japanese parentage are permitted to stay as long-term residents. They are referred to as "new comers".

The 1951 Immigration Control and Refugee

Recognition Act and the 1952 Aliens Registration Act constitute the basic legal framework for foreigners' entry and residence. The Japanese government has a fundamental policy to welcome highly skilled professional but refuse admission to unskilled workers. Over the past 50 years, these two acts have often been amended in order to bring them into conformity with the basic policy. For example, entrance procedures have been simplified and measures to combat illegal employment have been strengthened.

Foreigners are permitted to enter Japan under one of 27-residence status. The Certificate of Eligibility was introduced to expedite the entry procedures for foreigners who meet the residence requirements for landing in Japan. Having obtained this certificate, the person can easily obtain a visa at a Japanese consulate.

On the other hand, there are foreigners who work in violation of their visa or who overstay their visa, again, usually for the purposes of employment. The number of over stayers was 2,71,048 on 1 January 1999; the number has been decreasing since May 1993. Classified by the origin country, there were 62,577 from Korea, 40,420 from the Philippines, 34,800 from china, 30,065 from Thailand and 10320 from Peru.

This paper examines, from a legal point of view, the legal aspects of foreigners' integration into Japanese society. Specifically, the following issues will be examined: foreigners' registration and the provisions concerning foreigners in labour law, social security law, education law and criminal law.

2. FOREIGNERS' REGISTRATION

Foreign nationals are required to register at the office of local government where they reside within 90 days of the date of landing or within 60 days of their birth in Japan. Penalties can be imposed for failure to register. As foreigners may have difficulties in registering due to lack of mastery of the language, the offices have trained some of their personnel in foreign languages and have prepared foreign language guidebooks. Foreigners are permitted, moreover to be accompanied by someone who can understand Japanese. A foreigner generally receives the Alien Registration Card within approximately two weeks of making the application.

Local governments are required to maintain the original register book. When the foreigners have been registered, the local government must then send the information to the Governor of the local Prefecture who then forwards it to the Ministry of Justice. The original register book can only be consulted by the person her/himself or by an agent acting on her/his behalf, for example, a practicing lawyer.

The issue of using fingerprint records has been controversial. From 1951, providing fingerprints were compulsory for foreigners above 16 years of age wanting to stay for more than one year. This requirement was criticized from the point of view of human rights because foreigners were treated as offenders. A 1992 amendment to the Alien Registration act abolished the fingerprint requirement for permanent residents and special permanent residents only. Instead of fingerprints their identity can now be confirmed by their signature or photograph. After six years of implementation this measure was positively evaluated. The finger print requirement was, therefore, abolished for all foreigners on 1 January 2000. Foreigners are still obliged however to carry their Alien Registration Card with them at all times. This obligation has been criticized as being an excessive form of control. The Legal Committee of the Ministry of Justice will examine this issue.

Registered foreigners must report any change of nationality, name, address, occupation or office address to the municipal office within 14 days of the change. When registered, they obtain the right to participate in the national health insurance and national pension schemes, to live in a house built by the municipality (subject to availability), to enter their children in state schools and receive child benefits.

Even registered foreigners do not have the right to vote at every election however. Article 15 of the Constitution provides that Japanese nationals have the inalienable right to choose their public officials and to dismiss them. The Public Elections Act limits the right to vote to Japanese nationals. A permanent foreign resident has sued the Nation for damages because he was not permitted to vote at the Upper House elections. His grounds for the case were that the Public Elections Act violated the equality under the law stipulated under Article 14 of the Constitution. The Supreme Court did not accept this argument because limiting the right to vote to Japanese national was constitutional (Supreme Court Judgement, 22 January 1993). The Supreme Court adopted the same opinion in the case where permanent residents were not recorded on the election list for local level elections (Supreme Court judgement, 28 January 1995). The Supreme Court did state as *obiter dictum* however that whether the right to vote was limited to Japanese nationals or should be extended to foreigners at the local level elections depended on legislative policy because awarding permanent residents the right to vote at local level elections (and not other foreigners) was not prohibited by the Constitution. The reason for this being that the opinions of permanent residents had to be reflected in local government administration as it was closely related to their daily life. This judgement implicitly challenges an argument that only permanent residents may be given the right to vote at only local election.

It should not be forgotten that permanent residents are taxpayers. Foreigners having an address and living in Japan for more than one year must pay tax on their income tax. Foreigners who possess land or houses must also pay local taxes and property tax. Therefore, as taxpayers, the opinions of foreigners ought to be allowed to vote.

As with the right to vote, the issue of whether foreigners can take up employment in the public sector has also been discussed. Under the administrative regulations, only Japanese national can exercise public power or participate in central and local government decision-making. Foreigners can, therefore, only work in those public sector occupations, which are unrelated to the exercise of public power or participation in government decision-making. For example, Foreigners can be appointed as university teachers under the 1982 Foreign Teachers' Act. However, they cannot become a Faculty Dean, as this would involve them in the exercise of public power. For the same reason, whilst under the 1986 Research Exchange Promotion Act they can be employed as researchers in national research institutes, they cannot be promoted to managerial positions. In the case of local public service occupations, foreigners are increasingly taking up professional and operational posts (i.e. as doctors, nurses, medical technicians, bus drivers and teachers). It has recently been noticed that some local governments employ Koreans as regular local government officers. So far as appointments in the public sector are concerned, the differences between Japanese national and foreigners are gradually decreasing.

3. FOREIGNERS AND EMPLOYMENT LAW

Employment law and acts apply both to Japanese and to foreign nationals.. Under the Japanese Constitution, workers' rights are not limited to the Japanese people. Article 3 of the Labour Standards Act provides that an employer shall not engage in discriminatory treatment with respect to wages, working hours or other working conditions by reason of the worker's nationality, creed or social status. Under Article 5, Section 2 of the Trade Unions Act, the constitution of a trade union shall include that in no event shall anyone be disqualified for union membership on the basis of race, religion, sex, social status of family origin. Article 3 of the Employment Security Act stipulates that no one shall be discriminated against in employment placement, vocational guidance or the like, by reason of race, nationality, creed, sex, social status, family origin, previous profession, or membership in a trade union. Regarding the second point, the labour law acts are applied not only to genuine foreign legally staying workers, but also, under the Immigration Control and refugee Recognition Act, to illegal foreign workers.

Advisors for foreign workers are assigned to the Inspection Divisions of major Labour Standards Offices. They answer, in English, questions concerning working conditions and give proper guidance to foreign workers. Employment Service Centers for persons of Japanese descent have been established in Tokyo and Nagoya in order to give vocational advice, in Spanish and Portuguese, and to provide assistance in finding employment.

The Ministry of Labour issued administrative guidelines in May 1993 concerning the employment and working conditions of foreign workers. This was done in order to prevent trouble arising in the management of foreign workers and to promote proper working conditions and respect for safety at work.

(a) Recruitment and Employment of Foreigners

In Japan an employer is free to choose to employ foreigners on the basis of his company's needs, as he perceives them. The employer must however obey the restrictions regarding, for example, status of residence and the period of stay. An employer must affirm the foreigner's status of residence and the period of stay. An employer must affirm the foreigners' status of residence and the period of time for which the person will be an employee. Should the employer's business be outside the scope of the potential employee's residence status then the potential employee must first change residence status?

Foreigners legally residing in Japan can look for employment at the Public Employment Security Office; the office does not help illegal immigrants as they are violating the Immigration Control Act; owing to their legal status, this is interpreted to be non-discriminatory treatment.

Foreigners often obtain their employment through labour brokers. Fee-charging labour brokers are required to obtain authorization for their activities from the Ministry of Labour. Labour brokers will be punished if they are found to have engaged in labour recruitment or labour supply by means of violence, intimidation, imprisonment or other restraint on mental or physical freedom, or with an intention of having the workers engage in work injurious to public health or morals.

Person who employ illegal foreign workers or who keep them under their control with a view to letting them be engaged by others in illegal work are subject to up to 3 years imprisonment and/or fine of up to JPY 2 million. In addition to the employer, the company concerned might also be fined. Intermediation conducted abroad is also subject to punishment. A certificate of authorized employment is issued to foreign nationals on application. By verifying this certificate, the employer can inform himself of what type of employment the foreigner is permitted to be engaged in.

Under Article 21 of the Employment Measures Act, the employer must notify the Chief of the Public Employment Security Office if more than 30 persons are hired or dismissed within the course of one month. Since 1993, under the Executive Order of the Employment Security Act, employers of foreigners have been obliged to provide details on them to the Chief of the Public Employment Security Office on 1 June each year. The information to be provided includes the number of foreigners by origin country, occupation and status of residence. The purpose of this notification system is to gauge the extent and nature of foreigners' employment and to promote proper management of foreign workers.

Due to the recession, large number of foreign workers have been dismissed since 1992. Since 1993, all foreign workers (i.e. including illegal foreigners) have come within the scope of the Employment Insurance Act except when it is obvious that they will certainly return to their origin country upon completion of their contract. If they have been insured for more than six months during the twelve months prior to their dismissal they are eligible for unemployment benefit. It is estimated that over 50% of foreign workers have not joined the insurance scheme because neither they nor their employers wish to pay the contributions (which are equally split).

(b) Employment Contracts

With regard to the drafting of employment contracts, the question as to which country's law is to prevail is determined by the intention of the parties. In cases where the intention of the parties is unclear, the law where the employment contract is signed shall govern (Article 7 of the Act concerning the Application of Laws). So the Japanese law is, in general, applied when the foreigner works in Japan under contract.

In concluding the employment contract, the employer shall clearly state the wages, working hours and other working conditions to the employee. The employer shall clarify them in the language, which can be understood by the foreign workers. When the working conditions as stated differ from the actual fact, the worker may immediately cancel the employment contract. This is difficult however. The employer must bear the necessary travelling expenses when the foreign worker returns to his origin country within 14 days of the cancellation of the contract

In Japan, there is a practice under which employers make "informal decisions to employ" applicants before the employment contract is concluded. The aim of this practice is to secure better personnel at early stage from amongst school-leavers. According to the law, an employment contract is formed when the employer notifies the person of the informal decision to employ. This notice is deemed to be the employer's consent to hire the applicant. However, the employer has a right to rescind this informal decision before the applicant commences work. This must be done however with a proper reason. For example, the employer can withdraw the informal decision when the applicant is not a graduate from a school. A case of whether the employer can withdraw its decision because the applicant is a Korean student living in Japan has been disputed (Yokohama District Court, 19 June 1975). The applicant had both a Japanese name and a Korean name. He wrote his Japanese name in his curriculum vitae because he apprehended discriminative treatment; he informed the company (Hitachi Ltd.) that he was a Korean student residing in Japan once he had received from the company the informal decision to hire. The company insisted that it dismissed him because he reported false career details. The Court found that this decision to dismiss was made because the person was Korean and judged that is was a discriminatory treatment owing to nationality, which is prohibited under Article 3 of the Labour Standards Act. Sadly, employment discrimination against Koreans residing in Japan still takes place.

(c) Workplace Accidents

The rate of workplace accidents involving foreign workers is high, as they do not know Japanese well enough to understand safety rules and often do not receive safety education and training. Whether legal or illegal, under the worker's Accidents Compensation Act foreign workers must be treated the same as Japanese employees. So, illegal foreign workers cannot be protected unless the employer reports their insurance application to the Labour Standards Inspection Office. The government collects the contributions from only the employer whose duties are cancelled after a two-year prescription. So the employer has a duty to pay the contributions only for two years. There are however some violations of the act on the part of the employer.

For example, employers sometimes fail to report workplace accidents to the Labour Standards Inspection Office in order to hide the accident. False reports are submitted concerning the nature of the accident or the days of absence.

Illegal foreign workers do not like to apply for workplace accident benefits because they are afraid of being expelled from Japan. The Labour Standards Inspection Officers have a duty to report their illegal status to the Immigration Office. Normally, the officers abstain from reporting until the case has been examined. When it is expected that the case will take a long time to be resolved, the Ministry of Justice will give special status of residence to the person.

Workplace accident benefits are paid to foreign workers or his survivors on the same terms as for Japanese workers. When a foreign worker dies, the officer shall find his dependants. Bereaved family compensation, in the form of pension, must be sent to his dependants. However, unscrupulous employers sometimes divert the benefits into their own pockets. They are liable to punishment for theft.

In addition to the benefits due to them under the Worker's Accidents Compensation Act, foreign workers can also sue their employer for any pecuniary and non-pecuniary losses incurred under Article 415 or 709 of the Civil Code. The greatest problem concerns the calculation the appropriate damages. This problem was judged by the Supreme Court in the case of *Maqsood Ahmed Body* v. *Kaishinsha Ltd.*, in this case, the Pakistani worker was an illegal foreigner whose work was to ship and discharge goods, to use the automatic binding machines and to pack bound books. During his work of binding pamphlets using a binding machine his right forefinger was cut-off from the first articulation. It was established that there was a danger of pinching one's fingers in the machine if one did not have prior experience of using it: the binding machine did not have a safety device. The worker's manager did not warn him to be careful when using the machine. As his injury was judged to be one suffered in the course of duty, he was paid non-duty compensation and physical handicap compensation benefit under the worker's Accidents Compensation Act. But he sued for damages against the company under Articles 415 and 709 of the Civil Code.

The Supreme Court judged that the amount should be calculated by reference to the average income during his possible period of work in Japan; after that period it should be calculated by reference to the average income in his origin country. In principle, the amount of damages suffered from the after-effect of an injury should be decided on the basis of expected future earnings. So it is important to decide how many years he could have been expected to work in Japan, his illegal status not withstanding. The Supreme Court decided that the period would be 3 year because he would be subjected to compulsory deportation. This solution was thought to be wise. (Another idea was that the amount should be calculated by reference to his earnings in Japan because he was working in Japan. This idea was based on the premise that he would have worked until his mandatory retirement age, i.e. 60 years of age. However, in general, foreign workers come to Japan in the hope of just a few years of work. So this premise was different from the actual conditions of the foreign worker.)

4. FOREIGN NATIONALS AND SOCIAL SECURITY LAW

(a) Pension

The pension system is two-tiered: it includes the National Pension Plan and the Employees' Pension Insurance System. The National Pension pays basic pension benefits, while the Employees' Pension Insurance System pays additional pension benefits.

Under the revised National Pension Plan effective from 1 January 1982, all persons residing in Japan aged between 20 and 59 are covered. In case of foreigners, they must have stayed in Japan for more than one year before joining the National Pension Plan. It is not necessary for those insured under the Employees' Pension Insurance System to take any action to apply for National Pension Plan. The premiums are borne by the Employees' Pension Insurance. Other person (for example, farmers, the self-employed, students over 20 years of age) has to address an application to the local government office. The payment should be paid monthly. In 2000, they are JPY 13,300 per month.

The person has to fulfill the qualification period of 25 years in order to receive a pension. If a foreigner has contributed for 25 years, he can receive his pension abroad. If he pays into the National Pension Plan for less than 25 years and leaves Japan, the money is forfeited. However, under a 1994 amendment, a lump sum allowance maybe paid because in general many foreigners would not want to stay in Japan for more than 25 years. Recently some local governments have decided as part of their social welfare policies to pay some money on a monthly basis to foreigners who could not enter the National Pension Plan or have not qualified to receive a pension.

The employees' Pension Insurance System applies to employees at their respective place of work such as companies and factories. Every employee under 65 years of age must participate in this system as insured persons, regardless of nationality. Premiums are fixed at 16.5% of the monthly standard remuneration. Standard remuneration is divided into 30 bands ranging from JPY 92,000 to JPY 5,90,000 a month, which are classified under the monthly income of the insured employee. The benefits come under three categories: benefits for the aged, benefits for the disabled and benefits for the survivors. The insured person shall participate in the system for at least 20 years to be eligible for this pension. The eligible age for the benefits is to be raised erased gradually from 60 to 65 years. From 1 April 2013 the benefits shall be paid to those over 65 years old. But many foreigners withdraw from the system and leave the country before they have qualified to receive a pension. The money is forfeited. Under the 1994 amendment they can get a lump sum payment.

Bilateral arrangements—conventions—under which the value of the premium payment made in Japan can be received as a pension abroad has been concluded between Germany and Japan. The Japanese Ministry of Public welfare is negotiating a similar arrangement with the United States government. Given that the other country must have a pension scheme in order for it to be possible to conclude an arrangement, conventions cannot at present be signed with other Asian countries.

(b) Medical Care

In Japan the principal sources of medical care insurances are the National Health Insurance and the Employees' Health Insurance. Employees working in establishments where more than five persons are continuously employed must be insured at the Employees' Health Insurance. This applies to foreigners too. The employer and the insured in general, share the contribution rate fifty-fifty. So, in some cases the employers of foreign workers do not send the application form to Social Insurance Office because the employees will return to their origin countries after only two or three years.

The National Health Insurance is applicable to persons other than those insured through Employees' Health Insurance is · applicable to person other than those insured through Employees' Health Insurance: i.e. farmers, self-employed, employees of small-sized companies, and the unemployed. Foreigners have been eligible to be insured under this scheme since the 1 April 1986 amendment to the National Health Insurance Act. As a result, this insurance covers persons whose status of residence is cultural activities, college student, pre-college student, dependant or long-term residents. Foreigners are insured after one year of registration. So, this insurance cannot apply to foreigners who will stay in the country for less than one year.

Each municipal government on income proportion, asset proportion or equal proportion by household decides the National Health Insurance contribution rate. As it is difficult for foreigners to calculate their income and assets, the contribution rate is very low especially during the first year. In general, the minimum rate is applied to foreigners.

As illegal foreigners are not registered at local government offices they are not covered by either of the two types of health insurance. Foreigners from Asian countries sometimes suffer from tuberculosis and HIV. They do not go to a doctor because the doctor's fees are very high and they are in constant fear of being caught by the police. As a result, their illness becomes much more serious. They cannot pay hospital fees either. This is a big problem for the hospital because it cannot refuse to treat them because they are unable to pay the doctor's fees.

In October 1990 the Ministry of Public Health issued administrative guidance to the effect that public aid should be awarded only to legal foreigners. So illegal foreigners cannot be given medical aid under the Public Aid Act. But there are some means to save illegal foreigners. The first is to give medical treatment under the 1899 Ill Travelers in the Street Act. Local government may contribute to the treatment fees of illegal foreigners on the pretext that they are ill travelers. Some prefectures have created a budget for the hospital fees of illegal foreigners. Illegal foreigners can be treated without charges under the Social Welfare Institution Act. This act provides medical services to the poor for a low charge or without charge as a social welfare service. The funds available are very low however.

5. FOREIGNERS' EDUCATION

Education plays a major role in the integration of foreigners. The fundamental principles of education are presented below.

Under Article 26 of the Constitution, all people have the right to receive an education corresponding to their ability. All persons are obliged to have all boys and girls under their protection receive a 9-year general education as provided under Article 4 of the Fundament Law of Education. The compulsory education is free. Under the Constitution, Article 3 of the Fundamental Law on Education provides that people shall all be given an equal opportunity of receiving an education according to their ability, and they shall not be subject to educational discrimination on account of race, creed, sex, social status, economic position or family origin. It is now interpreted that these provisions apply to foreigners, whether legal or illegal, because social status includes eligibility to reside in Japan.

Since 1991, the Board of education at the local government informs foreigners that their children shall enter the elementary school or lower secondary school. This notification is made only to registered foreigners. The children of unregistered foreigners, therefore, have no possibility of entering the compulsory education system. There are increasing numbers of children from foreign countries that need help in learning Japanese at elementary and lower secondary schools. This notification is made only to registered foreigners. The children of unregistered foreigners, therefore, have no possibility of entering the compulsory education system. There are increasing numbers of children from foreign countries who need help in learning Japanese at elementary and lower secondary schools. To cope up with the situation, the Ministry of Education has been taking measures since 1992 such as allocating additional teachers and making available special teaching materials for learning Japanese.

There are many schools built for foreign children. At present, the local government permits 132 schools as miscellaneous schools, different from regular schools. The major ones are Korean schools, Chinese schools, International schools and American schools. These schools are not subject to the Course of Study issued by the Ministry of Education, but boys and girls who graduate from foreign schools have the possibility to enter high schools or private or municipal universities on the reason that they are judged to have the same level of attainment as graduates from Japanese schools. However, it has long been the legal interpretation that they are not qualified to take the entrance examination to the national university because applicants are required to have completed upper secondary school or 12-year formal school education. Graduates from foreign schools must, therefore, obtain special permission to take the entrance examination to enter the national university. This imposes a big burden on students learning at foreign schools. The question of how to introduce flexible qualifications for the entrance examination is being discussed at the Ministry of Education.

Students at foreigners' schools cannot participate in Inter-High School Sports Games because as a rule the participants must be students of Japanese high schools. Recently, however, this rule has been amended to involve students at foreigners' high schools, for example in games of soccer.

The number of foreign students studying in Japan had been increasing year by year prior to the financial crises in the region. At the end of 1998 they numbered 5,96,485. Since the crises the number has been stable. The Japanese government has a plan to receive 10,000 foreign students in colleges or universities. Given the economic situation it is now difficult to put the plan into practice. Foreign students come to Japan under a Japanese Government Scholarship Program or under the financial assistance from various kinds of organizations, or at their own expense. Most of the foreign students are studying at their own expenses. They are permitted to engage in paid work for only hours per a day by the Immigration Control Office; in fact they typically work for more than that.

Pre-college foreign students (*shugakusei*) study at high schools or advance vocational schools (*senshugakkou*) or miscellaneous schools (*kakushugakkou*) or Japanese language schools. They numbered just under 30,700 at the end of 1998; approximately 90% are from Asian countries. There have been problems concerning pre-college students. Their enrolment in school has sometimes been used as a pretext for them to come to Japan; in fact hey have come with the intention of working rather than studying. Some Japanese language schools do not have enough staff and facilities to teach Japanese. Many foreign students are not able to come to Japan because unscrupulous managers of schools have cheated them of their tuition fees. So, at present pre-college students can only enter Japanese language schools designated by the Minister of Justice and additionally found to be appropriate by the Minister of Education under the determination of the Association for the Promotion of Japanese Language education. These reforms are enabling pre-college students to come to Japan under the correct circumstances.

6. CRIMINAL PROCEDURES INVOLVING FOREIGNERS

There are many criminal cases related to foreigners, both as victims and as perpetrators. Under Article 31 of the Constitution, no person shall be deprived of life or liberty, nor shall any other criminal penalty be imposed, except according to legal procedures. In all criminal cases the accused has the right to a speedy and public trial by an impartial court. He is permitted the full opportunity to examine all witnesses and has the right to be assisted by competent counsel who shall, if the accused is unable to secure the same by his own efforts, be assigned to his use by the State (Article 36 of the Constitution). No person can be compelled to testify against himself. Confessions made under compulsion, torture or threat or after a prolonged period of detention are not admissible as evidence. No person can be convicted or punished in cases where the only proof against him is his own confession (Article 38 of the Constitution). These provisions are, of course, applied to foreigners whether they are legally or illegally resident as defined by the Immigration Control Act.

Under Article 74 of the Court Act, Japanese language is used in court. So the most important problem is how to obtain interpretation services at the stage of the criminal investigation and the court trial. Usually policemen, public prosecutors and judges have little knowledge of foreign languages. The accused often cannot completely understand Japanese language concerning legal procedures; this applies even to those who have an adequate knowledge of everyday Japanese.

Article 175 of the Criminal Procedure Act provides that in cases where a person not versed in the Japanese language is required to make a statement, an interpreter shall be present at the court. Under Article 223 of the Criminal Procedure Act, a public prosecutor, a secretary of the public prosecutor's office, or a policeman may, when it is necessary to investigate an offence, request the appearance of a person other than the accused, and examine him, or ask him to give an expert testimony, and to make interpretation or translation.

At the judicial examination of a foreigner, he should be beforehand notified by an interpreter that he shall not be required to make statement contrary to his will and that he can select and appoint a practicing lawyer. If not, the voluntarily nature of a written declaration made by the accused is considered as doubtful, and is not admissible as evidence.

The list of translators published in April 1999 included 2630 court translators who can interpret a total of 41 languages. However, interpreters who can speak minority languages are limited in number and their skills need to be improved to interpret verbal evidence and assist precisely in the cross-examination of witnesses. The Association of Court Interpreters has been organized for the purpose of sharing experience among them and promoting improvements in their

TABLE 1

Number of Registered Foreigners

	Total number	*% of total population*
1973	738410	0.68
1978	766894	0.67
1983	817129	0.68
1988	941005	0.77
1989	984455	0.80
1990	1075317	0.98
1991	1218891	0.98
1992	1281644	1.03
1993	1320748	1.06
1994	1354011	1.08
1995	1362371	1.08
1996	1415136	1.12
1997	1482707	1.18
1998	1512116	1.20

Source: Japan Immigration Association ed., Statistics on registered foreigners, 1999.

TABLE 2

Number of Registered Foreigners (by region of origin)

	1994	*1995*	*1997*	*1998*	*%*
Total number	1354011	1362371	1482707	1512116	
Asia	1050211	1039149	1086390	1123409	74.3
South America	203840	221865	284691	274442	18.2
North America	52317	52861	55312	54700	3.6
Europe	32529	33283	38200	39925	2.6
Oceania	8571	8365	9645	10514	0.7
Africa	4909	5202	6275	6940	0.5
Other	1634	1826	2194	2186	0.1

Source: Japan Immigration Association ed., Statistics on registered foreigners, 1999.

knowledge of the law. A Qualification test is to be introduced for professional court translators.

The expense of an interpreter is included in the costs of lawsuit. If found guilty, the court may order the foreigner to bear all or part of the interpretation expenses, but in practice it is not ordered if it is evident that the accused is unable to pay such costs owing to poverty as defined by Article 181 of the Criminal Procedure Act.

The courts have had various kinds of guidebooks and legal documents translated. However, they are written in only approximately 30 languages. The courts should arrange for the translation of these documents into more languages, not only for criminal cases, but also for civil cases.

The number of arrested foreigners is increasing year by year. The number was 13,436 in 1999, 14,660 in 2001 and 21,842 in 2004. The Ministry of Justice gives careful attention to foreigners in prison because their native customs and living circumstances are different from those in Japan. Special facilities are provided: i.e. special food and prayer time for the Muslims, different beds, showers or foreign books and magazines. Prisoners can get JPY 3500 per day when they receive vocational training. Strangely, this money is frequently used to sustain their families in their origin countries.

CONCLUSION

Foreigners ought to be accorded the same treatment as the Japanese nationals in the areas of labour, social security, education and criminal trials. After long discussions, the principle of equality is gradually being realized. There remains much to be done, however. The Japanese people have a tendency to exclude foreigners because in general Japan is thought to be an almost homogenous society. It is necessary to correct this way of thinking in order to cope with the internationalization of Japanese society.

{This original paper was printed at OECD ed., International Migration in Asia, 2001, OECD}.

References

Japanese National Committee ICSW ed., *Social Welfare Services in Japan*, Revised Edition. 1990.

Kozo Kagawa, *"Japan" in employment Term and Conditions Asia/ Pacific 1998/1999*, Watson Wyatt Worldwide, 1990.

Ministry of Education (1999), *Education in Japan—A Graphic Presentation*, Science and Culture ed.

Ministry of Justice ed., Immigration Control and Refugee Recognition Act, Nippon Kajo Shuppan Ltd., 1990.

Ministry of Labour ed., *Labour Laws of Japan*, The Institute of Labour Administration, 1995.

Social Insurance Agency ed., *Employees' Pension Insurance System Established in Japan for your Joining, 1995.*

Tanaka, H. *Foreigners Staying in Japan*, Revised edition, Yuwanamishinsho, 1995.

Tezuka Kazuaki, *Foreigners and Law*, 2nd ed., Yuhikaku, 1990.

CHAPTER

8

Movement of Corporate Social Responsibility

INTRODUCTION

Corporate social responsibility has been strongly emphasized from the late 1070s. The Principle of corporate conduct based on social responsibility has been claimed together with globalised economies. Namely expectations related to corporate social responsibility have been spread in a globalizing society. It is expected to promote responsible business practices that benefit business and society. Here we will discuss the background for promoting corporate social responsibility in the following order: (1) The content and meaning of corporate social responsibility, (2) the reason why corporate social responsibility has recently been promoted, (3) the reaction from Asian countries to corporate social responsibility. It is important to research these problems from global (global plus local) viewpoint.

1. THE CONTENT AND MEANING OF CORPORATE SOCIAL RESPONSIBILITY

The content of corporate social responsibility has not been defined clearly. There are debates on this problem from several viewpoints. One is the target to which a corporate shall realize social responsibility. It has naturally a responsibility fulfilling the requirements of shareholders. But now it is not enough to attain corporate social responsibility. It shall meet the demand of corporate stakeholders including shareholders. But no consensus can be found in the sphere of stakeholders. In general, it will comprise peoples and organizations affected by a corporate operation: e.g. workers, managers, customers, suppliers, trade unions, and local communities, central and local governments. (UNCTID ed., 1999; p. 7) There is a difference between shareholders and stakeholders. Shareholders want a corporate to attain high productivity in order to get profits in short-term, but stakeholders wish to have good partnership with a corporate for a long-term. In other words, stakeholders are more concerned in other interests than short-term profits of business enterprises. But this difference becomes narrower than before. Shareholders themselves will pursue socially responsible investment to business since shareholders begin to recognize that a corporate can get high profits if it would fulfil social responsibility as a reputable company and that profits would be lost if a corporate could not achieve social responsibility.

Naturally business must get profits. So getting profits are necessary conditions, but are not sufficient conditions to achieve corporate social responsibility. We must be careful to the process of getting profits for corporate social responsibility. Another is the content of corporate social responsibility. It has not strictly defined till now. A corporate has a duty to comply with laws and regulations proclaimed by central and local governments. Including these legal duties, it has social responsibility whose concept involves key problems, e.g.

human rights, workers' rights and environment problem. These are thought to be internationally accepted values especially in developed countries. But it is not limited to these key problems. Other unexpected problems affecting third parties may be targets covered by corporate social responsibility. They depend on the size, sector, production of businesses and present or future economic situations of a country where businesses are located. The scope of corporate social responsibility has been flexible, but it is commonly thought that a corporate shall make a contribution to the promotion of society. Concrete contribution has been changeable together with the wave of the times. At present human rights, workers' rights and environment are the main objectives to be achieved through corporate social responsibility.

There is a big problem when the legal regulations infringe internationally accepted principles relating to three important fields as mentioned above. For example, in developing countries the formation of trade unions or union activities is forbidden by laws as means to introduce multinational companies at duty-free zones. Have they demanded to comply with the legal regulations? Or can they ignore them? They shall be requested to disregard the laws from the viewpoint of corporate social responsibility. But can they keep continued existence at developing countries?

2. PROMOTION OF THE CORPORATE SOCIAL RESPONSIBILITY

The structure of world economies has undergone profound changes in the last three decades under the impact of the transnational movement of capitals. This deep-going trend towards borderless global economy is the most important factor to promote corporate social responsibility since the late 1970s. Globalization can be found in several developments: the growth of foreign direct investments providing a big role of multinational enterprises, the international extension of financial markets, and the development of communication and transport technology. These trends have prevailed under market-oriented economies especially after the collapse of communist countries

Global economies have helped to extend the size of world economies. But they have brought unfair division of world's wealth between the rich and poor peoples in one country and also developed and developing countries. Therefore, it is necessary to bring forth, fair division of wealth under the principles of social justice. Corporate social responsibility is expected to have a role to distribute wealth equally through the adherence to internationally accepted values.

From 1990s, corporate governance has been an important policy issue. In the wake of Asian economic crisis corporate governance has become a watchword in the development issues. Corporate governance deals with a problem of how a corporate shall be managed in order to create wealth to the stakeholders including investors, directors, managers and workers. For the purpose, creating more democratic forms of good corporate governance and corporate monitoring shall increase accountability. Various kinds of reformations are executed to improve corporate governance, involving a set of relationships among a corporate board, its shareholders and its stakeholders especially in the developed countries. The legal and institutional environment usually regulates the corporate governance framework. Furthermore, business ethics and corporate awareness of environmental and societal interests of the communities may have an impact on the reputation and profitable success of a company. In other words, corporate social responsibility has been recognized to develop good governance. Even from OECE Principles of Corporate Governance; we can understand that corporate governance has an impact to develop corporate social responsibility together with globalization of economies.

Next we must consider a big problem: how corporate social responsibility shall be enforced. There are two important corporate codes of conduct in international field: ILO Tripartite Declaration of Principles concerning Multinational Enterprises which has been revised in June 2000 including four fields of worker's rights incorporated under ILO Declaration of Principles on Fundamental Rights at Work in 1998. The problem is the little effectiveness of the Guidelines in which OECD can only make recommendations to multinational enterprises.

As the second type, there are voluntary frameworks on corporate social responsibility: for example, Global Compact launched by Mr. Kofi Annan, Sullivan Principle and SA 8000 developed by Council on Economic Priorities Accreditation Agency (Social Accountability International)

As the third type, there are a number of framework agreements negotiated by ICFTU (International Confederation of Free Trade Unions) and some, ITS which adopted "Basic Code of Labour Practices in 1997." Under the Basic Code, corporate code of labour practices is expected to conclude by the company and trade union. The purpose of basic code is to promote internationally recognized labour standards and to address the responsibility of a company for the labour practices of its contractors, sub-contractors and principal suppliers. For example, IMF-JC (Japan Council of Metalworkers' Unions) initiated Model Code of Conduct under the guidance of IMF. This model was made to suit Japanese conditions under IMF Model Code of Conduct.

As the fourth type, NGOs have advised a company to conclude with Corporate Code of Conduct modeled by NGOs like Campaign for Labour Rights and Clean Clothes Campaign. These four types of code of conducts are provided only as moral duty. These may be useful to measure corporate behaviour and to seek improvement to the companies. At most the companies will be attacked by customers who boycott engaging in social labeling movement. They shall be designed to increase the effectiveness and monitoring procedure of the code.

3. REACTION FROM ASIAN COUNTRIES TO CORPORATE SOCIAL RESPONSIBILITY

The movement of corporate social responsibility has been spread from developed countries to developing countries. We must check how the developing countries think of corporate social responsibility. Since all actors of developing countries do not have the same idea on this problem. And there can be seen sharp conflicts between developed and developing countries. We must consider this problem from local viewpoint especially from Asian position.

There are two good examples to know the content of this problem. One is Generalized System of Preferences (GSP) policy adopted by USA and EU. Especially USA demanded that GSP should be withdrawn from some products in developing countries if they would be produced under the working conditions violating minimum labour standards, for instance, freedom of association, free collective bargaining, minimum age of employment, labour safety and so on. This pressure to withdraw GSP was partly successful to level up minimum wages in Thailand and Indonesia because they were in the fear of reducing exports to the USA. NAFTA was concluded under the leadership of the USA, sanctioning violations of labour health and safety rules. So the USA partly succeeded to press for inclusion of enforceable labour standards in trade agreement only in North American areas. But the governments and employers in Asian developing countries opposed the USA that GSP policy did not aim to promote workers' rights, but to stop investments to developing countries for protecting national industries in USA.

Nevertheless, as a leader of developed countries the USA proposed social clause stipulated in the international trade agreements which would link labour standards with trade liberalization to GATT, later WTO. This social clause is another example to show reaction from Asian developing countries to the link with labour standards and international trade at the age of economic globalization.

For developed countries the main opinion is that unfair competition from imports of cheap goods produced by workers under low wages represents a great threat to unemployment at high wages countries, and also that low level wages will attract the capitals from developed countries to developing countries which will have a grave impact to the unemployment problem in the developed countries. This link of international trade and labour standards is not a new problem but has a long history as the issue of social dumping since 1930s. The same issue has been again presented as the title of "social clause" in the era of economic globalization.

The governments and employers associations in Asian developing countries opposed to introduce the social clause on the reason that it is motivated by protectionist intentions and that it is arranged as non-tariff barriers in trade in favour of developed countries. For example, a political leader of Southeast Asia, Mr. Mahatir bin Mohamad criticized the social clause on the following grounds.

"The newly industrialized countries are still disadvantaged. Other than lower-cost labour, they have no competitive advantage. They have to buy the technology and borrow the capital from the rich countries. The lower labour costs accord them only marginal advantages. Remove that and they would lose their only competitive advantage".

"Developing countries need stability and industrial peace in order to develop. Already the economics of many developing countries have been destroyed by irresponsible industrial action. If, because of instigation by unions in developed countries, the productivity of developing countries will remain poor forever. It is time that the powerful western unions and their governments cease their agitation for the so-called rights of the workers in the developing countries. What they really need is to be able to earn a living while contributing towards the development of their countries. Strikes and industrial action do not encourage investment and job creation." (ILO ed., 1994; pp. 176-77)

Mr. Mahatir's assertion is a typical opposition to the social clause problem. He argued that Asian developing countries had a right to develop their own countries because they were preoccupied with immediate challenges such as poverty. This right was recognized as a universal right in December 1986 in UN and also at the World Conference on Human Rights in Vienna in 1993.

For that purpose it is now important to achieve industrialization policy of economic growth while retaining political stability and industrial peace in order to invite direct foreign investments to developing countries. Political and social stability can be sustained under authoritative government to control political parties, trade unions and other organizations having possibilities of agitation and dissents to the ruling political and administrative power.

The ruling governments have a policy to get economic growth under developmental dictatorship, which has a possibility to curtail, rightly of associations and fundamental rights given to individuals and various kinds of groups. Therefore, the governments have an opinion that workers' rights under international labour standards should be achieved only after economic progress has been got. This assertion would negate an opinion that protecting workers' rights must become the basis of economic activity. This negative idea easily extends to human rights and environment problem. Politicians and administrators in power adopt the word of "Asian Value" as a symbol of negative idea.

Mr. Lee Kuan Yew said that one of driving forces making Singapore was that the majority of the people placed the importance of the welfare of society above the individual, which was a basic Confucian concept. The emphasis on group loyalty is suited to the needs of industrialization. The concern with providing for group members reinforces loyalty to group, for example, factory and establishment that might bring more efficiency of production. Individuals must always take a back seat to the interests of groups, which shall bring forth the dark side to human rights of individuals. So the rights of individuals are subordinate to the interests of groups. Brian Kelly and Mark London, 1989; p. 98) Workers' rights must be sacrificed for the sake of economic development and national survival. This way of thinking offers the ground for lower-cost labour to maintain competitive advantageous status in international trade and production.

Is there commonly "Asian Value" base on the interests of groups, which different from "European Value" based on the rights of individuals? Does "Asian Value" have a reasonable ground in socio-cultural context of Asia? And is there single "European Value" in European countries though she also has multiple cultures?

In theory it is so difficult to abstract "Asian Value" commonly seen in Asian world. In Asia there are many natives, religions and cultures in large and wide areas. Rather we can find various kinds of values in Asia. Therefore, some politicians often point that "Asian Value" can be found limitedly in East and South-East Asia. But there is much diversity only in East and South East Asia. So "Asian Value" can be situated. as a political slogan to maintain legitimacy of ruling authoritative power.

What is the assertion of trade unions in Asian developing countries? There is no total opinion. Some trade unions have the same opinions with the ruling government because they wish to be recognized as legal organizations by the government under the compulsory registration system of trade unions. On the other side some trade unions introduce the social clause because they can get better working conditions through collective bargaining under the guidance of ICFTU which insists to link social clause to international trade. ICFTU expected that the major beneficiaries from the social clause would be all the developing countries because the social clause would build a bottom floor below which competition was considered to be not only unfair but also unacceptable in terms of basic human rights, namely, workers' rights and human rights are considered to be international and universal standard by ICFTU.

Next we must check the opinions of multinational companies in developed countries. They have many companies in developing countries. The joint companies built in developing countries in general give no importance to the social clause because they want to continue to keep lower working conditions. And also the head quarters in developed countries have the same policy since they make inroads into foreign countries for lower wages, easy access to raw material and so on. There are complicated opinions on the social clause problem according to their own positions in the developed and developing countries. So unified way of thinking cannot be found even in Asian developing countries. We cannot say that the social clause problem simply brings about the conflicts only between the developed and developing countries.

After discussions and negotiations at ILO, this problem was compromised under the Declaration of 1998 on Fundamental Principles and Rights at Work and its follow-up to promote the implementation of these principles and rights. This Declaration has two important meanings: core labour standards shall be implemented though treaties are not ratified and technical help shall be given to the developing countries which cannot implement these treaties. It is compromised that core labour standards shall be universally kept both at the developed and developing countries. Core labour standards must be one of the most important factors kept by companies as corporate social responsibility. But there is a problem in the sphere of core labour standards. At present they cover the rights of (a) freedom of association and collective bargaining (ILO Convention No. 87 and 98), (b) elimination of all forms of compulsory labour (ILO

Convention No. 29 and 105), (c) abolition of child labour (ILO Nos. 138 and 182), and (d) abolition of discrimination in respect of employment and occupation (ILO Nos. 100 and 111) the content of core labour standards has been decided in political situation. Theoretically they are not limited to four fields. For example, minimum wages and labour safety will be involved in core labour standard because they are important working conditions.

At least Asian developing countries have agreed to follow this Declaration though they have not ratified all eight ILO Conventions. Therefore, core labour standard shows a tendency to be involved in corporate code of conduct represented as corporate social responsibility.

CONCLUSION

Corporate social responsibility has been spread under the globalization of economies and corporate governance since 1970s. The content has been politically compromised with the actors and stakeholders concerned. It has positively been allocated by those getting profits, but rejected by those losing profits from corporate social responsibility. It reflects complicate international politics and economics. And it brings forth the conflicts between the developed and developing countries. This means that global viewpoint is necessary to research this problem. Namely we must study international standards not only from the point of universal interests but also local interests including Asian ones. From both points we must consider how we can make universally accepted content of corporate social responsibility in these circumstances and we may put it into practice effectively.

{This original paper was printed at Raoul Wallenberg Institute, French Ministry of Foreign Affairs and Asia-Europe Foundation ed., Human Rights and Economic Relations, 2004, Sia-Europe Foundation}.

References

ICFTU ed., *A Trade Union Guide to Globalization*, ICFTU, 2001.

UNCTAD ed., *The Social Responsibility of Transnational Corporation*, United Nations, 1999.

ILO ed., *Vision of the Future of Social Justice*, ILO, 1994.

Brian Kelly and Mark London ed., *The Four Little Dragon*, Simon and Schunster, 1989.

Kozo Kagawa, "Legal Cultural Research on Social Clause Problem in South and South-East Asian Countries" in the Proceedings of 1995 Annual Meeting Research on Sociology of Law, International Sociological Association, Tokyo, 1995.

Kozo Kagawa ed., *Fair Labour Standards in Asia*, Special Seminar at International Industrial Relations Association 12th World Congress, Tokyo, 2000.

Kozo Kagawa, "Code of Conduct regarding Labour and Employment pertaining to Overseas Business Practices initiated by IMF-JC", *Social Sciences Journal* No. 66, Doshisha University, Kyoto, 2003.

CHAPTER

9

Labour and Employment

Code of Conduct

INTRODUCTION

This paper deals with Corporate Code of Conduct promoted by Japan Council of Metal Workers' Unions (IMF-JCX). As Japanese branch of International Metal Workers' Federation, IMF-JC was organized in 1964 when Olympic Games was held in Tokyo and Japan was admitted to the Article 8 of the International Monetary Fund (IMF). Since that time IMF-JC has been active in 4 key industries, automobile, electronic machinery, steel and shipbuilding and heavy machinery and has developed the concentrated wage struggles (Shunto) annually. IMF=JC has 7 affiliated industry-wide unions, namely, the Japanese Electrical, Electronics and Information Union (JEIU), Japan Federation of Steel Workers' Unions (JAW), Japan Federation of Electric Wire Workers' Unions (JEWU), Japan Confederation of Shipbuilding and Engineering Workers' Unions (JSEU) and Japanese Association of Metal, Machinery and Manufacturing Workers (JAM). The number of membership is 2.36 million occupying one third of members of Rengo (Japanese Trade Union Confederation, JTUC) known as the biggest national center in Japan and the third largest organization in the world. IMF-JC has a big power in Japanese labour movement. So IMF-JC Model Code of Conduct is a good example to consider corporate social responsibility in Japan from the viewpoint of trade unions.

In Japan union density is decreasing from 35.4% in 1970 to 20.7% in 2001. So union activities do not become intense in harmony with Japanese matured and stable economies. In general, Japanese unions are now cooperative with management though there remain some unions that often cause disturbances in the workplace. But the trade unions always pursue social justice and try to attain full employment, establish basic trade union rights, improve working conditions and living standards for the construction of equal, fair and peaceful society. Therefore, IMF-JC Model Code of Conduct is targeted to attain union purposes to establish a fair society.

Beside IMF-JC, Zensen (The Japanese Federation of Textile, Garment, Chemical, Commercial, Food and Allied Industries Workers' Unions) whose name is changed into UI Zensen from 19 September 2002 is eager to make the Guideline on the Code of Conduct. Under this Guideline, some companies (e.g. Joshin Electric Appliances Sales Company) made the Code of Conduct in consultation with the trade unions. But this case cannot be discussed in my paper.

1. THE REASON AND PROCESS OF MAKING IMF-JC MODEL CODE OF CONDUCT

Under the Action Program adopted at the 29th World Congress of IMF held on May 1997 in San Francisco, it was approved to deal with multinational enterprises through negotiating corporate code of conduct in order to secure fundamental rights of workers in the process of economic globalization. Economic globalization has been having minus impacts on weak parts of workers and the poor. So we can see the growing movement against globalization that favours only transnational corporations. And IMF has adopted the policies to seek a social dimension to globalization. One of them is to draw up a Model Code of Conduct. IMF World Councils are expected to play a leading role in international collective bargaining to push the adoption of the code of conduct.

From 1990s, corporate governance has been an important policy to promote more democratic forms of good governance in the corporations. Various kinds of reformations are executed to improve corporate governance, involving a set of relationships among a corporate board, its shareholders and stakeholders. The corporate governance framework usually is regulated by legal and institutional environment. Furthermore, business ethics and corporate awareness of environmental and societal interests of the communities may have an impact on the reputation and profitable success of the company. In other words, corporate social responsibility has been recognized to develop good corporate governance together with globalization of economies.

In December 1998 IMF Model of Code of Conduct was confirmed at the executive committee. The Code was made on references of ILO Declaration on Fundamental Principles and Rights at Work in 1997, OECD Guidelines on Multinational Enterprises in 1976 and Social Charter for Democratic Development framed by ICFTU-APRO in 1994. IMF-JC made a draft of Code of Conduct suited to Japanese companies in August 1999 and discussed it at the meeting with Nikkeren (Japan Federation of Employers' Association) and Labour Management Committee in Metal Industry. And finally, IMFD-JC decided to approve it as Model Code of Conduct proposed to the company in July 2000. And under the policy of IMF-JC, company-wide labour unions have tried to negotiate with the company in order to conclude the code of conduct.

2. THE CONTENT OF IMF-JC MODEL CODE OF CONDUCT

There are some features in Model Code of Conduct framed by IMF-JC. It is made in due consideration of Japanese companies. So it is not the same to Code of Conduct made by IMF. The characteristics are the followings:

(1) Core labour standards shall be recognized and honoured by the multinational companies, regardless of whether the country has ratified the relative conventions. Namely they shall not adopt forced labour, child labour and discriminatory treatment of employment or promotion based on race, colour, sex, religion, nationality, social origin, political opinion or other distinguishing characteristics. And the company shall recognize the right of all workers to form and join trade unions, the right to bargain collectively and other rights to act collectively.

(2) Adequate safety and health shall be secured in the workplace by providing and improving the work environment by the company. The company shall promote and improve occupational health to the extent possible under the standards of the general knowledge in the industry. Safety and health does not become core labour standard, but it is included in both Code of Conduct because IMF and IMF-JC thinks of it as one of core labour standards because it is the most important working condition.

(3) Core labour standards and adequate safety and health is only minimum standards. The company does not intend to, and will not, use these minimum standards and conditions as maximum standards, or as the only applicable

conditions. Nor shall the company use these minimum standards as the basis for restraining the workers' rights in any way.

(4) But minimum wage and working hour is not included in IMF-JC Code of Conduct though both are written in IMF Code of Conduct. IMF-JC thinks that working conditions including wages shall be determined on the consent of the employers and employees in accordance with the degree of economic development. Namely it separates minimum wages and working hours from core labour standards.

(5) This Code shall be applicable to all workers who are working at overseas business facilities, including contractual workers, dispatched workers, temporary workers and so forth. "Overseas business facilities" shall mean any overseas local business facilities established by the company and oversea subsidiaries and sister corporations, which are included in the consolidated settlement of account of the company. But IMF Code shall be applicable to all suppliers and sub-contractors in spite of the amount of investment and does not limit the sphere of application to all workers at overseas enterprises, subsidiaries and sister corporation including in the consolidated settlement of accounts. So IMF Code shall be applicable to wider range of workers than JMF-JC Code. But under IMF-JC Code, the company shall promote this Code to overseas capital participating companies, which are excluded from the consolidated settlement of accounts.

(6) There are some measures to secure implementation of the Code. At first, the company shall strive to increase awareness the provisions and term of this Code of Conduct among overseas business facilities.

> Then the company shall exercise due care in constant manner whether this Code of Conduct is upheld at overseas business facilities. Whenever a violation of any provisions of this Code of Conduct is reported, or there are any problems arising out of the provisions or terms of this Code of Conduct, the company shall immediately investigate the case, and take measures to ensure that this Code of Conduct shall be upheld and problems shall be resolved.

As the third measure, the company shall promote this Code of Conduct to oversea capital participating corporations, which are excluded from the consolidated settlement of accounts, to the direct trade connections and to the overseas business facilities, in order to urge them to observe this Code of conduct. Whenever there is a violation of this Code of Conduct by one of the corporations, the company and the trade union shall, in corporation with the overseas business facilities, take measures to have the corporation respect the provisions of this Code of Conduct.

In these measures it is the most difficult problem how to monitor a violation of the provisions of the Code of Conduct. Under IMF Model a monitoring group, consisting of an equal number of management and union representatives must be created. In the case of deadlock, the ILO will handle arbitration or a neutral party agreed upon management and the union side. Management shall bear the cost of all monitoring activities.

In IMF-JC Code the company shall have a responsibility to investigate the case. So is it premised that the company shall bear expenses for monitoring? Does the trade union not have expenses at all? There is another possibility that monitoring committee composed of representative members from both the parties can investigate the case. Furthermore, there shall be the third way of monitoring conducted by the third party, foe example, NGO or voluntary association. This problem must be decided through collective bargaining between both the parties.

What measures can the company take when a violation of the provisions of the Code is reported? This Code does not provide concretely the provisions on measures. Is any sanction to the corporation included in the consolidated settlement of accounts possible when its violation of the Code is reported? Or does the company take sanction to the corporation excluded from the consolidated settlement of accounts if its violation of the Code is found by some monitoring? IMF Model Code of Conduct provides that the company does not transact with the contactor, but under the IMF-JC model, there is no provision on the concrete sanction. In other words, IMF-JC mode Code has some ambiguity in the provisions. It is thought that the ambiguous provisions shall be negotiated through collective bargaining between the company and the workers' union.

3. HOW MANY COMPANIES HAVE SIGNED THE CODE OF CONDUCT?

IMF has campaigned for the adoption of the Code in all corporations where affiliates have members under Action Program 220-2005 decided at the 30th Congress in Sydney. At present three group companies have signed IMF Model Code of Conduct in the world.

As the first case, the statement of agreement was signed between Merloni Elettrodomestice S.P.A. and the national FIM-FIOM-UILM in Italy in December 2001. In this agreement the company undertakes to respect fundamental human rights and core labour standards. In particular, the company shall be oriented toward promoting positive action to support the principles of trade union freedom and to correct non-compliance to eliminate child labour and forced labour. The company shall monitor its own production for the compliance. But the monitoring shall be entrusted to the National

Joint Commission. When the violation should be found at its own direct suppliers, the company reserves the right to institute sanctions against the said suppliers including cancellation of the contract.

On 6 June 2002, Volkswagen AG, the Group Global Works Council of Volkswagen AG and the International Metalworkers' Federation agreed to sign the Declaration on Social Rights and Industrial Relationships at Volkswagen. Besides core labour standards, Volkswagen shall meet national legal minimum requirement on wages (compensation and benefits), work hours and occupational safety and health protection. Volkswagen supports and encourages its contractors to take this declaration into account in their own respective corporate policy. Appropriate measures will be agreed at the meeting of Volkswagen Group Global Works Council in order to realize this declaration.

As the third case, top management of Daimler Chrysler and representatives of the Daimler Chrysler Worlds Employee Committee signed "Social Responsibility Principles of Daimler Chrysler" in September 2002. In this Code the company supports the principles on human and workers' rights and the environment, which make the basis for the United States' Global Compact Initiative advocated by Mr. Annan. It expects its suppliers to apply these principles as a favourable basis for enduring business relations.

How is the situation in Japan? It is so regrettable that there is no company signing the IMF-JC Model Code of Conduct in Japan. IMF-JC has organized the head quarter to promote the Code of Conduct whose members are President and three key officials of IMF-JC. They have a responsibility to decide the concrete program to conclude the Code with the company through information exchange and consultation with company-wide trade unions and company group-based trade unions.

Toyota is the most profitable and excellent company. So Toyota is targeted to be the first company to sign IMF-JC Model Code of Conduct. Joint consultation will be expected to hold soon between Toyota trade union and the company. The other companies will follow after Toyota if it will sign the Code of Conduct because Japanese companies, in general, make a move to stand one behind another. But, the management of Toyota refused to submit this problem to joint-consultation at the present stage.

A group of major economic organizations in Japan published the "Guidelines for Investment Activities in Developing Countries" in June 1973. But these Guidelines were revised in April 1978 to be welcomed by the host countries, whether in developing or developed countries, and contribute towards its development and national welfare. They provide corporate ethics to avoid tensions and frictions within the political, economic, social and cultural sectors of the host countries. In Art. 4 of the Guidelines, Japanese companies establish sound and fair labour-management relations by opening both knowledge and understanding of labour union organizations and labour practices of the host country and by promoting mutual understanding between labour and management through exchange of information and opinions. And they take into consideration local circumstances when deciding working conditions and to improve the work environment so as to ensure safety and hygiene for employees under Art. 5. These Guidelines do not neglect working conditions and labour management relations relating to core labour standards. Therefore, it is thought that these Guidelines have the similar sphere with IMF-JC Model Code of Conduct. So Japanese companies cannot completely deny the Code of Conduct. Rather there shall be found room for compromise to admit the Code of Conduct. But we must recognize that there are some differences between them in which IMF-JC has more effective scheme and Guidelines, which they have not applied to contractors in both host countries and Japan.

4. IMF-JC MODEL CODE OF CONDUCT APPLIED TO CHINA

Japanese companies have invested direct capitals in China so rapidly especially since 1992. According to "Overseas Direct Investment Directory in 2002" published by Toyo Keiuza Shinposha, Japan-affiliated companies in China (Joint companies between China and Japan and the companies invested by only Japanese corporations) are 2500 in number and employ about 580,000 labourers mainly working in manufacturing industries, e.g. electric and electronics, textile, automobile, food, machinery and chemical industry. Recently they begin to found department of development works in China.

In the future direct investment to China is expected to increase since China has a big market. After China entered into WTO, direct investment from Japan will grow in the following grounds: (1) the Chinese Government has a policy to positively introduce foreign direct investment, (2) there are many workers receiving lower wages than in Japan though their wages are increasing every year, (3) Legal system is being arranged on investment environment, for example, intellectual property and Contract Act.

Are there no problems in applying IMF-JC Code of Conduct to Chinese joint companies and contractors? We must investigate factual conditions on the right to organize trade unions, to bargain collectively, and to do industrial actions (strikes) among core labour standards under Trade Unions Act amended in 2001.

At first we must check whether workers can organize trade unions freely or not. It is understood that only trade unions can be permitted to be organized which can join in All-China Federation of Trade Union. They are to be used within the existing structure of socialist political system. So it is questionable whether freedom of association is guaranteed in China.

And we must consider whether Chinese trade unions based on an enterprise are playing the same role with ones in capitalistic countries. They are expected to maintain the present political system together with the Communist Party of China. So they are inclined to have political character and dislike to protest the company on behalf of the employees.

In China the right to strikes is not formally guaranteed in order to maintain socialistic market economies. But in fact we can find many strikes and demonstrations especially in nation-owned enterprises. In this case trade union shall try to settle the problem with the establishment in order to recover production and industrial peace under the Trade Unions Act of 2001. Is this changing the role of trade unions in China? So we must be careful in applying Code of Conduct relating to freedom of association, their right to collective bargaining and to do industrial actions and strikes because social and economic structure is different from that of capitalistic countries like Japan.

Child labour has been seen in urban areas. Children from poor rural area are often working in urban factories. For example, MacDonald China was criticized that its contractor employed children to make premiums attracting customers. According to the statistics of ILO, there are 9,224,000 working children between 10 and 14 years old in China. Japanese-affiliated companies will not directly employ children, but we must check whether the sub-contractors employ child labourers. They shall be careful to the children employed by the sub-contractors and forced labour is discussed only at Chinese prisons. Therefore, we think that forced labour cannot be found in Japanese-affiliated companies. In China it is formally thought that there cannot be found discriminative treatment of labourers based on sex. But we must examine whether discrimination can be seen based on sex and the other reasons, for example, political opinions. There are many rules and regulations to maintain labour safety and health in China. But their implementations cannot be assumed because the companies are not willing to spend money to protect their workers. So it is necessary to examine labour accidents and occupational diseases in Japan-owned or funded companies.

CONCLUSION

IMF-JC Model Code of Conduct is discussed in this paper. It is not yet concluded between a company and trade union. It is reported that NIPPON KEIDANREN organized in May 2002 began to study on "Global Compact" initiated by Mr. Annan, General Secretary of the UN because it can be monitored by the leadership of each company. If Toyota will enter Global Compact, other Japanese companies will follow it. So IMF-JC cannot be successful to conclude Code of Conduct.

If the company will conclude on the Code of Conduct, what problems are there in China where many Japanese companies are in operation? It is a good example how multinational companies shall fulfil social responsibility in foreign countries. And we can find that there are peculiar problems relating to core labour standards in China because she is now promoting socialist market economy.

{This original paper was submitted to the workshop on corporate social responsibility relating to labour dimension held in China Peoples University, Peking, China, November 2002}.

References

ICFTU ed., *A Trade Union Guide to Globalization*, ICFTU, 2001.

UNCTAD ed., *The Social Responsibility of Transnational Corporation*, United Nations, 1999.

Japanese Trade Union Confederation ed., *Creating Constructive Labour-Management Relations in Multinationals*, May 2002.

Marvin J. Levine, *Worker Rights and Labour Standards in Asia's Four New Tigers*, Plenum Press, New York, 1997.

Kozo Kagawa, "Legal Cultural Research on Social Clause Problem in South and South-East Asian Countries", in the Proceedings of 1995 Annual Meeting Research Committee on Sociology of Law, International Sociological Association, Tokyo, 1995

Kozo Kagawa ed., *Fair Labour Standards in Asia,* Special Seminar at International Industrial Relations Association, 12th World Congress, Tokyo, 2000.

Part III

SUPREME COURT JUDGEMENTS ON LABOUR RELATIONS: CASE COMMENTS

CHAPTER

10

Individual-Employment Relationship

(1) LABOUR CONTRACT

Michiko Kitada
v.
Hyougo Prefectual Labour Relations Commission

Supreme Court (Third Petty Bench)

Michiko Kitada
v.
Hyougo Prefectual Labour Relations Commission

Legality of employment contract of local public employee renewable day by day refusal to renew contract after four years' employment

HEADNOTES

Facts

The appellant was employed at Hyogo Prefectural Institute of Hygiene from April 1974 as a part-time employee whose contract would be renewed day by day. Her task was to clean test tubes and to pigeonhole data. From January 1977, she was engaged in pigeonholing books at the library of the Institute. On 31 March 1978 she was refused further renewal of her contract. She filed an unfair labour practice complaint with Hyogo Local Labour Relations Commission on the ground that she had been dismissed because of her activity in organizing part-time public employees in Hyogo Prefecture.

The Commission rejected the complaint on 31 July 1984. It considered that the chief of the Institute had reasonable grounds for refusing to renew the contract and that there was no evidence that the refusal was designed to prevent her form playing an active part in union activities.

Kobe District Court and Osaka High Court upheld the order of the Commission for the following different reasons: (1) Although there was no provision regarding part-time public employees in the Local Public Service Act—except as regards a temporary employee whose contract could not exceed six months in duration and might be renewed only for one further period of six months—a local public government was permitted to employ a part-time worker whose contract was renewed day by day when there was a special reason for such employment, namely, when there was no need for a permanent employee and a part-time employee sufficed to meet temporary needs for a time. (2) Even if the contract of a part-time public employee had been renewed day by day for a long period, her status could not be changed to that of a permanent public employee, because she had not been selected on the basis of competitive examination and under the strict procedure of appointment required for a permanent employee by the Local Public Service Act. (3) Accordingly she had to lose her position if her contract was not renewed, and it was within the discretion of a person who had the power of appointment to renew it or not. There was thus no scope for discussion of whether the failure to renew the contract amounted to an unfair labour practice or not.

The appellant submitted the following arguments to the Supreme Court: (1) it was agreed at the initial stage of appointment that she was to be employed for an indefinite period as a temporary employee. This was not permitted by article 22, paragraph 2 of the Local Public Service Act. Since the violation was due to the illegal personnel policy of the local government, that government should protect the employee's status. (2) A temporary public employee should be treated like an employee in a private company as regards recruitment, because a competitive examination and a strict procedure of selection was not necessary for employing her; the argument that she should be selected by such procedure violated the principle of equality under the law laid down in article 14 of the Constitution.

Decision

The appeal was dismissed.

Law Applied

Local Public Service Act

Article 22: . . . (2) At the local government establishment personnel committee an appointing officer, as provided by rules of the committee, may, with the approval of the committee, engage a person for temporary employment, not to exceed six months in duration, in emergencies, for temporary government positions or in instances when there is no list of eligible candidates. In such cases, the employment may, with the approval of the committee, be renewed for a period of six months, but may not be renewed a second time.

(3) For the purpose of the preceding paragraph, the committee may specify the qualifications of persons to be given temporary employment.

(4) The committee may cancel any temporary employment, which does not comply with the provisions of the preceding two paragraphs.

JUDGEMENT

This court considers the finding and the judgement of the lower court rational and appropriate in the light of all the evidence in this case. Although the appellant alleged a violation of article 14 of the Constitution, her claim can be interpreted as amounting, in substance, to the assertion of a violation of the Local Public Service Act. However, that assertion cannot be admitted and the appeal is accordingly dismissed. [*Source*: No. (Gyou-Tsu) 140 of 1991, decided on 3 December 1991. Reported at Rodohanrei No. 609: 16.]

ANNOTATION

1. The reported case poses two main problems. One is whether a fixed-term employment contract is permissible in the local public service and whether it can be renewed day by day. Another is whether such a contract can be changed into one without limit of time after four years' employment. The appellant filed a complaint of unfair labour practice, but the High Court and the Supreme Court focused on the abovementioned two main problems and did not directly deal with the problem whether the refusal to renew the contract amounted to an unfair labour practice.

2. A public employee is usually employed for an indefinite period of time. Fixed-term employment is not regulated under the Local Public Service Act, except as provided in article 22 (see above, Law Applied). Hence, the question arises whether fixed-term employment is otherwise permitted under the Act.

There are two opinions on this problem. According to the negative opinion, fixed-term employment is not permitted because the Act does not provide for it even though the legislature would have anticipated the need for such employment. According to the positive opinion, fixed-term employment is permitted, though only when it is practically necessary to have recourse to it, and the status of public employee is guaranteed, because the Act does not prohibit it. The Supreme Court accepts the positive view and admits the legality of one-day employment contracts when there is a shortage of permanent skilled employees at the Institute.

3. Let us consider the second problem. With respect to private companies it has been held that a fixed-term employment contract, after repeated automatic renewals, continued in existence substantially as if it were a contract for an indefinite period (*Tokyo Shibaura Denki K.K. v. Tatsuko Maeda et al.*, 1 ILLR 95). In the cited case, the Supreme Court did not say clearly that the fixed-term contract was changed into one for an indefinite period. However, it was understood that, as a result of repeated renewal, the employee had become entitled to expect renewal of the contract as if it were one for an indefinite period. In the present case, dealing with a local public employee, the Supreme Court was not prepared to apply that legal theory.

A permanent local public employee is engaged after a strict procedure of selection under the Local Public Service Act. The appellant had not been selected though this procedure. If her contract could be changed to one for an indefinite period, she would obtain permanent status without going through the strict procedure of selection. The judgement must accordingly be considered to be a consequence of the Local Public Service Act.

(2) POLITICAL RIGHT

Kansai Electric Power Co.
v.
Jiro Hayami *et al.*

Supreme Court (Third Petty Bench)

Kansai Electric Power Co.
v.
Jiro Hayami *et al.*

Company watching and shadowing employees because of their membership in or sympathy with Japanese Communist party—damages

HEADNOTES

Facts

The four respondents were employees of the appellant company and members of the Kansai Electric Power Labour Union, which was organized in 1953 after the dissolution of the Communist, controlled Electric Power Industrial Union. The Kansai Electric Power Labour Union in 1958 concluded a collective agreement with the company, according to which it intended to cooperate in promoting productivity and smoothing management of the company in mutual understanding: in 1968 it passed a resolution to support the Democratic Socialist Party. However, the respondents continued to be members or sympathizers of the Japanese Communist party; they thus belonged to a minority radical group in the enterprise-based labour union.

The treaty of Mutual Cooperation and Security between Japan and the United States of America was concluded in 1960 and automatically renewed in 1970. At the time of renewal, radical groups were expected to mount an opposition movement. The appellant company feared that radical members of the labour union might destroy the facilities for power supplies and production. The Kobe branch of the company accordingly had a policy of opposing the communist group, on the assumption that the strategy of the group was to crush the company through violent revolution. The company distributed pamphlets to employees and supervisors to propagate anti-communism; it also held classes to educate employees in the matter.

The following harassment tactics were applied to the four respondents. They were transferred to posts were they could easily be watched by supervisors. Supervisors were ordered to shadow them after working hours, to check whether they stopped-off anywhere on there way home. The company directed other employees to avoid personal contact with them during commuting, so that they might be isolated. The company checked who telephoned to them from the outside. And one-day supervisors opened their lockers without their consent and checked the contents, wearing gloves so as to avoid leaving fingerprints.

The respondents demanded 2,871,000 yen each as compensation, on the ground that their freedom of belief was violated and their right to keep their honour and good character was impaired by the company's policy of labour management. They also asked that a letter of apology be posted on a notice board for one week and published in an internal house organ on 2 December 1971.

Kobe District Court, by decision of 18 May 1984, only awarded moral damages and lawyer's fees. Its reasoning was as follows: (1) According to Article 3 of the Labour Standards Act, an employer shall not engage in discriminatory treatment with respect to wages, working hours or other working conditions by reason of the nationality, creed or social status of any worker. This stipulation must be interpreted so as to prohibit an employer from violating an employee's freedom of belief, except on reasonable grounds relating to order in the establishment or the promotion of productivity. Therefore, an employer may infringe freedom of belief only when there is a concrete possibility of danger to order in the establishment or the promotion of productivity. Also, the procedure and means must be reasonable, because it is public policy that the employee be not deprived of freedom of belief by the unilateral conduct of an employer. (2) In this case it could not be found that the respondents had a concrete possibility of interfering with order in the establishment or the promotion of productivity. Nevertheless, the company watched them and isolated them from other employees. They suffered social ostracism at the workplace. Thus, the company's conduct violated the respondents' freedom of belief and their right to keep their honour and good character. This amounted to tortuous conduct under articles 709 and 710 of the Civil Code. On this basis, the Court awarded each of the respondents 300.000 yen as "consolation money" and 100.000 yen as lawyers' fees. However, the Court did not order the employer to post and publish a letter of apology.

Osaka High Court affirmed the judgement of Kobe District court on 24 September 1991. The company then appealed to the Supreme Court.

Decision

The appeal was dismissed.

Law Applied

The Labour Standards Acts

Article 3: No employer shall discriminate against or in favour of any worker, as regards wages, working hours and other working conditions, by reason of nationality, creed or social status.

Civil Code

Article 417: In the absence of any contrary

agreement, the amount of compensation for damages shall be assessed in money.

Article 709: Any person who intentionally or negligently violates the rights of another is obliged to compensate the damages arising therefrom.

Article 710: A person who is liable for damages in accordance with the provisions of the preceding article must compensate even non-pecuniary damage, whether the injury was to the person, liberty or reputation of another or to the latter's property rights.

Article 722: (1) The provisions of article 417 shall apply *mutatis mutandis* to compensation for damages arising from a tort.

Article 723: If any person has defamed another, the court may, on the application of the latter, order the former to take suitable measures for the restoration of the latter's reputation, either *in lieu* of together with compensation for damages.

JUDGEMENT

Although it could be seen that there was no real possibility for the respondents to destroy the order of the enterprise, the company continued to watch them merely because they were members of or sympathizers with the Communist Party. Also, the company directed other employees not to contact them or associate with them, on the ground that they were left-wing extremists and did not try to work together in pursuance of management policy. As a result, the respondents were isolated from other employees. This conduct infringed the respondents' right to communicate with other employees at the workplace.

In addition, the supervisors opened lockers without the permission of the respondents and took a photograph of their pocketbooks, showing that they were members of the Communist Party. This conduct brought disgrace on them and infringed their right to privacy. As a result, it could be judged that the conduct amounted to a tort under articles 709 and 710 of the Civil Code.

[*Source*: Case No. (o) 10 of 1992, decided on 5 September 1995, reported at Rodohanrei No. 630:28.]

ANNOTATION

1. In Japan, the Communist party was first allowed to organize after the Second World War, to promote democratization. But communists were purged from government and from private companies after 1950, because of a change in policy in relation to the party by General Headquarters of the Supreme Commander, Allied Powers, under the cold war system. Generally, the courts held that the dismissals resulting from the purge were valid, because the orders of General headquarters overrode the Constitution.'

After the end of the occupation, in 1952, Japanese companies were afraid of communist activities in the enterprise, since they thought that the communists had a strategy to destroy the companies in order to build a communist nation. The case here reported occurred in 1970, when the Treaty of Mutual Cooperation and Security between Japan and the United States was amended. The company feared that the communist group of employees would impair its interests in order to protest against the Treaty, in recent cases concerning the Tokyo Electric Power Co., the issue was whether discriminatory payment of wages amounted to discriminatory treatment on the ground of political thought of employees who were members of the Communist party (see, for instance, *Masuo Aoki et al.* v. *Tokyo Electric Power Co.*, decided on 24 August 1993 by Maebashi District Court, reported in Rodohanrei 635:22). In Japan, companies continue to be afraid of the destructive activities by communists after the Second World War.

2. Under article 3 of the Labour Standards Act, employers are prohibited from engaging in discriminatory treatment with respect to wages, working hours and other working conditions by reason of the nationality, creed or social status of any worker. A

person who has violated the provisions of that article shall be sentenced to imprisonment of not more than six months or to a fine of not more than 300,000 yen.

The word "creed" means religious thought or political belief or other ways of thinking. It is a widespread interpretation that article 3 forbids discriminatory treatment based solely on an employee's thought or belief. But discriminatory treatment may be permitted when an employee, in pursuance of his political or religious belief, engages in actions, which are detrimental to order in the enterprise. The nature and extent of the treatment must be proportionate to the degree of interference with order in the enterprise. If it is not, the treatment is deemed to violate article 3 of the labour Standards Act.

It is now understood that the term "other working conditions" includes the conditions for dismissal. Therefore, this provision is often invoked in labour cases on the effect of dismissal. The dismissal becomes *null and void* when it is found to come under discriminatory treatment by reason of creed. However, "other working conditions" do not include conduct of the company in watching and shadowing employees. Hence the provisions of article 3 could not be directly applied to the conduct of the company in the reported case, and the respondents had sued for damages under articles 709 and 710 of the Civil Code.

3. Article 709 of the Civil Code provides that a person who intentionally or negligently violates the rights of another is obliged to compensate the damages arising there from. It is an established interpretation that "the rights of another" are not only concrete right such as ownership, but also interests, which should come under the protection of the law.

In this case, the Supreme Court denied that there was a possibility that the respondents would impair the company's interests in pursuance of their political thought. It found that the company was engaged in watching and shadowing the respondents only because they were members or sympathizers of the Communist party. As a result, the company infringed the respondents' right to communicate freely with other employees and their right to keep their honour and good character. Also, the company invaded their right to privacy. This conduct was tantamount to a violation of "the rights of another" in the meaning of articles 709 and 710 of the Civil Code.

4. Compensation is usually paid in monetary from. Article 722, paragraph 1 of the Civil Code establishes that rule as the most proper form of compensation. Compensation in money is used also for non-property damage. However, other forms of remedy are exceptionally allowed: article 723 provides that, where the victim requests, the court can order measures for the restoration of the reputation of the defamed party and/or compensation in money. The following court order is deemed to be a proper measure for this purpose (Zentaro Kitagawa ed., *Doing Business in Japan*, Vol. 8, p. 27):

(a) A letter of apology from the wrongdoer to the defamed;
(b) A notice of apology or withdrawal of the statement in the place where it was made; and
(c) Publication of an apology and withdrawal in a newspaper.

In the reported case, the Supreme Court did not admit other forms of remedy. It judged that compensation in money was sufficient to restore the reputation of the defamed. In general, the Court orders other forms of remedy only where the wrongdoer's conduct is extremely pernicious to the defamed.

(3) SEXUAL HARASSMENT

Otoko Kouda
v.
Otoda Construction Company and its President

Supreme Court (Second Petty Bench)

Otoko Kouda
v.
Otoda Construction Company and its President

Sexual harassment—damages suffered

HEADNOTES

Facts

Appellant was a female employee at the respondent company as from 21 January 1991. The company employed some ten employees and engaged in construction and snowplowing. The president, separated from his wife, lived alone. The appellant was divorced and had one child. She worked in the president's house where she cooked, cleaned, tended the garden, answered the phone and brought mail to his office. She managed 100,000 yen per month for household expenses and her monthly wage was 105,000 yen. She was allowed to take lunch with the president with no charge. During meals she sometimes enjoyed sexual conversation with him. From the end of January, the president began to touch her body and breasts. He also tried to kiss her. He used many words with sexual meanings and proposed having sexual relations with her. He removed her trousers and tried to force her down on 27 March 1991. But she refused to submit. Thereafter he began to mistreat her with a view to dismissing her. He stopped taking meals at home, and no longer allowed her to manage the household funds. He slapped her face with anger when she blamed him for his sexual approaches. He did not pay a bonus to her.

She complained to him orally and in writing. He knew that she was disclosing his conduct to other persons. He dismissed her on 14 September 1991 and she sued for five million yen for moral damages resulting from his sexual harassment.

The District Court found that the president's conduct had damaged her work environment and amounted to sexual harassment, because his action gave displeasure to her. The Court ordered the president and the company, jointly and severally, to pay 800,000 yen to her as consolation money. However, the Court found that the dismissal was based on reasonable grounds owing to her defiant attitude and her carelessness in managing the household affairs; furthermore, she refused to obey his orders after 27 March. Thus nothing was due as consolation money for the dismissal as such.

The decision was appealed to the High Court to increase the amount of consolation money due her. The president and the company also appealed to dismiss that part of the judgement favouring the appellant. The high Court ruled that it was not always illegal for a male superior to engage in sexual remarks and behaviour towards a female subordinate, even against her will. But it encroaches on the right to sexual self-determination or freedom when such speech and behaviour is found to be totally inappropriate, judged on the basis of the status and age of the male superior, the age and matrimonial status of the female subordinate, the existing relationship between the two of them, the place where, and the situation in which, the remarks and behaviour occur, the reaction of the female subordinate, and the frequency of the sexual remarks and behaviour.

On the basis of the above principles, the High Court found that the employer's remarks and conduct, between February and April, infringed the personal rights of the appellant, and ordered the president and the company, jointly and severally, to pay 1.2 million yen as consolation money. However, after April, the president treated the appellant only an employee and in a business-like manner. She had insufficient ability to handle the household affairs and confidence between them was lost. Thus, dismissal was not abusive and hence not grounds as such for consolation money.

Appellant appealed to increase the amount of consolation money on the grounds that the dismissal was *null and void.* The president and the company appealed to reverse the judgement of the High Court.

Decision

The appeal was dismissed.

Law Applied

Civil Code: Art. 44, Sec. 1. A juridical person is liable for compensation for any damage to other parties by its directors or other representatives in the performance of their duties.

Art. 709. Any person who intentionally or negligently violates the rights of another is obliged to compensate the damages arising there from.

JUDGEMENT

The Supreme Court found that the judgement of the High Court, ordering 1.2 million yen as consolation money for suffering arising out of sexual harassment, was rational and appropriate in the light of all the evidence presented to the High Court. There was no error in the judgement and the appeal was accordingly dismissed.

[*Source*: Case No. (0) 293 of 1997 decided on 16 July 1999; reported at Dodohanrei No. 767:14]

ANNOTATION

This is the second judgement on sexual harassment rendered by the Supreme Court. The first was the Osaka City Tennoji case in June 1999. In that case a male colleague teacher repeatedly harassed a female teacher with sexual remarks. This was found to be illegal in the lower courts as violating her personal rights. The appeal to the Supreme Court was not receivable on procedural grounds. Hence the judgement reported here is substantively the first Supreme Court pronouncement on the question.

Sexual harassment includes both the "quid pro quo" type and the "environmental" type. In the former, a female worker suffers a job disadvantage owing to her reaction to sexual speech or behaviour by a male worker. In the latter, the environment becomes distasteful to the female worker owing to such speech or behaviour in the workplace. This case reported on here is in the latter category.

When this case arose, there was no special provision on sexual harassment in the field of labour law. Thus the only course open to the appellant was to sue for damages under the Civil Code, either under ART. 709 as a tort or under Art. 415 as a default in an obligation to protect female employees from sexual harassment. The former provision was used in this case.

A feature of the facts in this case was that it took place at a special workplace. Her work combined official and private matters, because her workplace was the president's own house.

In Japan there are many cases of sexual harassment of female subordinates by male superiors. But there has been no case of sexual harassment by a female superior of a male subordinate, *inter alia* because there are few female managers. And same-sex sexual harassment has not come before the courts.

There were two important points in this Supreme Court judgement. First is the standard applied to determine whether the action of the male superior constitutes illegal sexual harassment under Art. 709 of the Civil Code. The Supreme Court endorsed the principles enunciated by the High Court. The following should be considered in their entirety in judging sexual harassment cases: status and age of the male superior; age and matrimonial status of the female subordinate; frequency of sexual remarks and behaviour. These standards are flexible and will have to be clarified in future cases.

The second important point concerns the company's obligation under Art. 44, Sec. 1 of the Civil Code. In this case the employee's work was done not only for the president's own interests, but also for the company's business. For example, she received business telephone calls from the company and from outside. Thus the company had an obligation to pay damages jointly and severally with the president. This interpretation is based on reasonable grounds.

Under an amendment to the Equal Employment Opportunity Act effective as from April 1999, employers have a duty to endeavour to prevent sexual harassment in the workplace. The Ministry of Labour has issued guidelines concerning the derailed content of this duty. Under these guidelines, employers are required to give consideration to the following: (1) establishing a policy against sexual harassment, making it known to workers, and providing related education; (2) responding to representations and complaints in an appropriate manner based on their nature; (3) responding promptly and properly in sexual harassment cases. The company would not be liable for damages if these three points are put into practice, as the employer's duty to "endeavour" to prevent harassment has been met.

(4) PART-TIME WORKER

Heiankaku Co.
v.
Uta Tamurea and Sumire Warashina

Supreme Court (Second Petty Bench)

Heiankaku Co.
v.
Uta Tamurea and Sumire Warashina

Contract of employment of part-time worker for fixed term-effect of repeated renewal - dismissal of part-time worker

HEADNOTES

Facts

Heiankaku Co. manages a wedding and funeral hall. The appellant company engaged Tamura as a part-timer on February 1971. Warashina was engaged as a part-timer on November 1974. At the time of hiring they did not conclude a contract in written form. Tamura's work was to cook food and to wash dishes. Warashina was employed to arrange clothes for marriage and funeral ceremonies. In 1980 they concluded a contract of employment for a one-year term in written form. After that the contracts were renewed twice. The appellees were engaged on the same working conditions as the regular employees. But the company refused to renew the contracts of employment at the expiration of their duration in April 1983. There was no promise that the contracts would be renewed at the expiration of the duration. But the employment contract was expected by the appellees to continue in force. Therefore, the appellees appealed for a provisional disposition to the effect that an employer-employee relationship existed provisionally between the company and the appellees.

They were successful in Shizuoka District Court on 16 August 1983. After this judgement they agreed to a compromise that they would be employed from 21 July 1984 to 20 May 1985. But they were ordered to work in a different job. Their work was to weed a garden and to sweep the floors and lawns. So they fell ill and were obliged to absent from work. After they recovered, they offered to work again. But the company refused to accept their work. Therefore, they sued for a declaratory judgement to the effect that an employer-employee relationship existed between the company and appellees. And they demanded wages, which were earned after they offered to work again, and consolation money.

Shizuoka District Court and Shizuoka High Court accepted the appellees' assertion. According to the reasoning of Shizuoka High Court, the employment contracts, in fact, had been renewed on the cessation of a given period unless the contrary intent was represented. These employment contracts were not to be treated as contracts for an indefinite period. Nevertheless, the cessation of employment was substantially tantamount to an expression of an intention to discharge the defendants. Therefore, the employer's refusal to renew the contracts should be subject to restriction in the light of either the principle of good faith or the doctrine of abuse of exercise of his right to discharge his employees. The company did not present food reasons to refuse renewal. So the contracts continued to exist between the company and the employees. The company did not present good reasons to effuse renewal. So the contracts continued to exist between the company and the employees. The company should pay wages to the appellees. The company ordered the appellees to do a job, which was not provided for in the employment contracts. This order caused mental anguish to the appellees. So the company should pay consolation money.

JUDGEMENT

This court finds the finding and the judgement of the court below rational and appropriate in the light of all the evidence in this case. There is no error in its conclusion. The appeal of the appellant shall accordingly be dismissed.

[*Source*: Case No. (0) 871 of 1987, decided on 16 October 1987]

ANNOTATION

1. Part-time workers have recently increased in number, particularly among housewives (about 5 million in 1987). At present there is no legislation in Japan, which specifically deals with part-time workers. Consequently, laws, which apply to regular full-time workers, also apply to part-time workers. Therefore, some problems may arise. Although Article 15 of the Labour Standards Act provides that the employer must specify the wages and working conditions at the time of concluding the labour contract, some part-time workers are employed only with an oral and insufficient explanation of their working conditions. Such obscurity at the time of hiring often results in trouble. So, in 1982, the Ministry of Labour introduced a standard form on "employment notice" for part-time workers and has been guiding employers to clarify the main working conditions of part-time workers. But the attempt to pass the new Bill on part-time workers failed in 1988. So the Ministry of Labour decided to strengthen the administrative guidance for protecting part-time workers.

2. There are some problems in this case. One is the definition of part-time workers. There is no clear definition of part-time workers in Japan. In general, there are two types of definitions. One definition is that part-time workers are those whose prescribed working hours are shorter than those of regular full-time workers on a daily, weekly or monthly basis. The other

defines them as those who are called part-time workers in the company. The former definition ignores the existence of part-time workers in the company. The former definition ignores the existence of part-time workers who are working the same hours and days as regular full-time workers. In this case the latter definition is adopted, because the defendants are part-time workers who are working the same hours and days as permanent workers.

3. Part-time workers are considered as workers of a temporary nature. So part-time workers have the same role as temporary workers in the Japanese industrial relations system. Namely, part-time workers are expected to play the role of safety valve in maintaining a lifelong employment system for permanent employees. Therefore, part-time workers are expected to discharge more easily than regular employees. But many courts hold that it is unfair that part-time workers and temporary workers who are engaged in the same job as regular workers should be treated less favourably in the termination of employment than permanent workers.

Therefore, when part-time workers are employed with no provision regarding the term of employment, they are treated in the same manner as regular employees who are employed for an indefinite term. For example, those part-time workers must be discharged in the same manner as permanent employees. If the discharge is an abuse of the right to dismiss, it is *null and void.*

Where part-time workers are employed for a definite term, the employment contract is automatically terminated at the expiration of the term. Therefore, the problem of discharge does not arise. However, the employer continues to hire part-time workers by repeating the renewal of their employment contract. The Supreme Court supports the judgement of the High Court that the employment contract is not to be treated as a contract for an indefinite term when the contract for a definite term has been renewed repeatedly. But the fact that it has been repeatedly renewed gives rise to a mutual trust relationship where under part-time workers expect the employer not to refuse renewal of the employment contract without a fair and appropriate reason. In other words, part-time workers expect the employer not to refuse renewal of the employment contract without a fair and appropriate reason. In other words, part-time workers have become entitled to expect renewal of the contract. Therefore, if the employer refuses to renew the employment contract at the expiration, this may be considered as identical with discharge in substance and the existence of just cause for the refusal of renewal may be required. So the refusal to renew the contract is *null and void* as an abuse of right unless grounds such as the presence of excess personnel or other reasons were found to justify refusal of the renewal. This judgement is influenced by that of the Supreme Court dealing with temporary workers (*Tokyo Shibaura Denki K.K.* v. *Tatsuko Maeda et al.* 1 International Labour Law Reports 95).

(5) TRANSFER

Koji Aiko et al.
v.
Nissan Motor Co.

Supreme Court (First Petty Bench)

Koji Aiko et al.
v.
Nissan Motor Co.

Employer's right to change employee's job

HEADNOTES

Facts

Fuji Precision Machines Co. and Prince Motor Co. had employed the seven appellants respectively. After the amalgamation of these companies with Nissan Motor Co., they worked as machinists for over 10 years at the latter's Murayama Factory. At the Murayama factory three kinds of motor cars (Sunny, Violet, Austin) were manufactured. In April 1980, the company made plans to produce FF cars instead of FR cars, so as to adapt to the trend of the world motor industry. After investigation, it became evident that the Murayama factory was too small for changing three kinds of motorcars into FF cars. So the company decided that FF cars would be produced at its Tochigi factory and that at the Murayama factory other kinds of motorcars*Skyline, Laurel, (March) would be manufactured as FR cars. It was supposed that as a result about 800 new employees would be needed in mechanical pressing assembly, coating and fitting to produce the new motorcar, "March". Therefore, the company decided to transfer almost all machinists to work in mechanical pressing, assembly, coating and fitting. This plan was executed in 1982 and 1983. The company automatically changed the assignments of 495 machinists—except for elderly or sickly persons—in the production department of "March", without any consideration for their careers, their experience, their skills and their individual expectations. The seven appellants refused to change their jobs because they considered that these transfers were *null and void.* They sued for a declaration affirming their status as machinists and for damages on the ground that the transfers were unfair labour practices and torts.

Yokohama District Court allowed the claims in part for the following reasons.

(1) In the company, works rules provided that the company might order an employee to change his job and workplace in case of business necessity and that the employee could not refuse to obey this order without reasonable grounds. The plaintiffs (appellants) were considered to have given prior consent to changes of workplace and type of work. So the company could determine these unilaterally without the plaintiffs' consent. Nevertheless, the employer's right did not give him an absolute discretion; the exercise of the right was subject to the general rule of good faith and public order. In particular, the company had to give sufficient consideration to the personal circumstances of the employee as well as the needs of the company. In other words, the Court had to judge the effect of the employer's order by comparing the company's need and their personal inconvenience caused by the order. In this case the plaintiffs' inconvenience was the more serious because the company did not give consideration to the plaintiffs' skill, experience and adaptability to the new job, and accordingly their skill and experience could not be used in the new type of work. Furthermore the working conditions became worse and became the work was simpler and harder. The company's order to change the type of work then amounted to an abusive exercise of rights. The District Court held that the seven plaintiffs had no obligation to work at the workplace and job to which they had been transferred.

(2) There ware two labour unions in the company. Many members of the two unions, including the seven plaintiffs, were ordered to change their workplace and type of work. Hence it was not found that only the company treated the seven plaintiffs disadvantageously. The orders to change the workplace and type of work did not amount to unfair labour practices. And there was no evidence that these orders were given in order to injure the plaintiffs. So the Court denied damages, because the orders did not constitute torts.

Tokyo High Court revised the judgement of the District Court on the following grounds. (1) The seven appellants had been working as machinists for more than ten years. It could not be deduced directly from this fact that their work was restricted to that of machinist under the employment contract. (2) In the company there was a provision in the works rules permitting the company to change the workplace and type of work in case of business necessity. And there were some cases of transfer between different jobs in the company. In general, changes of workplace and jobs have become more necessary to respond to economic growth and changes of industrial structure. So the company reserved the right to change the workplace and job without the individual consent of the employee in case of business necessity. Abusive exercise of the right should not be permitted. However, in this case transfers were not ordered for an unfair purpose or in order to weaken the labour union or to treat the members of the labour union disadvantageously. Rather there was the business necessity of maintaining the company's position in the worldwide competitive motor industry. It was not unreasonable for the company to transfer almost all machinists to a different type of work without any consideration for their individual skills and experience.

These transfers were the result of the need to achieve efficient work arrangements and the smooth management of the business. The appellants were not working in an environment, which was difficult to endure though their work became harder than that of machinists. So they did not suffer greater disadvantages than they could normally be expected to bear. The High Court accordingly considered that the order to transfer to another workplace and job was not an abusive exercise of the employer's right.

The seven appellants appealed to the Supreme Court.

Decision

The appeal was rejected.

JUDGEMENT

This Court considers the finding and the judgement of the High Court rational and appropriate in the light of all the evidence in this case. There is no error in the conclusion. Accordingly the appeal must be dismissed.

[*Source*: Case (0) of 513 of 1988, decided on 7 December 1989; reported at Rodohanrei No. 554:7].

ANNOTATION

1. In Japan transfer from one job to another, and from one workplace to another has been regarded as a matter of course connected with the lifetime employment system. Frequent transfers can give an employee the possibility to learn different types of job and to become a multi-skilled worker. This has led to flexible job assignments, to correspond with technological change and business fluctuations. But many cases concerned with transfer have been brought to the Courts and the Labour Relations Commissions because the workers take more interest in their own family life hand happiness than in a sense of loyalty and devoted service to the company. The first relevant judgement of the Supreme Court is that given in *Toa Paints Co.* v. *Yoshida* (6 ILLR 131), the legal framework of which is applied to the present case.

2. In this case the workplace was not changed though the job was changed from that of machinist to a different type of work. The Supreme Court upheld the right of the company to decide the appellants' jobs without their individual consent on the following grounds: (1) Though the appellants had worked as machinists for more than 10 years, the Court could not find an agreement that the appellants could not be transferred to other jobs. Their jobs were not narrowly specialized as machinists. (2) There were provisions in the works rules specifying that the company might order an employee to change his job and workplace in case of operational necessity and that he could not refuse to obey the order without reasonable grounds. (3) There were some previous instances of transfer between different jobs, including those of machinists, in this company. (4) Transfer was necessary to cope with economic growth and raped change of industrial structures.

Among these four reasons, the first is questionable. It completely disregards the fact that the appellants worked as machinists for more than ten years. Are their jobs supposed to be specialized as a result? If so, the company's order would be considered to be a proposal to change their job. The appellants have the right to effuse the proposal, but may not exercise the right abusively. If there were found to be abusive exercise of the right, one might reach the same decision as the Supreme Court.

3. Even under the decision of the Supreme Court, the employer's authority may not be exercised abusively. The standard by which to judge abusive exercise of the right to transfer the employee to another job is almost he same as in the judgement in the Toa Paints Co. case. The Court finds there to be an abusive exercise of the right in the exceptional cases where there is no business necessity, or where the employer has an improper purpose in ordering the transfer even though there is business necessity, or where the transfer inflicts greater hardship on the employee than he should

normally be expected to bear. The Court weighs the extent of the damage inflicted on the employee against the business need for the transfer.

4. In the present case the appellants were ordered to change their job. But there was no necessity to change their homes. So their personal circumstances were judged not to affect by the transfer. And the Court considered that change from one skilled worker's job to another did not harm their occupational career. In Japan it is common even for skilled employees to be transferred from one job to another because of rationalization or relocation of plants. The judgement of the Court is influenced by this custom of flexible job assignment.

There remains the problem, in judging the abusive exercise of the employer's right, whether it is reasonable to transfer almost all the machinists without any consideration for their respective skills and experience. The High Court and the Supreme Court answered this in the affirmative, from the viewpoint of efficient use of labour and smooth management of business. Their judgements attached more importance to business necessities than to personal circumstances affected by the employer's order to transfer jobs.

(6) WAGES

(i) **Kozato Machine Materials Co.**
v.
Ikeda ***et al.***

(ii) **Masami Arai**
v.
The Hong Kong and Shanghai Banking Corporation

(iii) **Minoru Amano**
v.
Nisshin Steel Co. and Hiroshi Watanabe

(iv) **H. Inoue and others**
v.
Kochi Sightseeing Ltd.

(v) **Toho Gakuen School**
v.
Yukiko Sagara

Supreme Court (First Petty Bench)

(i) Kozato Machine Materials Co. *v.* Ikeda *et al.*

Calculation of overtime allowance

HEADNOTES

Facts

The appellant company makes and sells industrial leather and asbestos for insulation. The company employs the four appellees. They work from 8:30 a.m. to 5 p.m., except for one hour's rest time. So their working time is 7 hours and 30 minutes. Overtime allowance is paid for extended working times at this company.

The company must pay wage rates increased by at least 25 percent of the normal wages under the Labour

Standards Act, Article 37. Article 37(2) stipulates that family allowance; commutation allowance and other remuneration prescribed by Ordinance are excluded from the normal wage upon which increased wage rates should be computed. The Labour Standards Enforcement Ordinance, Article 21, stipulates that the following items shall not in addition to family and commutation allowance, be included in the wages on which increased wage rates should be based; (1) separation allowance, (2) allowance for educational expenses of children, (3) extraordinary wages, and (4) wages paid periodically at periods of more than one month.

At this company, employees' wages consist of basic wage, housing allowance, perfect attendance allowance, allowance for driving license, allowance for responsible position (YAKUSHOKUTEATE), commutation allowance, family allowance and incentive allowance. Housing allowance is paid to an employee who is the head of a household, whether married or unmarried. The amount is 5000 yen per month irrespective of family number, 3000 yen per month is paid as perfect attendance allowance to an employee who is not late for work and does not leave work earlier than usual. Allowance for driving license is paid to an employee who has a license to drive a four-wheel motorcar. The amount is 3000 yen per month. 3000 yen per month is paid to a team leader as allowance for responsible position.

In calculating overtime allowance, the company excluded housing allowance, perfect attendance allowance, allowance for driving license, and allowance for responsible position from the normal wages upon which increased wage rates are computed. But the appellees asserted that these allowances should be included when the company calculated overtime allowances. So they claimed that the company should pay the difference between the amount of overtime allowance actually paid and the amount recalculated by the method, which they asserted.

Tokyo District Court and Tokyo High Court both held that the assertion of the appellees was right, and that the six items under Article 21 of Labour Standards Enforcement Ordinance should be interpreted restrictively, because overtime allowance is designed to compensate overtime work. According to this interpretation, the allowances in question do not correspond to the six items. Therefore, these allowances should be included in the normal wages on which increase wage rates should be calculated.

JUDGEMENT

This Court finds the finding and the judgement of the court below rational and appropriate in light of all the evidence in this case. There is no error in its conclusion. The appeal should accordingly be dismissed.

[*Source*: Case No. (0) 267 of 1988, decided 14 July 1988]

ANNOTATION

1. An employer must pay wages for overtime work, work on rest days and midnight work at a rate increased by at least 25 percent of the normal wages, under Article 37 of Labour Standards Act. 25 percent is lower than the international standard provided by international convention. The purpose of this provision is to pay compensation to an employee doing overtime work and indirectly to restrict overtime work.

To calculate extra wages for overtime work, wages are divided into two parts. First part is not required to pay at the increased rate. Therefore, it is not included in the normal wages on which the increased rate is based. It consists of family allowance, commutation allowance, separation allowance, allowance for educational expenses of children, extraordinary wages and wages paid periodically at periods of more than one month, such as bonuses under Article 21 of Labour Standards Enforcement Ordinance. Another part must be paid at the increased rate. So it must be included in the normal wages, this provision is made on the ground that it is not rational to calculate overtime wages on the ground that it is not rational to calculate overtime wages on personal conditions, irrespective of the content of work and skill of jobs.

2. In Japan, wages are almost always calculated monthly, even in employment contracts for production workers. Monthly regular wages are composed of basic wages and certain allowances. Basic wages and allowances both include the portion earned for the employee's work and the portion paid by virtue of being an employee. So there is a question as to which allowances correspond to the six items under Article 21 of the Ordinance. This is the first judgement of Supreme Court on the question.

3. In this judgement Supreme Court held that the six items must be interpreted restrictively from the viewpoint of the aim of the provisions mentioned above. This opinion is approved in general. Therefore, it must be judged in each case whether particular allowances correspond to the six items, regardless of the title of the allowances. Commutation allowance is excluded from the normal wages under the Act. But when it is paid uniformly, irrespective of commuting distance, it is interpreted as being included in the normal wages, because the commutation allowance is then not decided on personal conditions. Family allowance, also, must be included in the normal wages when it is paid uniformly independently of family numbers. But family allowance must be excluded from the normal wages if it is paid in proportion to family numbers, under the Act and Ordinance.

4. In the case at issue housing allowance is paid uniformly irrespective of family numbers, and of whether the employee is married or unmarried. Allowance for driving license is paid at a flat rate to an employee who holds a motorcar license. Allowance for responsible position, also, is paid uniformly to an employee who occupies the responsible position.

Therefore, these three allowances should be included in the normal wages. Perfect attendance allowance is paid for the employee's work. Therefore, it is rational that this allowance should be included in the normal wages.

Supreme Court (First Petty Bench)

(ii) Masami Arai

v.

The Hongkong and Shanghai Banking Corporation

Determination of amount of retirement allowance after collective agreement became ineffective

HEADNOTES

Facts

The appellant was an employee of the appellee band, whose head office is located in Hong Kong. The appellant had worked at Osaka branch as a temporary employee since 7 December 1978. Before then, he was employed by another company and was despatched to the appellee bank to serve as a messenger form 16 June 1977. In the contract between the band and the appellant, it was agreed that length of service at the bank should be calculated from 16 June 1977 and that the contract should be renewed every year.

The appellant retired from the bank on 30 June 1980 because he had reached the mandatory retirement age. He had the right to receive a retirement allowance. But there was a difference of opinion on the amount of the retirement allowance, owing to the following circumstances.

Rules of employment made by the bank stipulated that the amount of retirement allowance should be calculated in accordance with the provisions of the collective agreement valid at the time paying it. There were two labour unions at the bank. The appellant was a member of labour union "A", a minority union. Labour union "B", a majority union, agreed terms of retirement allowance with the bank on 26 June 1975. On the same day an identical agreement was concluded between labour union "A" and the bank. And so as to include the relevant part of the agreement into the rules of employment, an amendment of the rules of employment was submitted to Osaka Central Labour Standards Inspection Office with a copy of the agreement on retirement allowance, under Art. 89 of Labour Standards Act. The agreement was renewed every year. But the agreement between labour union "A" and the bank lost effect at the end of December 1978 because an amendment on calculation of retirement allowance could not be agreed. Union "A" rejected the proposal made by the employer, which reduced the amount of retirement allowance. But labour union "B" and the bank agreed to amend the agreement on 16 December 1980 and to give effect to the amendment retroactively to 16 January 1979. In other words, labour union "B" agreed to worsen the working conditions on retirement allowance. And the amendment of the rules of employment was also submitted to the Labour Standards Inspection Office.

In these circumstances, the bank calculated the retirement allowance of the appellant by reference to the basic salary at the end of December 1978, when the agreement then in force became ineffective. But the appellant asserted that it should be computed by reference to the basic salary at the time of retirement (June 1980), because the content of the ineffective agreement had become a part of his contract of employment until a new agreement could be concluded. In consequence he refused to receive the allowance offered by the bank and requested the bank the sum that he claimed.

Osaka District Court upheld the appellant's claim, declaring that the content of a collective agreement on working conditions remained effective even after its termination as part of individual contracts of employment. In other works, 'working conditions prescribed by the agreement were integrated into individual contracts of employment and could not be terminated even after the agreement had become ineffective.

Osaka High Court held that (1) the agreement, which became void on 31 December 1978, did not apply the appellant but (2) Art. 17 of the Labour Unions Act applied to a member of a minority union when the agreement between the minority union and the employer became ineffective and a new agreement was not concluded. Under this reasoning the agreement between labour union "B" and the bank, of 16 December 1980, which had effect retroactively for the members of labour union "A". The High Court accordingly ordered the bank to pay the sum in question in accordance with the provisions of the amended agreement.

Law Applied

Labour Unions Act

Article 17: When three-fourths or more of a particular category of workers normally employed in a factory or other work place are covered by a single collective agreement, the remaining workers of that category employed in that factory or work place shall *ipso fac*t be bound by the same agreement.

JUDGEMENT

(1) Under his contract of employment the appellant has a right to claim retirement allowance. The rules of employment stipulate that the amount of retirement allowance shall be computed in accordance with the collective agreement valid at the time of retirement. But the agreement became ineffective before the time of retirement. This circumstance cannot serve to deny the right of the appellant to receive the retirement allowance. Therefore, the amount must be computed on the basis of a reasonable interpretation of

the contract of employment and the rules of employment.

(2) The amendment of the rules of employment was submitted to the Labour Standards Inspection Office with a copy of the agreement on retirement allowance. So the standard of calculation of the retirement allowance became a part of the rules of employment. The rules of employment represent a uniform determination and collective treatment of working conditions. Therefore, it is a function of the rules of employment to supplement the content ineffective. Considering these circumstances, the standard of computing retirement allowance under the rules of employment, which became void on 31 December 1978, must apply to the appellant.

(3) The right to receive retirement allowance cannot be changed retroactively by the agreement concluded after the right has come into existence. Therefore, the agreement between labour union "B" and the bank does not apply to the appellant. Similarly, the amendment of the rules of employment based on the agreement in 1980 and 1981 between labour union "B" and the bank does not apply retroactively to the appellant.

[*Source*: Case (0) 728 and 729 of 1985, decided 7 September 1989: reported at Rodohanrei No. 546:6].

ANNOTATION

1. In this case the disputed point is how a sum of retirement allowance shall be computed after a collective agreement becomes ineffective. Three courts—District Court, High Court, and Supreme Court—each followed different reasoning.

The District Court judged on the ground of the so-called "after-effect" (*Nachwirkung*) of the agreement. In Japan the Labour Union Act does not include provisions regarding the effect of a collective agreement after its termination. But the majority view holds that the content of an agreement remains effective after its termination as part of individual contracts of employment. In other words, the conditions of employment laid down in an agreement were integrated into the individual contracts of employment during the effective term of the agreement. Therefore, these conditions remain binding on the employer and the workers, although only until a new agreement or a new individual contract of employment is drawn up.

The High Court judged on the basis of the extensive effect of the collective agreement under Art. 17, Section 1 of the Labour Unions Act. This article stipulates that when three fourths or more of a particular category of workers normally employed in a factory or other work place are covered by a single collective agreement, the remaining workers of that category employed at that factory or work place must *ipso fact* be bound by the same agreement. But it has been considered that this provision does not apply to a minority union unless its members agree to be covered by the agreement entered into by the majority union, because the minority union can itself conclude an agreement. This interpretation has been adopted even when the members of the minority union are less than one-fourth and those of the majority union are more than three-fourths of a particular category of workers normally employed in a factory. But the High Court held that an agreement between the majority union and the employer which applies to more than three-fourths of the workers must be applied to member of a minority union as long as it has not yet concluded an agreement on working conditions or when the agreement it has concluded becomes ineffective. This view differs from the interpretation of the majority. If the new agreement between the majority union and the employer worsened working conditions, members of the minority union would suffer worse working conditions. This conclusion cannot be supported.

There is another problem in the High Court judgement. In this case, members of the majority union "B" were 52 in number. Minority union "A" members numbered 19 and non-union members 6. The agreement between union "B" and the bank covered Non-union members. Therefore, the High Court considered that the agreement applied to more than three fourths of the employees of Osaka branch. This judgement is open to doubt. For example, when a majority union organizes only 20 percent of employees and a minority union 15 percent, the High Court's reasoning, taking account of the fact that the agreement between the majority union and the employer applies to the non-unionized 65 percent of employees, would seem to be inappropriate because the agreement concluded by the labour union organizing only 20 percent of employees would decide the working conditions of all the employees in the establishment. Therefore, the Supreme Court based its judgement on different reasons.

2. The Supreme Court dealt with this case as a matter of interpretation of rules of employment. Normally, rules of employment have detailed provisions on retirement allowance. In general these establish the method to calculate the amount of the allowance, the date at which and the means by which the allowance must be paid. In this case, the rules of employment only stipulated that the allowance should be computed in accordance with the provisions of the collective agreement. Therefore, they did not have a provision to clarify the content of the right and obligation regarding retirement allowance. But the content of the right becomes evident when the rules of employment are read together with the agreement. This conclusion comes from the fact that the agreement on retirement allowance in substance becomes a part of the rules of employment.

3. The Labour Unions Act lays down that the terms of a collective agreement have a mandatory effect upon contracts of employment. This system is derived from the German system. According to Art. 14 of the Act, the collective agreement between a labour union and the employer or the employer's organization concerning working conditions and other matters takes effect when the agreement is put in writing, either with

signatures or with names affixed with seals, by both of the parties concerned. This effect is called the normative effect. Thought the collective agreement has normative effect, the right to claim retirement allowance cannot be changed retroactively by an agreement concluded after the right has come into existence. This is one example of the limitation of the normative effect (*Grenzen der Tarifoutonomie*)

Supreme Court (Second Petty Bench)

(iii) Minoru Amano
v.
Nisshin Steel Co. and Hiroshi Watanabe

Legal effect of the offsetting of debts to the employer against wages with the consent of employer and employee—right of voidance under Bankruptcy Act

HEADNOTES

Facts

The appellant is a trustee in bankruptcy of Mr. Hiroshi Watanabe, who is an employee of Nisshin Steel Co. Mr. Watanabe had borrowed from the appellees company, from a bank and from B labourers' bank in order to build a house. The loans were not secured by mortgages. Mr. Watanabe made monthly repayments to the appellees by deduction from his monthly salary and bonuses. Monthly repayments to the two banks were made by the appellees on behalf of Mr. Watanabe, again by deduction from the latter's salary and bonuses. There was also a promise that any loan outstanding when Mr. Watanabe ceased to be an employee would be repaid in a lump sum from his retirement allowances. These deductions were permitted under the collective agreement between the appellees company and the labour union organizing a majority of the employees in the establishment to which Mr. Watanabe belonged. But that agreement only covered the loans from the appellees company and the B labourers' bank: the loan from a bank was not covered.

Mr. Watanabe subsequently borrowed more than 70 million yen, in addition to the housing loans, and in due course went bankrupt. He, therefore, applied for retirement from the appellees company and gave the latter a procreation entrusting it with the repayment of the remaining housing loans. In pursuance of that power, the appellees cleared the loans by deductions from salary, bonuses and retirement allowances.

The appellant, who was appointed a trustee in bankruptcy when Mr. Watanabe was declared bankrupt, sought to obtain the amounts which had been deducted from salary, bonuses and retirement allowances, on the ground that these deductions were contrary to article 24, section I of the Labour Standards Act which provides that the employer must pay wages in full directly to the employees themselves. Moreover, the appellant contended that under the Bankruptcy Act he was entitled to void the bankrupt's action in entrusting the employer with the repayment of loans out of salaries, bonuses and retirement allowances.

Osaka District Court denied that there was violation of article 24, section I of the Labour Standards Act, but upheld the right to void the bankrupt's action on the ground of his malicious to harm other obliges. Osaka High Court denied that assertion.

Decision

The appeal was dismissed.

Law Applied

Labour Standards Act

Article 24, section 1: Wages must be paid in cash and in full directly to the workers: Provided that payment other than in cash may be permitted when otherwise provided for by law and regulation or labour agreement; and that partial deduction from wages may be permitted when otherwise provided for by law or regulation or when there exists a written agreement with the labour union—when there is a union which is composed of a majority of the workers at the place of work or with persons representing a majority of the workers when there is no such union.

Bankruptcy Act

Article 72, section 1: The trustee can set aside an act of the bankrupt if the bankrupt had malicious intent to harm other obliges and if the beneficiary knew that such a legal act would harm the other obliges.

Civil Code

Article 649: If any expenses are required for the management of the affairs entrusted to the mandatory, the mandatory shall upon demand pay them to the mandatory in advance.

JUDGEMENT

1. The purpose of the principle of full payment of wages laid down in article 24, section of the Labour Standards Act is to ensure that workers will indeed receive full wages by prohibiting the unilateral deduction of the whole or of a part of wages by the employer. Thus employers may not set off wages against amounts, which they are entitled to demand. However, when employees freely agree to the offset, the offset does not violate the principle of full wages. Strict and careful consideration must be given to the question whether the employee's consent was freely given. In this case Mr. Watanabe spontaneously requested the employer to take the steps necessary to repay the remaining loans in a lump sum from his salaries, bonuses and retirement allowances when he left his

employment. There was thus a reasonable ground for a finding that his consent was freely given. In these circumstances the offset in this case did not violate article 24, section 1 of the Labour Standards Act.

2. The offset was made pursuant to the right of the appellees company to call in its outstanding loans and also the right of the company under article 649 of the Civil Code to request in advance the expenses for the repayment, entrusted to the company, of the loans made by the two banks to Mr. Watanabe. Mr. Watanabe agreed of his free will that the company exercises the right of setoff against remuneration. Therefore, the trustee cannot exercise the right to void the employer's rights to setoff before or after the declaration of bankruptcy.

[*Source*: Case No. (0) 4 of 1988, decided on 26 November 1990. Reported at Rodohanrei No. 584: 6].

ANNOTATION

1. The judgement of the Supreme Court, to the effect that partial deductions from wages with the employee's consent do not violate the principle, regarding full payment of wages laid down in article 24, section 1 of the Labour Standards Act, is significant. The section is interpreted as prohibiting the employer from setting off wages unilaterally. For example, the employer may not unilaterally set off against wages his right to compensation by the employee for damage caused by the employee's tortuous act or contractual non-performance. On the other hand, according to the Supreme Court, an offset pursuant to the employee's free consent can be excluded from the principle of full payment of wages.

The background of the judgement is as follows. In Japan, companies have housing loan programmes as a fringe benefit, in order to promote home ownership by employees. Under these programmes employees can borrow money at low rates of interest, and loans are repaid in monthly installments to the employer or to banks. When the employee retires from the company, he must repay the loans still outstanding from his retirement allowances. In general, retirement allowances of permanent employees represent a large sum. According to a survey by the Labour Ministry at the end of 1989, the average lump sum payable in the case of mandatory retirement of university graduate white-collar employees in companies with more than 10,000 workers is 24.13 million yen. These large sums support the housing loan programme of the company. Therefore, the judgement of the Supreme Court serves to ensure that repayment of loans can easily be secured by offset against retirement allowances.

2. Partial deductions from wages are permissible when there exists a written agreement with the labour union—when there is a union which is a union which is composed of a majority of the workers at the work place or with persons representing a majority of the workers when there is no such union. In the present case there was an agreement permitting partial deductions from wages to repay the loans from the appellee company and the B laboures' bank. But there was no agreement regarding the repayment of loans from the A bank. This was a mistake of both the appellee company and the union.

What was at issue, therefore, was not whether the deductions from wages to repay the loans from the appellee company and the B labourers' bank violated the principle of full payment of wages, since there was an agreement permitting an exception to that principle. The problem arose because of the offset to repay the loans from the A bank. The judgement of the Supreme Court as analyzed under 1. above is meaningful in cases in which there is no agreement under the proviso of article 24, section I of the Labour Standards Act. Partial deductions may be permitted with the worker's free consent even when there is no agreement permitting them. Of course, the worker's consent must be shown, to have been freely given. In this case it was found that the worker had his free will given a procuration. This conclusion poses the problem whether it is reasonable that the legal prescriptions of the Labour Standards Act, subject to financial penalties for any violation. Yet the worker's consent can release an employer from his responsibility under the Act.

3. The right of voidance is intended to be exercised by the trustee in bankruptcy, on behalf of the obligor, to recover decreases in the bankruptcy estate affected by the bankrupt himself. In this case, the appellee company was an obligee of the bankruptcy estate. A partial deduction from retirement allowances was made by the company as such and was not an action by the bankrupt. Accordingly that deduction was not covered by article 72 of the Bankruptcy Act, which only empowers the trustee to void legal acts by the bankrupt himself. The company action could not be a target of the right of voidance exercised by the trustee.

The Supreme Court adduces another consideration. From the procuration it was found that Mr. Watanabe agreed that the company should take the steps necessary to repay loans by lump sums from his retirement allowances. The procuration gave the company the right to request in advance the expenses for the repayment of loans the company the right to request in advance the expenses for the repayment of loans entrusted to it. This meant that it was not detrimental to the obligees of the bankruptcy estate and, accordingly, the consent of the worker given by the procuration could not be a target of the right of voidance of the trustee.

Supreme Court (Second Petty Bench)

(iv) H. Inoue and others
v.
Kochi Sightseeing Ltd.

Payment of overtime and midnight work allowances to taxi drivers whose wages are calculated as a percentage of turnover

HEADNOTES

Facts

1. The four appellants were taxi drivers employed by the appellee company. Their working hours were from 8 a.m. to 2 a.m., including two hours rest break, every other day. According to the work rule, normal working hours were from 8 a.m. to 5 p.m. that rule was amended in November 1986, following the conclusion of a collective agreement with the labour union representing a majority of the employees, to permit a flexible working hours system under which average working hours, spread over four weeks, did not exceed 48 hours per week; in working hours, spread over four weeks, did not exceed 48 hours per week; in application of this system the drivers worked from 8 a.m. to 2 p.m. every other day. However, the four appellants were not member of the union. Accordingly, their working hours remained subject to the former rule; the flexible working hour's system could not apply to them.

The wages of the drivers were calculated as a percentage of turnovers from the beginning to the end of a month. The percentage was 42% in case of a probationary employee, 45% in case of a regular employee and 46% in case of an employee with long service. They were not paid overtime or midnight work allowances. And they could not distinguish, in the wages received, between amounts for normal hours and amounts for overtime and midnight work. The four appellants sued for allowances, at increased rates, for overtime work after 2 a.m. and midnight work between 10 p.m. and 5 a.m. during the period from 1 June 1985 to 28 February 1987, as well as for an equivalent amount as additional payment under Article 114 of the Labour Standards Act. The appellee company contended that these allowances were included in their wages calculated as a percentage of turnovers.

Kochi District Court found for the drivers. It held that it was necessary to distinguish between wages for normal hours and wages for overtime and midnight work, because an employer had to pay the balance between increased rate allowances and normal amounts. At the same time, in this case the wage system could not be regarded as in contravention of Article 37 of the Labour Standards Act, providing for increased wages for overtime and midnight work.

Takamatsu High Court partially amended the judgement of the District Court, negativing the demand for midnight work allowances after 2 a.m., it did so on the ground that in the company there was no custom of work from 2 a.m. to 8 a.m.; the appellants were not required by work rules or collective agreements to work overtime after 2 a.m. and the company did not permit drivers to work after that time.

The four appellants appealed to the Supreme Court.

Decision

The Supreme Court partially allowed the appeal. It declared that the company had to pay overtime and midnight work allowances under Article 37 of the Labour Standards Act and Article 19, paragraph 1(6) of the Enforcement Ordinance.

Law Applied

Labour Standards Act (prior to the amendment of April 1994).

Article 37: (1) When an employer extends working hours, or calls on a worker to work on rest days in virtue of the provisions of Articles 33 or of the preceding Article, or requires a worker to work between 10 p.m. and 5 a.m. (or between 11 p.m. and 6 a.m. when the competent Minister of Labour deems it necessary to apply this variant to a certain area or during a certain time of the year), the employer shall pay an increase in wages for work during such hours or on such days at a rate of at least 25 percent of normal wages.

Article 114: At the request of a worker, a court may order an employer who has violated the provisions of Article 20, 26 or 37, or an employer who has not paid wages in accordance with the provisions of Article 39, paragraph 6, to make an additional payment of the same amount in addition to the unpaid portion of the amount he was required to pay under these provisions: Provided that such a request shall be made within two years of the violation.

Enforcement Ordinance of Labour Standards Act

Article 19: (1) The amount of wages to be paid for normal working hours or working days under the provisions of Article 37, paragraph 1 of the Act shall be the amount obtained by multiplying the amount in each of the following items by the number of overtime working hours in pursuance of Article 33 or Article 36 of the Act, by the number of working hours on rest days or by the number of working hours between 10 p.m. and 5 a.m. (or 11 p.m. and 6 a.m. ...):

. . .

(vi) The amount obtained by dividing the sum total of wages calculated on the basis of a piece work system or other contract system during the wage calculation period . . . by the number of aggregate working hours during the said calculation period, in the case of wages to be paid on the basis of piece work or other contract system.

1. It was evident from the assertions of both parties that the appellants had worked after 2 a.m. under their employment contracts. Hence the High Court judgement was in error in concluding that their work was not performed under these contracts.

2. In this piece-rated wage system the appellants were not paid an increased amount even if they performed overtime and midnight work. Also, it was impossible to distinguish the part of the wages to be

ascribed to normal working hours from that to be ascribed to overtime and midnight work. Therefore, this Court finds it difficult to hold that overtime and midnight work allowances had already been paid to the appellants. Accordingly the appellee company has an obligation to pay these allowances under Article 37 of the Labour Standards Act and Article 19, paragraph 1(6) of the Enforcement Ordinance of the Act.

3. The appellee company had to pay an equivalent amount as additional payment, in addition to the unpaid wages it was required to pay, on condition that the request for such payment is made within two years from the date of the violation, according to Article 114 of the Labour Standards Act. Insofar as more than two years had elapsed at the date of the request, the relevant potion of the request had to be rejected.

[*Source*: Case No. (0) 63 of 1991, decided on 13 June 1994. Rodo-hanrei 653-12]

ANNOTATION

This is the first judgement of the Supreme Court admitting an employer's obligation to pay overtime and midnight work allowances under the piece-rated wage system at a taxicab company. The judgement thus has considerable influence on the practical business affairs of the taxicab companies in Japan.

There are three points in the above-mentioned judgement. Each will be considered below.

1. One point was whether the appellants had worked after 2 a.m. It was not disputed that their working hours were from 8 a.m. to 2 a.m. every other day. As a result overtime-working hours were from 2 a.m. to 8 a.m. and midnight working hours were from 10 p.m. to 5 a.m. under Article 37 of the Labour Standards Act.

The High Court denied that the appellants had driven taxis as overtime work after 2 a.m. But the Supreme Court concluded from the assertions of both parties that they had in fact performed overtime work after 2 a.m. under their employment contracts.

It was not clear whether there was a written agreement on overtime work. Such an agreement is required under Article 36 of the Labour Standards Act in order to legalize overtime in excess of the legal standards for working hours laid down in Article 32 of the Act. Employers may not order employees to work overtime without an agreement concluded with the majority labour union or with the representative of the majority of the employees in the absence of a majority union. An employer should be punished if he orders overtime work without an agreement. But even if an employee is ready to work overtime without an agreement, the employer must not be relieved of the obligation to pay overtime allowances. In other words, an employer must pay wages when an employee actually provides work during a time period when he does not have a duty to work under the employment contract. In the present case, it was not decided whether the company ordered overtime work under an agreement. But the Supreme Court found that the appellants had actually provided work after 2 a.m.

2. The Supreme Court held that the company did not pay overtime and midnight work allowances on the following two grounds. First, the amounts of piece rated wages were not increased even when the appellants actually provided overtime and midnight work. Second, it was difficult to distinguish the part of the wages to be ascribed to normal working hours from that to be ascribed to overtime and midnight work.

These two points may be considered to be reasonable. These are some cases on the question whether it is valid to consent to the inclusion of the increases for overtime and rest day work in basic wages. For example, in the Ori Materials Co. case, decided on 14 July 1988 (Rodo-hanrei 523-6), the Supreme Court considered that the consent was valid if the overtime work allowances could be clearly determined within the basic wages, since it would be necessary to check whether the increased wages were calculated in conformity with Article 37 of the Labour

Standards Act. In the present case the Supreme Court followed the reasoning of that precedent.

3. Under the Act as amended from 1 April 1994, employers must pay premiums at a rate of at least 25% and not more than 505 over nominal wages for overtime work. The percentage is to be decided by Ministerial Order, taking into consideration workers' welfare, the trend of overtime and rest day work and other circumstances. At the present time it is 25% for overtime work on weed-days, and 35% for work on holidays. As the case here reported occurred before 1 April 1994, 25% was applied to both overtime work and work on holidays. An employer must now also pay wages increased by 50% or more for overtime work at midnight.

An employer who does not pay these allowances may be required by the Court to pay an equivalent amount, in addition to the unpaid allowances, under Article 114 of the Act. This system was inspired by punitive damages in the United States. The request for such additional payments must be made within two years from the date of violation. Therefore, an employer cannot be requested to make the additional payments later than two years from the date of violation.

Supreme Court (First Petty Bench)

(v) Toho Gakuen School
v.
Yukiko Sagara

Effect of work rules on non-payment of bonus to an employee attending on fewer than 90 percent of workdays because of maternity leave

Facts

The appellee was an officer at the appellant private educational school. The appellee gave birth on 8 June 1994 and took maternity leaves for 8 weeks after childbirth. After that, she chose to work shorter working hours (less one hour and 15 minutes per day) from 6 October 1994 to 8 July 1995 under the Child, Ill Parents and Spouses Care Leaves Act.

She was not at all paid winter bonus of 1994 and summer bonus of 1995. Under the work rules, bonus is paid in June and December to employees continuing to work on paid day and attending on more than 90 percent of workdays (hereafter referred to as the 90 percent rule). Bonus is to be calculated under a certain formula. Wages cannot be paid to a female employee taking maternity leaves during six weeks before childbirth and eight weeks after childbirth. An officer requesting shorter work hours to take care of a child less than one year old can work from 9 am. to 4:30 pm. Wages are to be reduced in proportion to working hours.

According to a circular paper relating to winter bonus of 1994, it was to be paid only to employees attending more than 90 percent of workdays. Therefore, winter bonus cannot be paid to employees absent for more than 13 days during six months from June to November 1994. Maternity leaves and menstruation leaves are to be treated as non-working days under the circular paper. So the appellee was not paid the winter bonus since she took maternity leaves for 40 days.

As to the summer bonus of 1995, the 90 percent rule was also applied to the appellee. Her working hours were six hours and 15 minutes per day. But regular working hours were 7 hours and 30 minutes. So her working hours were about 83 percent of regular working hours. As a result she was not paid the summer bonus according to the 90 percent rule.

The appellee requested that bonuses, compensation money and lawyers fees be paid because of breach of duty on the part of the appellant private school. She also requested, as an alternative assertion that damages be paid owing to torts of the appellant. The Tokyo District Court ordered the appellant school to pay 1,260,000 yen as two bonuses. The District Court judged that the 90 percent rule violated public policy and was null and void because it would substantially restrain the exercise of rights under Art. 65 of the Labour Standards Act and Art. 10 of the Child, Ill Parents and Spouses Care Leaves Acts. So the District Court ruled that the total amount of the two bonuses be paid.

The Tokyo High Court maintained the result of the District Court. The reason is the following. The 90 percent rule was economically reasonable because it had a purpose to prevent high absenteeism. But it brought about unreasonably disadvantageous treatment for the appellee to lose her right to receive the total amount of the bonuses. So it resulted in a bad influence not to exercise employee rights granted by the Act. As a result, this 90 percent rule violated public policy and was null and void under Art. 90 of the Civil Code. Therefore, it would be null and void that the periods during maternity leaves and non-working hours during childcare were not treated as working days and hours in order to calculate the amount of the bonus. So the appellant school should pay the total amount of the winter bonus in 1994 and the summer bonus in 1995. But other compensation money could not be awarded because the payment of both bonuses would repair the economical and spiritual loss. And damages under torts could not be awarded since it could not be found that the appellant had an intention to discriminate and retaliate against the female appellee.

Decision

The appeal was partially rejected; the case was sent to the Tokyo High Court.

Law Applied

Labour Standards Act

Art. 65:

1. In the event a woman who is expected to give birth within six weeks, or within fourteen weeks in the case of twins or greater, requests rest days, the employer shall not have such person work.
2. An employer shall not have a woman work within eight weeks after childbirth; however, this shall not prevent an employer from having a woman work who has so requested after six weeks have passed since childbirth, in duties which a doctor has recognized would not adversely affect her.
3. In the event a pregnant woman has requested, an employer shall transfer her to other light duties.

Child, Ill Parents and Spouses Care Leave Act

Art. 10: An employer shall be prohibited from discriminating or dismissing employees for taking child; ill parents and spouses care leave.

Civil Code

Art. 90: An act, which has for its objects such matters, as are contrary to public policy or good morals is null and void.

JUDGEMENT

. There is no clause under Art. 65 of Labour Standards Act that an employer shall pay wages during maternity leave. So Non-payment of wages is not illegal under the Act because does not provide work. But an employer may have the choice to pay wages during maternity leave. Thus, wages during maternity leave are left to the labour contract or the work rules or the collective agreement.

An employer is to take the necessary steps to induce an employee to take child care leave. If he or she cannot take all-day childcare leave, an employer may allow him or her to reduce working hours. In this case, a wage cut can be possible under the no-work, no-pay principle. But wages can be paid for non-working hours under the special provisions of the labour contract, work rules or collective agreement.

2. Under this 90 percent rule, a bonus cannot be paid at all to an employee attending less than 90 percent of normal working hours. This rule gives, economically, a big disadvantage to the employee. Therefore, the 90 percent rule can be found to substantially restrain him or her in the exercise of rights to take maternity and childcare leaves. Thus, the 90 percent rule is judged to be null and void because it violates public policy.

3. But in this case, wages are not be paid for non-working hours during maternity leave and reduction of working hours for taking care of a child under the work rules of the appellant school. This stipulation cannot be found to be null and void because it does not breach public policy. In other words, this stipulation is reasonable because it would not restrict the exercise of rights under the Labour Standards Act and Child, Ill Parents and Spouses Care Leaves Act. Therefore, it would be natural that the attendance rate shall be calculated to decide the amount of bonuses. But the High Court decided pays the total amount of bonuses. The High Court shall consider how the reasonable amount of bonuses can be calculated under the formula. In this point the judgement of the High Court showed an erroneous interpretation. As a result, the Supreme Court sends back this case to the High Court.

[*Source*: Case No. 1066 of 2001, decided 4 December 2003, Reported at Rodohanrei No. 862-14].

ANNOTATION

The Supreme Court showed a different result to that of the High Court and District Court. The problem is how to assess the difference. The High Court and

District Court decided to pay the total amount of the two bonuses, but the Supreme Court objected to this judgement. The Supreme Court did not decide the issue by itself but sent the case back to the High Court. There is a difference in the content of the remedy among these Courts.

All the three Courts considered that the 90 percent rule was null and void because of the breach of public policy. The High Court and District Court judged to pay the total amount of bonuses on the assumption that the employee had worked during maternity leave and the reduction of working hours to take care of child. But the Supreme Court questioned this assumption.

It is now an established interpretation that the 90 percent rule is null and void. For example, in the N.B.C. Industry Co. case, an employee was denied a wage increase when she attended on fewer than 80 percent of workdays owing to menstruation leave granted under the Labour Standards Act. In that case it was judged that the 80 percent rule was null and void because heavy economic loss resulted from taking menstruation leave, so that the statutory purpose of the menstruation leave system was jeopardized (see 5 ILLR190). The same legal framework of judgement was adopted in the Japan Schering case (see 9 ILLR 227).

But the Supreme Court disagreed with the judgements of the High and District Court. These courts held that the 90 percent rule was totally *null and void.* But the Supreme Court considered that the 90 percent rule was partially null and void. This different point is important.

The Supreme Court decided that the partial invalidity of the 90 percent rule did not mean that it cased to be valid in its entirety in relation to the bonus payment clause. Partial invalidity did not affect the bonus payment clause itself. It was null and void that the provision of the work rules would treat maternity leave and reduction of working hours to take childcare as absence in calculating the attendance rate.

The Supreme Court pointed to another ground to decide that the 90 percent rule was partially null and void. There is no stipulation that an employer shall pay wages during maternity leave under Art. 65 of Labour Standards Act. So an employer is not to be punished even if he or she does not pay wages during maternity leave. But an employer must pay wages when the payment is promised under the employment contract, work rules or collective agreement. A bonus can also be paid under the conditions provided by the employment contract, work ruled or collective agreement. The 90 percent rule is partly effective to calculate the attendance rate. For example, absence from work owing to truancy, illness, injury or hospitalization resulting in non-employment can be reasonably treated as absence in calculating the attendance rate. Therefore, the Supreme Court judged that the High Court was erroneous in interpreting that the 90 percent rule totally was ineffective as being in violation of public policy and that the total amount of bonus should be paid to the appellee under the work rule without the 90 percent rule.

Under the judgement of the Supreme Court, the Appellant school must decide properly how the amount of bonuses should be reduced not to obstruct the appellee in the exercise of her right to take maternity and child care leaves under the Acts. So the Supreme Court would impose a hard obligation to decide the proper reduced amount of bonuses.

(7) EMPLOYEE'S INTERVENTION

Olympus Optical Co.
v.
Shunpei Tanaka

Supreme Court (Third Petty Bench)

Olympus Optical Co.
v.
Shumpei Tanaka

Employee's invention—adequate remuneration when patent is transferred to a company

HEADNOTES

Facts

Appellant was a company manufacturing and selling optical instruments. Appellee was employed in May 1969 and retired in November 1994. During 1973 and 1978 he was engaged in improving videodisc quality and invented a "Pick Up Apparatus" which was granted a patent. This patent was the employee's inventions stipulating that an employee could get remuneration for transferring the right of patent. Under the work rule the amount was set at the ceiling of up to one million yen if the company would attain profits continuously from the other companies with which it contracted to grant an ordinary license. The remuneration is paid only during two years from the date of the contract.

Under the work rule the appellee was paid 3000 yen on 5 January 1978 as remuneration for filing the patent, 8000 yen on 14 March 1989 for the remuneration for the registration of the patent, and 200,000 yen on 1 October 1992 as remuneration from profits from ordinary licenses. The remuneration was paid three times separately. Total amount was 210,000 yen. But he requested the company to pay 200 million yen with 5% per year interest because the remuneration was not reasonable.

The Tokyo District and Tokyo High Courts both admitted that the total 210,000 yen remuneration was inadequate. The reasons are the following:

(1) The company had a work rule on the remuneration for transferring the patent. The former employee has submitted a written oath to obey the rule. It could not be concluded from this fact that he gave up his right to request the reasonable remuneration.

(2) The former employee had received 210,000 yen as the remuneration for transferring the patent. But this fact could not be interpreted that he had an intention to give up his right to demand the reasonable remuneration.

(3) It was reasonable to estimate 50 million yen as the profits the company gained from the employee's invention. The rate of contribution made by the company was estimated to be 95% in order to help the former employee to make the invention. Therefore, the appellee's contribution was only 5%. The former employee could get 2 million yen, namely 5% of the profits as the remuneration. The former employee could request the difference in payment if the amount already paid under the work rule was less than 2 million yen.

(4) The right to pay is extinguished after the lapse of ten years under Article 167 of the Civil Code. The former employee was paid the remuneration on 1 October 1992 because until that day the remuneration could not be calculated. So the period of prescription started from that day. Thus the period was not expired when he claimed to the Court on 3 March 1995.

Decision

The appeal was dismissed and the appellant company was ordered to pay 2,289,000 yen to the appellee.

Law applied

The Patent Act, Art. 35:

(1) An employer, a legal entity or a state or local public entity (hereinafter referred to as the "employer, etc.") shall have a non-exclusive license on the patent right concerned, where an employee, an executive officer of a legal entity or a national or local public official (hereinafter referred to as the "employee, etc.") has obtained a patent for an invention which by reason of its nature falls within the scope of the business of the employer, etc. and an act or acts resulting in the invention were part of the present or past duties of the employee, etc. performed on behalf of the employer, etc. (hereinafter referred to as an "employee's invention") or where a successor in title to the right to obtain a patent from an employee's invention has obtained a patent therefor.

(2) In the case of an employee's invention made by an employee, etc. which is not an employee's invention, any contractual provision, service regulation or other stipulation providing in advance that the right to obtain a patent or the patent right shall pass to the employer, etc. or that he shall have an exclusive license on such invention shall be null and void.

(3) The employee, etc., shall have the right to a reasonable remuneration when he has enabled the right to obtain a patent or the patent right with respect to an employee's to pass to the employer, etc., or has given the employer, etc. an exclusive right to such invention in accordance with the contract, service regulations or other stipulations.

(4) The amount of such remuneration shall be decided by reference to the profits that the employer, etc. will make from the invention and to the amount of contribution the employer, etc. made to the making of the invention.

Civil Code: Article 167:

(1) A claim shall lapse if it is not exercised for ten years.

JUDGEMENT

1. The amount of remuneration cannot be confirmed in advance before the content and value of patent will be concretely evident. Therefore, it cannot be interpreted that the remuneration provided by a work rule is always equal to the adequate remuneration under Section 3 and 4, Article 35 of the Patent Act. If the remuneration calculated under a work rule will be less than the adequate amount of remuneration, the appellee can request to be paid the difference in the amount. Sa the maximum amount of the remuneration, one million yen, can be paid to the employee under the work rule of this appellant company, therefore, it can be judged that the appellee can demand the difference in the amount if the adequate amount of the remuneration is more than the amount paid under the work rule.

2. As the time limit of the remuneration is provided under the work rule, the amount of remuneration cannot be calculated until the time limit day. Therefore, the appellee cannot request to pay more remuneration until the time limit day. As a result, the prescription can start from the time limit day. The last remuneration was paid to the appellee on 1 October 1992. So the period of prescription started from that day. So the period of prescription was not expired when he brought a suit to the Court on 3 March 1995.

[*Source*: Case (ju) 1256 of 2001, decided on 22 April 2003; reported at Rodohanrei 846: 5].

ANNOTATION

1. Recently, the lawsuit has drawn wide attention to the amount of remuneration given to an employee inventor for the transfer of patent rights to the company. As background, the Japanese government has a policy to give importance to intellectual property in order to promote high technology inventions. And also engineers begin to have the tendency to claim his or her right of inventions more strongly because the remuneration for the transfer of the patent, in general, is very low as provided under the work rule in spite of big profits gained by the company.

Under Article 35 of the Japanese Patent Act, when an employee makes an invention falling within the scope of his or her employer's business, the invention is named as an employee's invention. The right to obtain a patent belongs to the employee. But, the patent is subject to a royalty-free nonexclusive license given to the employer by the operation of law. And also the employee invention may be assigned or exclusively licensed by the employee to his or her employer by an agreement or the employer's work rule in advance. When the employee has transferred the right to gain patent for an employee's invention, or granted the employer an exclusive right to use the invention in accordance with the contract or work rule, the employee is to be granted a reasonable remuneration.

2. The point of contention is how to calculate a reasonable remuneration. The amount of remuneration is to be decided by the consideration of the profits, which the employer can get from the employee's invention, and of the degree of the employee's contribution to make the invention and of the degree of the employee's contribution to make the invention. But it is very difficult to calculate a reasonable amount concretely.

There are two points in this Supreme Court judgement on the calculation of reasonable amount. As the first point, the Supreme Court ruled that the company could not decided unilaterally how much to pay an employee for the invention. Namely the Court can intervene to judge to determine the adequate remuneration.

As the second point the Supreme Court decided that though the company could predetermine the amount of remuneration under the work rule, it could not automatically be considered to be reasonable. Therefore, the Court admitted that the employee could demand the difference between the adequate remuneration and that already paid to him or her.

In Japan an employee can be given some kind of remuneration for transferring the patent right in addition to a reasonable one provided under Article 35, Section 3 of the Paten Act. One is a high bonus paid twice per year. Another is monthly or annually high salary based on good performance and outcomes of his or her work. It is a problem to neglect bonuses and salary based on performance and outcomes when calculating a reasonable remuneration.

In case of an employee's invention, the company provides materials and funds to the employee. And other employees often help the employee to make inventions as members of an inventing group. So the degree of contribution from the company and other employees is to be considered to estimate a reasonable remuneration. From these points it becomes very difficult to determine a reasonable remuneration.

3. Recently the amount of remuneration has become higher through the judgements of courts. For example, the Tokyo High Court ordered Hitachi Ltd. To pay 162.84 million yen, about four times that awarded by the Tokyo District Court, to a former employee for his invention of three technologies enabling to read information on optical disks such as CDs.

In a second recent case, the Tokyo District Court ordered Nichia Corp. to pay 20 billion yen to the inventor of a blue light-emitting diode for his transfer of the patent rights to the company. He had received only 20,000 yen for his contribution. The Court ordered to pay a million times of the initial amount that he had demanded in the suit. But the company appealed to ht Tokyo High Court on the reason that the district court failed assesses fairly the contribution of the company and many other researchers.

4. In USA and EU work rules or the individual contract has detailed provisions on the calculation of the remuneration in advance when the right of patent is transferred to a company. Considering the recent judgements, in Japan, a work rule or individual agreement has been reconsidered in order to avoid conflicts on the remuneration and also to promote incentives of engineers to make inventions.

Besides the work rules, labour unions can intervene to decide a reasonable remuneration through collective agreement or collective bargaining. But in Japan almost no labour unions have been interested in employees' inventions.

And the employers' associations now propose an amendment of the Patent Act that the remuneration shall be consented only under an individual contract between the inventors and the company in order to exclude judicial intervention.

(8) OVERTIME WORK

Tookoro Company
v.
Masashi Dehara

Supreme Court (Second Petty Bench)

Tookoro Company
v.
Masahi Dehara

Agreement on overtime work—selecting employee representative

HEADNOTES

Facts

Appellant was a printing company making mainly memorial albums of school graduations. At the headquarters employing 70 workers, appellee was employed as a computer operator of photo type setting from 11 July 1991. In this company overtime work was necessary from November until March every year because graduation took place in February or March. Appellee quit work at 5:30 p.m. until September 1991. From October he did overtime work for thirty minutes or one and three quarters hours under the arrangements that overtime work could be done until 7.00 p.m. But some employees worked until midnight to meet the time limits for delivery. This was an infringement of the Labour Standards Act. So appellee began to criticize the overtime work system.

In this company the agreement on overtime work was conclude between the company and a person representing employees at the workplace. There was no trade union, but a "friendship" Association was organized in which appellee participated at the time of joining the company. Under Art. 36 of the Labour

Standards Act, the employer shall enter into a written agreement with either a trade union organized by a majority of the workers at the workplace concerned where such a trade union exists, or with a person representing a majority of the workers where no such trade union exists, in order to regulate overtime work. So a representative of the friendship association signed the agreement as a person representing a majority of workers. In this agreement it was stipulated that overtime work per week was limited to 3 hours for male workers and 1 hour for female workers from April until October, and 6 hours for male and 2 hours for female workers from November until March.

Appellant company emphasized the necessity of overtime work. But appellee criticized the overtime system, which violated the Labour Standards Act. The company advised him to obey overtime work order and that his attitude was not cooperative and gave troubles to other workers doing overtime work. But from January 1992 appellee refused to do overtime work owing to fatigue of eyes. On 20 February 1992 the company submitted him to disciplinary dismissal because he violated the work rules that he should obey orders by the company. So he sued for unpaid wages and a declaratory judgement that the dismissal was null and void. He also sued for consolation money of one million yen.

The Tokyo District Court judged on 25 October 1994 that the dismissal was null and void, but denied the request to pay consolation money. The reason was that he had no duty to obey overtime work because the agreement on overtime work was *null and void*. The District Court judged that a person representing a majority of workers was not properly selected under Art. 36 of the Labour Standards Act because a representative of the friendship association was selected automatically as a person representing employees at the concerned workplace. The Court decided that declaratory judgement was enough to console the appellee. The company appealed to the Tokyo High Court.

The Tokyo High Court affirmed the judgement with that of the District Court on 17 November 1997. A representative of the friendship association was treated automatically as a person representing workers at the workplace. But this manner of election was not democratic enough to lead to proper representation of the interests of workers. And evidence could not be found that the representative asked the workers whether the content of the agreement should be concluded or not and also that the representative issued the pamphlets or documents of the content of the agreement to the workers. Therefore, the appellee had no duty to obey the overtime work order because the agreement was null and void. At another point the Court found that there was a reasonable reason not to obey the overtime work order as the appellee suffered from fatigue of the eyes, which was certified medically. As a result, the dismissal was found to be null and void. The appellant company appealed to the Supreme Court.

Decision

The appeal was dismissed.

Law Applied

The Labour Standards Act: Art. 36. In the event that the employer has entered a written agreement with either a trade union organized by a majority of the workers at the workplace concerned, where such a trade union exists, or with a person representing a majority of the workers where no such trade union exists and has filled such agreement with the administrative office, the employer may, in accordance with the provisions of such agreement, and regardless of the provisions of Articles 32 through 32-5 and Article 40 with respect to working hours . . . and the provisions of the preceding Article with respect rest days . . ., extend the working hours or have workers work on rest days.

JUDGEMENT

In the facts found by the High Court the agreement was null and void because a person representing workers was not properly elected. Therefore, the appellee had no duty to obey an overtime work order. This Court found that the judgement of the High Court, declaring that the disciplinary dismissal was null and void, was rational and appropriate in the light of all the evidences presented to the High Court. There was no error in the judgement appeal was accordingly dismissed.

[*Source*: Case (0) 555 of 1998, decided on 22 July 2001; reported at Rodohanrei 808:11]

ANNOTATION

This is the first judgement to consider whether a person representing workers at the workplace is elected properly to conclude an agreement on overtime work under Article 36 of the Labour Standards Act. In Japan two requirements at least must be satisfied for the employer to order overtime work. One is the agreement on overtime work, and another is the labour contract in which the employee agrees to obey overtime work orders. A provision in work rules to order the employees to work in excess of the regular hours constitutes a term of the labour contract between the employee and the employer (*Tanaka* v. *Hitachi Ltd.*, 12 ILLR 150). In this case the former point was discussed. This agreement named a "36" agreement after Art. 36 of the Labour Standards Act.

All the employees joined the friendship association at the company. This association aimed to promote mutual friendship and welfare among members. This was different from a trade union defined under the Trade Unions Act as organizations for the main purposes of maintaining and improving working conditions and raising the economic status of the workers. Can a representative of the friendship association be a person representing workers at the workplace under Art. 36 of the Labour Standards Act?

There is no provision how to elect properly a person representing workers under the Labour Standards Act. There is, however, an administrative interpretation issued by the Ministry of Welfare and Labour. Two points are required under it. One is that a chance shall be given to a representative to judge whether the content of the agreement is proper or not in favour of the concerned workers at the workplace. Another is that democratic procedures must be adopted so as to demonstrate that a representative is supported by a majority of the concerned workers at the workplace.

Under this interpretation circular, the Ministry of Welfare and Labour regarding proper procedures of election issue notices. A person representing a majority of workers must be one who is qualified to conclude the agreement of behalf of the concerned workers. For example, a person appointed unilaterally by the employer and a person occupying a managerial post is not qualified. And a representative of a friendship association is not qualified when he is automatically elected as a person representing a majority of workers. In this case a representative of the friendship association was elected by the vote of its members. But the judgement of three Courts found that the election was not the procedure to select a person representing workers under Art. 36.

But there is a possibility for a representative of a friendship association to be qualified for concluding an agreement on overtime work. He or she can be on another occasion selected by voting, show of hands, making a list of candidates or summing up of approvals at the workplace. In this case there was a problem in that he was treated automatically as a person representing a majority of workers at the workplace.

The next problem is whether the representative asked the workers their view of the draft of the agreement. The agreement must include the reason needed for overtime work, the type of work, the number of workers and the period during which the extension of normal working hours would be admitted. A representative must sound out the workers before he or she can decide to conclude the agreement. In this case this democratic procedure was not followed.

Subsequently there is a problem whether the agreement shall be null and void for the reason that the necessary democratic procedure was not adopted. In this case, an unqualified person concluded the agreement, and he or she did not comply with the procedure to obtain the opinions of the workers. So the agreement violated Article 36 of the Labour Standards Act. As a result, it is natural that the agreement was found to be null and void.

After the judgement of the Tokyo High Court was issued, the amendment of the enforcement regulation for the Labour Standards Act became effective as from 1 April 1999. This stipulated that an agreement shall be made known to the workers by displaying or posting it at all times in a conspicuous location in the workplace or by other methods; and that a person representing the workers shall be selected by vote, or show of hands or other methods, making clear the selection procedure required by the Labour Standards Act; and also that a person shall be protected from discriminatory treatment. These amendments aim to promote the degree of democratization in the process of selection. It is sure that the judgement of the Supreme Court was influenced by this regulation.

The agreement has an effect to exempt the employer from criminal liability. If the employer should order overtime work under an invalid agreement, he or she shall be sentenced to penal servitude or to a fine. But he or she shall be exempted from punishment in the case that he or she has not the intention to conclude the agreement with the unqualified person representing a majority of workers. In any event the employer must be careful regarding the qualification of a person representing a majority of workers. The employer must pay increased wages to the workers working overtime even under an invalid agreement.

(9) ANNUAL LEAVE

(i) **Fumio Murata *et al.***
v.
Nippon Telephone and Telegraph Public Cooperation

(ii) **Jiji News Agency Co.**
v.
Toshiaki Yamnaguchi

(iii) **Nippon Telegraph and Telephone Co.**
v.
Aoi Nogata

Supreme Court (Third Petty Bench)

(i) Fumio Murata *et al.*
v.
Nippon Telephone and Telegraph Public Corporation

Employer's right to change designated period of annual leave with pay

HEADNOTES

Facts

The three appellants were employees of the appellee public corporation. Appellant "A" asked for paid annual leave on 16 September 1978 (Saturday). Appellants "B" and "C" asked for annual leave on 17 September 1978 (Sunday). Their purpose was to use annual leave to participate in a meeting against the building of the New Tokyo International Airport. The appellee exercised the right to change the designated day of annual leave because of obstruction of the normal operation of business. The three appellants were nevertheless absent on the day in question. The appellee then gave them a sanction of warning and reduced their wages for one day. The three appellants sought to have the sanction annulled and to obtain the unpaid amount of wages as well as damages for an illegal sanction.

In the appellee corporation, the employees were working on a monthly roster. In this roster two employees were scheduled to work on Saturday at the section where "A" worked. This number was a minimum. When Saturday was designated as annual leave, it was an established practice that other employees—except for managers—were not to be ordered to work as substitute. Normally the appellee ordered a manager to work on Saturday as a substitute. But on the day that "A" designated as annual leave, the manager could not work as a substitute because he was obliged to prepare to safeguard machines from vandalism by a group of radicals who opposed the opening of the New Tokyo International Airport. So the appellee did not try to look further for a substitute and exercised the right to change the designated day, which "A" asked for as annual leave. At the section where "B" designated as annual leave. At the section where "C" worked, one employee had to work on Sunday under the roster. The manager looked for a substitute. But no one agreed to work on Sunday. Therefore, the appellee exercised his right to change the designated day of annual leave because of obstruction of normal business operations.

The District Court held that the right to change the designated annual vacation was exercised illegally because the appellee did not consider whether a substitute could be secured for the day, which "A" designated as leave. So the sanction on "A" was judged as void, and the District Court ordered the employer to pay the amount of unpaid wages as well as 100,000 yen in damages to "A". But the District Court ordered the employer to pay the amount of unpaid wages as well as 100,000 yen in damages to "A". But the District Court held the sanctions imposed on "B" and "C" to be valid. The reason was that the appellee tried to find a substitute, but did not succeed, i.e. it was found that the appellee endeavored give annual leave to "B" and

"C", but no one agreed to work as a substitute. This meant that the conditions required for a change of the designated leave were met.

On appeal to the High Court, the sanction on all three appellants was held to be valid. The High Court recognized that it was impossible for the employer to secure a substitute from the employees of the sanction where "A" worked, because the appellee could not order the manager who had to protect the machines from radical activities to work as a substitute, and at the section where "A" worked the roster on Saturday and Sunday was not usually changed even if an employee asked for annual leave on Saturday or Sunday to work as a substitute, they would suffer from unfavourable treatment. The circumstances would have obliged the appellee to make strenuous efforts to find a substitute. It was natural for the employer to change the designated leave without investigating whether a substitute could be secured. The employer's exercise of the right to change the leave designated by "A" was judged to be legal under Article 39, Section 4 of this Labour Standards Act. The High Court had the same judgement regarding the annual leave designated by "B" and "C".

Decision

The appeal was dismissed.

Law Applied

Labour Standard Act

Article 39, Section 4: The employer shall grant the leave provided for in the preceding two paragraphs at the time requested by the workers: Provided that, when it would prevent the normal operation of the enterprise to give the leave at the required time, the employer may change the time.

JUDGEMENT

Under Article 39, Section 4 of the Labour Standard Act, an employer has the right to make a change in the dates, which the employee designates when it would prevent the normal operation of business to give the leave at the designated time. In judging whether normal operations would be obstructed, the Court should estimate the difficulty or ease of substituting another employee [for the one taking leave], especially when the employees are working on a roster. If the employer does not make arrangements to assign a substitute, although it would objectively be possible for him to get a substitute and to change the roster, he may not change the designated leave for the reason that it would obstruct the normal operation of business. The employer must consider the following circumstances when he judges whether it would be objectively possible to secure a substitute or to change the roster:

(1) How can the roster be changed when annual leave is designated?
(2) What arrangements have been made by the employer to offer the designated leave?
(3) Can other employees work as substitutes from the point of view of content and nature of the work?
(4) Does the employer have time to judge in advance whether or not to exercise his right to change the designated leave?
(5) How is the weekly [rest] day system put into practice?

When it is found objectively that the employer cannot secure a substitute and change the roster, he can exercise his right to change the designated leave legally even though he does not make a concrete arrangement to secure a substitute.

In this case, it was agreed between the labour union and the employer that the weekly day of rest should not be changed when an employee designated a rest day on which he add to work as annual leave. Therefore, the appellee could not change the roster. He had to order a manager to work as substitute. But this was impossible owing to the extraordinary situation cased by radicals. So the Supreme Court finds that the employer could not secure a substitute, and that the annual leave of "A" interfered with the normal operation of business. The Supreme Court considers the findings and the judgement of the High Court rational and appropriate as regards the annual vacation designated by "B" and "C".

[*Source*: Case No. (0) 1555 of 1985, decided on 4 July 1989: reported at Rodohanrei No. 543:7]

ANNOTATION

1. Under an amendment of the Labour Standards Act in 1988, an employer must offer at least 10 days of annual paid vacation to employees who have worked continuously for a year and attended for more than 80 percent of entire working days. Before this amendment, the minimum number of days of annual paid leave was 6. The employer must also grant one additional day of leave with pay per year to employees who have worked for two or more years. The maximum number of days of leave is 20. Large-scale employers give more annual leave than prescribed by law. But many small firms tend to offer no more than is so prescribed.

An employee can take paid leave "consecutively or separately", whenever he likes. In Japan, annual leave is usually taken one or two days at a time. They are used for various private purposes such as shopping, going to one's home city, going to a hospital, visiting the children's school, holding a Buddhist service for the dead or attending a funeral or marriage ceremony and so on. So some of the paid leave is left unused at the end of the year. At present only 60.8 percent of days of leave are used by workers in enterprises with 300 employees or more. To promote full use of vacations, an employer may conclude a labour management agreement with a majority union or a representative of the majority of employees, in which the schedule of annual leaves (except for five days which must be reserved for private use) can be planned with biding effect upon individual employees under the amendment of the Labour Standards Act in 1988. This new system has been introduced to shorten the long working hours criticized by American and European countries since they unfavourably affect their balance of trade. But this case reported here happened before the amendment of the Act. The appellants took only one day of leave with pay.

2. When an employee wants to take a day of paid leave, he must first designate the day chosen by him. But under Article 39, Section 4 of the Labour Standards Act the employer can exercise his right to change the designated date, when it would prevent the normal operation of business to give the leave on the designated day. In such case the point to be discussed is whether an obstruction of the normal operation of business would occur under the working system at the company. As the appellants were working on a roster, the answer depended upon how the appellee could endeavor to find a substitute for the designated day.

According to earlier Supreme Court judgements, it is understood that lack of the requisite number of employees only does not constitute obstruction of the normal operation if the employer does not try to find a substitute even though it would be objectively possible for him to find a substitute who is working on the roster (*Toshihiro Hanada v. Nippon Telephone and Telegraph Public Corporation*, decided on 10 July 1987 by the Supreme Court: reported at Rodohanrei No. 499:19). The Supreme Court followed the same line of thinking in this case. And five points are indicated as a standard by reference to which the employer can judge whether it would be objectively possible to secure a substitute. These five points are characteristic in comparison with the former Supreme Court judgements.

The annual paid leave system requires that the necessary number of employees should be available to assure the normal operation of the business. But it is difficult always to secure the necessary number of employees. In Japan life-time (long-time) employment system has been established. So it is difficult for an employer to dismiss employees at a time of economic and business depression. Therefore, in normal times an employer will show a tendency to employ the minimum number of employees and not to secure the number of employees necessary in order to grant all the holidays requested by all the employees. When an employee wants to take leave, this would then create problems for the work of his fellow employees; as a result there will be some difficulty in taking the leave with pay. Also, the employer cannot easily find a substitute. This gives rise to disputes as in the case reported. To solve the problem the Supreme Court indicated that an employer should do his best to secure a substitute, so as to offer paid leave to the employees.

3. Nippon Telephone and Telegraph Public Corporation were privatized in April 1985. It is now a private company. But the Labour Standards Act is applied to it as a public corporation and a private company.

Supreme Court (Third Petty Bench)

(ii) Jiji News Agency Co.

v.

Tohiaki Yamaguchi

Employer's right to change long period of annual leave designated by employee

HEADNOTES

Facts

The appellant was a journalist employed by the

appellee news agency. He belonged to the section concerned with local news, which consisted of 41 journalists. Of these 31 worked outside. The appellant had been attached as a journalist to the Ministry of Science and Technology since 1978; from 1979 he was the only one so assigned. To cover his field, he had acquired professional knowledge and experience regarding science and technology, particularly atomic energy.

In July 1980 he proposed taking paid annual leave from 20 August to 20 September, to collect materials on atomic power generation in Europe. At that time he had a right to 40 days of paid annual holiday. Of these he planned to take 24 days during the designated period. The chief of the local news section agreed to part of his proposal, i.e. to take leave form 20 August to 3 September, but ordered him to perform his normal duties from 4 to 20 September. In the view of the chief, the activities of the news agency would be crippled by the appellant's absence for one month, while the agency could not afford to assign another journalist from the local news section to his position.

The union to which the appellant belonged discussed the matter with the news agency, but a compromise solution could not be reached. In spite of the order of his chief, the appellant took the holiday as originally proposed. During his absence, an assistant normally concerned with meteorology reported on science and technology. The appellant was given a reprimand for not obeying the order to perform his duties, and 47,638 yen were deducted from his bonuses on the ground of ten days' absence without permission, the appellant sought a judgement declaring the reprimand invalid and ordering payment of the amount withheld from his bonuses as well as damages for the injury suffered as a result of the disciplinary sanction.

Tokyo District Court gave judgement for the news agency on the ground that it reasonably exercised its right to change the paid annual leave designated by the appellant. It reasoned as follows: when one journalist was absent for along time, his post was usually occupied by another one form the same section, it accordingly had to be determined within the local news section whether annual leave at the designated time would prevent the normal operation of the enterprise. It was reasonable to find that paid leave for one month would do so, since there was only one journalist assigned to the Ministry of Science and Technology and the appellee could not find any one having the knowledge and experience to take over within the local news section in summer.

Tokyo High Court reversed. It considered that the employer's right to change the designated paid holiday was exercised illegally, on the ground that it would not be difficult to find a substitute (for instance, form an assistant desk or a free roving reporter) and that obstruction of the normal business operation was due to the improper policy of the new agency to assign only one journalist to a post requiring professional knowledge. The Court accordingly declared the reprimand invalid and ordered payment of some damages.

Decision

The Supreme Court reversed the judgement and referred the case back to the High Court.

Law Applied

Labour Standards Act

Article 39: (1) An employer shall grant annual leave with pay of ten days, either consecutive or divided into portions, to workers who have been employed continuously for one year and who have reported for work on at least 80 percent of the total working days.

(2) To workers who have been employed continuously for two or more years, an employer shall grant one day of annual leave with pay additional to the

number of days specified in the preceding paragraph for each additional year of continuous service beyond one year: Provided that, if the total number of days of annual leave with pay would exceed 20 days, the employer shall not be required to grant annual leave with pay for such excess days.

(3) (Omitted)

(4) The employer shall grant the leave provided for in the preceding two paragraph at the time requested by the worker: Provided that, when it would prevent the normal operation of the enterprise to give the leave at the required period, the employer may grant the leave at another period.

JUDGEMENT

1. An employee may have a right to take annual leave if he meets the conditions laid down in article 39, paragraphs 1 and 2 of the Labour Standards Act. When he specifically designates the days for taking annual leave with pay, he is exempted from the obligation to perform his duties unless the employer properly exercises his right to change the designated period. The provisions in question require the employer to make, as soon as possible; arrangements to enable the employee to take leave at the designated time. However, if it proves difficult for the employer, despite his efforts, to secure a substitute, he may change the designated days on the ground that it would prevent the normal operation of the enterprise to give the leave at the required time.

2. A long period of consecutive days of annual leave raises the possibility of interference with the normal operation of the business. It accordingly becomes necessary to adjust the designated days of leave in advance. When a long period of leave is designated without such adjustment, the employer must have a discretionary power to change the designated time because it would be difficult to make an accurate estimate of the extent of the obstruction caused to

normal business operations by the leave. The discretionary power must, however, be exercised properly in light of the purpose of article 39 of the Labour Standards Act. If the employer exercised his right without considering how a period of annual leave could be facilitated, this would have to be judged illegal.

3. The appellant had considerable professional knowledge and experience for reporting on science and technology, particularly as regards problems of atomic energy. It was accordingly difficult to find a substitute for one month among journalists of the local new section.

In that section, it was not unusual to assign only one journalist to a particular job, because for business reasons there were few journalists posted at the section. The policy was accordingly not improper.

In this case, the appellant proposed taking annual leave for one month without adequately adjusting the period and the time in advance. In the circumstances, the chief of the local news section gave him enough consideration in changing the required days of annual leave.

In light of the above, it can be held that the appellee reasonably exercised the discretionary power to change the designated period and time. The decision of Tokyo High Court accordingly has to be reversed and the case sent back for a decision as to whether the change and the reprimand constituted an unfair labour practice.

[*Source*: Case No. (0) 399 of 1989, decided on 23 June 1992. Reported at Hanreiji Ho No. 1426:35].

ANNOTATION

1. In Japan annual leave with pay has not been taken in the same way in industrialized European or American countries. Usually only one or two days of leave are taken at a time; it is rare for a large number of days to be take consecutively. This has meant that

45.4 percent of annual leave is left unused at the enc of the year (Ministry of Labour, General Survey of Wages and Working Hours Systems in 1991). However, Japan is now trying to reduce the hours actually worked per year, so that workers may be able to enjoy life comfortably in good economic conditions. One of the means to attain this end is to promote full use of annual holidays.

For this purpose an employer can conclude an agreement with either a labour union organized by a majority of the workers at the workplace, or with a person representing a majority of these workers where there is no union. In such an agreement a schedule of annual leave can, under the amendment of the Labour Standards Act in 1988, be established with binding effect upon employees at the workplace concerned. There are three types of leave plans under such agreements. According to one, all employees at the workplace would take their holidays simultaneously, in summer or winter. According to a second type, leave would be taken by alternating squads of employees. Under the third, an individual employee would take his annual vacation in accordance with the planned schedule.

The case here reported is analogous to the third type, but, because the events occurred before the amendment of the Labour Standards Acts, the appellant did not designate the beginning and end of the leave under a schedule.

2. This is the first case in which the Supreme Court has given a judgement concerning a paid holiday for a long period. As lengthy annual holidays will be more frequent in the future, the judgement is significant as a precedent. The prevalent view has been that, when an employee designates the beginning and end of his annual leave, the designation is effective unless the employer exercises his right to change the time because of obstruction of the normal business operations (*Public Prosecutor v. Tadaaki Ono*, decided on 2 March 1973 by the Supreme Court and reported at

Minshu, Vol. 27, No. 2, p. 191; *Shozo Kokubu et al. v. Japan National Railway Corporation*, decided on 2 March 1973 by the Supreme Court and reported at Minshu, Vol. 27, No. 2, p. 210).

3. The judgement makes two particular points. One is that it is necessary to arrive at an adjustment, as between employer and employee, of the designated annual leave before the employee can in fact take leave for a long period. However, it is not fully explained why such adjustment is necessary despite the fact that article 39 of the Labour Standards Act does not provide for such a requirement.

The term "period" used in paragraph 4 of article 39 of the Labour Standards Act has two meanings, namely "a season and a definite periok" (Kazuo Sugeno, Japanese Labour Law, translated by Leo Kanowitz, University of Washington Press, 1992, p. 274). When an employee designates the beginning and end of a definite period, he can take leave on the basis of his unilateral action unless the employer changes the period. On the other hand, when an employee designates a season, he can take the leave after the specification of the actual days of absence has been reasonably adjusted in light of the employer's business needs and the leave proposals of other workers. In the reported case, the appellant designated the beginning and end of one month's continuous leave, i.e. of a definite period. The view of the Supreme Court is thus that, in case of leave for a long time, it is necessary for the designated days to be adjusted on an individual basis between the employer and the employee even as regards a definite period, whereas such adjustment is not necessary in case of the designation of a definite period of leave for a short time.

The other point is that an employer may have a discretionary power to change the days designated for lengthy annual leave without adjustment in advance. This is a new opinion, not previously found in the case law of the Court. The discretionary power is limited to determining the extent of obstruction of normal business operations and the consequent amendment of the timing and length of the leave. The power cannot be altogether denied, because there is a strong possibility that the designation of a substantial number of consecutive days of leave will involve the obstruction of normal business operations. However, it may naturally not be so exercised as to conflict with the purpose of article 39.

4. The crucial difference between the High Court and the Supreme Court is their view regarding the appropriateness of assigning only one person to a particular post. The High Court considered that it was improper to do so, because the employer had to secure the number of employees necessary to permit the grant of an annual leave designated by all the employees. However in practice it is difficult always to secure the necessary number and the judgement of the High Court thus imposed an impossible or at least difficult duty on the employer. The Supreme Court, on the other hand, considered that it was difficult to secure a substitute, on the premise that the existing assignment was proper. Having found further that the appellant designated the timing and period of long leave without full adjustment in advance, and that the employer nevertheless exercised his right to change the designated days only as regards the latter part of the period, the Court held that the employer's discretionary power was not unreasonably exercised in light of article 39.

Supreme Court (Second Petty Bench)

(iii) Nippon Telegraph and Telephone Co.
v.
Aoi Nagata

Effect of taking paid annual leave during vocational training—time off for purposes of union activity

HEADNOTES

Facts

The appellant is an employer of Nippon Telegraph and Telephone Co. (referred to as NTT) whose work is to maintain telephone machinery as chief of section at Tachikawa Network Center. NTT began to introduce digitalized telephony and the appellant was ordered to undergo vocational training for the maintenance of digitalized telephones for a period of 29 days. He was expected to teach the contents of the training to his section members.

He was a member of executive committee of the Telecommunication Workers' Union belonging to the National Confederation of Trade Unions (Zenroren), which was close to Japanese Communist Party. He wanted to participate in the opening ceremony of Zenroren during his training period and proposed taking annual paid leave therefor. But NTT exercised its right to change the paid annual leave designated by the appellant because annual leave could not be granted during the vocational training. The appellant attended the ceremony and did not participate in vocational training on that day. His wage was not paid for that day and he was subjected to a reprimand as a disciplinary sanction.

The appellant sought a judgement declaring the reprimand invalid and ordering the payment of unpaid wages for the following reasons: (1) NTT acted illegally when it changed the annual leave designated by the appellant; (2) it was an unfair labour practice for NTT to change his designated annual leave because the appellant was a member of the Telecommunication Workers' Union; (3) NTT made improper use of its right to impose disciplinary action (the reprimand) if (1) and (2) were not maintained.

The Tokyo District Court gave judgement for the appellant that the reprimand was null and void because NTT abused its right to administer disciplinary punishment. The District Court found that annual leave had usually been permitted even during vocational training and that the reprimand was too extreme. But the District Court denied that NTT exercised its right illegally to change the annual leave designated by the appellant for the following reasons: promotion of vocational ability to cope with rapid technical change is necessary to operate business smoothly; in the process of training the appellant could not be replaced by someone else. Thus, the annual leave designated by the appellant was found to prevent normal operation of the enterprise at NTT. As a result, NTT could legally change the designated leave day, but the reprimand was judged to be null and void. The District Court ordered NTT to pay the amount of the reduced wages.

The Tokyo High Court found NTT's proposal to change annual leave illegal, and the reprimand null and void because the appellant had the possibility to get knowledge and technical skill through supplementary lectures and other means even if the appellant was absent during the vocational training. So it could not be said that annual leave during the vocational training would always impede the normal operation of the enterprise. Legality of the employer's right to change designated annual leave should be judged from the viewpoint of how annual leave would prevent attaining the purpose of the vocational training. To this end all the following points should be considered: the content, the purpose and the period of vocational training, the level of knowledge and skill of the trainee, the period of annual leave, the content of the missed lecture, existence of supplementary means to make up for the missed lecture, and all other relevant circumstances. In this case the period of annual leave was only one day. On that day the appellant could not attend lectures on the management of signals at telephone switchboard for four hours although trainees were expected to take the lectures on that totally for six hours.

But the Court found that the appellant could make it up by his endeavor to read the textbook and through his own acquired knowledge and skill. So it could not be said that one-day's leave made it difficult to get the import of the vocational training. In fact the appellant could finish the training course with good marks. As a result NTT could not legally change the designated annual leave. Consequently the appellant could take one day's leave legally and the reprimand could be found to be null and void. NTT appealed to the Supreme Court.

Decision

The Supreme Court quashed the judgement and sent the case back to the Tokyo High Court.

Law Applied

Labour Standards Act

Article 39(4): The employer shall grant the annual leave provided for in the preceding two paragraphs at the time requested by the workers: provided that, when it would prevent the normal operation of the enterprise to give the leave at the required period, the employer may grant the leave at another period.

JUDGEMENT

1. As a representative of employees in the workshop, the appellant was ordered to undergo vocational training whose purpose was to promote his ability relating to maintenance of digitalized telephony and to improve operations in the workshop by his knowledge and skill. The purpose of the training would not be attained if he was partly absent from the training course, unless there were special circumstances. Therefore, the employer could propose to change the designated annual leave if it was found that the appellant would not be short of his knowledge and skill even if he were absent from the course of training during his annual leave. Furthermore someone else instead of him could not receive this training.

The lecture was scheduled for a total of six hours and was intended to improve his ability to manage signals at telephone switchboards. But he was absent form the lecture for four hours. There was a high possibility for him to become short of knowledge and skill because of absence from the lecture and also his workshop would receive bad influence from his unsatisfactory training.

2. It would be difficult to compensate for the missed lectures through self-training using a textbook. It was not certain that the appellant could execute his self-training when the employer decided to propose to change the designated annual leave. . . . Therefore, the employer could consider whether it would impede the normal operation of the enterprise to give the leave for the requested period. . . .

It cannot be concluded that the appellant had already the knowledge and skill scheduled to be attained in the training course from his past job career. And it could not be predicted that the appellant would get good marks when the employer decided to propose to change the designated annual paid leave.

3. From the above-mentioned, the Court finds that the judgement of the lower court made a wrongful interpretation and application of the Labour Standards Act Art. 39(4). Accordingly, the judgement of the lower court is dismissed.

But at the lower court it will be necessary to consider whether the appellant had already knowledge and skill scheduled to be attained in the training course and also whether the employer could propose to change the designated leave. And it should be judged again whether it is an unfair labour practice for the employer to propose to change the designated leave, and whether the employer abused his right to order the reprimand to the appellant as disciplinary punishment.

[*Source*: Case No. (0) 1026 of 1996, decided on March 31, 2000: Rodohanrei 781-18].

ANNOTATION

(1) This case deals with the legality of the employer's right to change the designated annual leave during a period of vocational training. This is the first judgement of the Supreme Court on annual leave during off-the-job training. In this case there can be found some particularities of annual leave with pay in Japan. As the first point, only one day of leave was taken at one time. The Labour Standards Act permits an employee to parcel out one day at a time. This reveals that annual leaves can be used in small pieces. As the second point, the Act does not regulate the purpose for which annual leave can be used. So annual leave can be freely used by an employee and may not be interfered with by an employer. In fact annual leave may be used for various kinds of purposes. . . . In this case it was used for trade union activity. If the employer proposed to change the designated leave on account of trade union activity, it would amount to an unfair labour practice under the Trade Union Act, Art. 7(3) that prohibits control or interference in the management of the labour union. The Supreme Court sent this point to the lower court for reconsideration.

(2) When an employee designates a period of annual leave with the dates of commencement and termination, his or her obligation to provide labour during the leave is erased unless the employer exercises the right to change the designated leave under the Labour Standards Act Art. 39(4). The employer can change the period designated if it would obstruct the normal operation of the business. However, the employer must give the employee annual leave at some other time.

It would usually obstruct the operation of business unless a substitute employee was assigned to fill the vacancy. So the employer has a duty to assign someone to the job before the employer exercises his or her right to change the designated leave. But in this case the District Court, High Court and Supreme Court all judged that someone else instead of the appellant could not receive this vocational training. So the employer could not assign a substitute employee to receive the training course during his annual leave. If so, would annual leave during vocational training necessarily obstruct the normal operation of business? Cannot the employee take annual leave at all during vocational training?

(3) The judgement of the Supreme Court was different from that of the High Court on the problem of whether annual leave during vocational training would obstruct the normal operation of business. The Supreme Court pointed out the problems of the High Court judgement.

The first point was the time when the employer would decide whether the leave could obstruct the normal operation of business. The Supreme Court judged that the employer could decide the question just at the time when he would propose to change the designated leave. Therefore, it is not reasonable that the employer be requested to consider whether the operation of the business would be obstructed after the leave had been used. But the High Court said that only one-day leave did not obstruct the normal operation of business and that the appellant could finish the training course with good marks. Those circumstances mentioned in the judgement of the High Court took place only after the leave was used. So they could not be predicted at the time when the employer proposed to change the designated leave. As a result the Supreme Court overruled the judgement of the High Court.

The second point was whether the cut lectures could be replaced by self-study of the textbook. The Supreme Court rejected this premise. And the Supreme Court had doubts that the appellant had already acquired the knowledge and skills scheduled to be taught in the training course form his past job career. Thus the Supreme Court sent this case to the High Court for reconsideration.

(4) In this case the period of the training was about one month. In one month there could be unexpected incidents during the training period, which compelled an employee to take annual leaves. For example his or her parents could die in a plane crash for this occasion the employer should arrange to offer supplementary lectures in order to secure annual leave with payment to an employee. In the present case it would have been easy to arrange for a supplementary lecture for only four hours. This is an employer's duty to give a consideration to an employee who wants to take annual, even during vocational training. This point is neglected in the judgement of the Supreme Court.

(10) EMPLOYMENT ACCIDENT

(i) **Maqsood Ahmed Body**
v.
Kaishinsha Ltd.

(ii) **Noriko Suzuki**
v.
Yohohama City

Supreme Court (Third Petty Bench)

(i) Maqsood Ahmed Boby v. Kaishinsha Ltd.

Illegal foreign worker—employment accident—calculation of damages

HEADNOTES

Facts

Pakistani appellant came to Japan as a temporary visitor for sightseeing on 28 November 1988 when he was 23 years old. He was employed on 29 November by the appellee bookbinding company where in total 5 persons were working. He was an illegal foreign worker under the Immigration Control and Refugee Recognition Act 1951. His work was to ship and discharge goods and to set papers at the automatic binding machines and to pack bound books. On 30 March 1990 his right forefinger was cut from the first articulation during his work binding pamphlets by using a binding machine. There was a danger of pinching fingers in the machine when a user was not experienced in using this machine. The binding machine did not have a safety device. And the appellant had never used this binding machine before. His manager did not warn him to be careful of using the machine. After the injury he did not work at the appellee company, but attended a hospital till 19

April 1990. After that he worked at another bookbinding company (Sakushin Ltd.) till 23 August 1990. Thereafter he changed his address frequently and worked as a temporary worker at many places.

The Labour Standards Inspection Office judged his injury to be one suffered in the course of duty. So the appellant was paid 132.972 yen as non-duty compensation benefit and 1,644,725 yen as physical handicap compensation benefit under the Workmen's Accident Compensation Insurance Act. And also the appellee company paid him 178,133 yen. But he sued for damages against the company under Article 415 of the Civil Code and against the president of the company under Article 709 of the Civil Code.

The judgement of Tokyo District Court was the following:

(1) This claim should be judged on the basis of Japanese law under Article 7, section 1 and Article 11, Section 1 of the Act concerning the Application of Laws.

(2) The company had responsibility to pay damages under Article 415 of the Civil Code because the company did not perform the obligations to warn the appellant to be careful in using the binding machine and to instruct him how to work safely. The president of the company negligently violated the obligation to take care of him under tort law. Therefore, the president should compensate the damage under Article 709 of the Civil Code.

(3) The amount of damages was estimated as follows. 120,428 yen should be counted as the damages for inability to work from 31 March to 18 April. Though he was an illegal foreign worker, his work was not contrary to public order and morals because he was not a smuggler. So inability to work could be an object for damages. As damages for after-effect of the injury, 2,222,622 yen was ordered to be paid to the appellant. The Court judged that he could work in Japan only for 3 years from 23 August 1990 when he retired from Sakushin Ltd. So the amount of damages during these 3 years for after-effect of the injury should be calculated

by reference to the real incomes level (7,500 yen per day) in Japan. Thereafter it should be calculated by reference to the standard of income (30,000 yen per month) in Pakistan, till he was 67 years old, because he should go back to his mother country.

(4) Considering the degree of the injury and the process of treatment, the District Court judged that it was worth 2,500,000 yen to console the appellant. So, in total, the amount for damages was 4,843,050 yen.

(5) If there is any fault on the part of the injured party, the court may take such fault into account in assessing the amount of damages. The District Court found that the appellant partly contribute to the injury. He worked in a desultory manner though he should have been careful not to pinch the finger. Therefore, for contributory negligence the amount of damages should be reduced to 70%, namely, 3,390,135 yen (1,640,135 yen for pecuniary loss and 1,750,000 yen for non-pecuniary loss)

(6) The appellant was altogether paid 1,777,697 yen as non-duty and physical handicap compensation benefit under the Workmen's Accident Compensation Insurance Act.

The amount included special supplement allowances for non-duty and physical handicap provided by labour welfare services under the Workman's Accident Compensation Insurance Act. The government provides labour welfare services to promote the smooth social re-integration of the injured workers, and to support injured workers and bereaved families. So these special supplement allowances were judged to be compensation for economic and pecuniary loss. Thus his pecuniary loss was offset by non-duty and physical handicap compensation benefits did not make up for non-pecuniary damages. Namely, 1,750,000 yen had to be paid to the appellant as non-pecuniary damages and 200,000 yen at attorney's fee. In conclusion, the District Court ordered the appellees to pay 1,950,000 yen to the appellant with 5% interest.

The Tokyo High Court endorsed the judgement of

the District Court. The appellee company appealed to the Supreme Court.

Decision

The appeal was rejected.

Law Applied

Act concerning the Application of Laws

Article 7, Section 1: With regard to the formation and effect of a legal act, the question as to which country's law is to govern shall be determined by the intention of the parties.

Article 11, Section 1; The formation and effect of obligation rights arising from the voluntary management of affairs, unjust enrichment or torts, shall be governed by the law of the place where the events giving rise to such obligation rights have occurred.

The Civil Code

Article 415: If an obligor fails to perform in accordance with the main intent of the obligation duty, the oblige may demand compensation for damages; the same shall apply in the case where performance becomes impossible for any reason imputable to the obligor.

Article 709: A person who intentionally or negligently violates the rights of another is obliged to compensate any damages arising there from.

Workmen's Accident Compensation Insurance Act

Article 23: In order to promote the welfare of workers in the undertakings covered by this insurance and their bereaved families, the Government may undertake the following services as labour welfare services:

(1) Establishment and operation of facilities for medical treatment and rehabilitation, and other services necessary to promote the smooth return to society of workers having suffered employment injury or commutation injury.

JUDGEMENT

1. *Calculation of damages for loss suffered by after-effect of the injury*

The amount of damages must be calculated by reference to an income earned in the future by the injured person concerned. The appellant is a foreign worker who wishes to work wishes to work in Japan for a short time. Therefore, the Court in estimating his future income, must consider how long he will work in Japan, and to which country he will come after his work in Japan. It is natural that the Court should judge the amount of damages by reference to his level of income during his possible period of work in Japan and also his possible income earned in his mother country after his departure from Japan. His possible period of work shall be deduced from such points as, his intention to stay in Japan, certification of eligibility to enter Japan, the period of stay in Japan, the situation of his work and etc.

Over-stay foreign workers are subject to deportation under the Immigration and Refugee Recognition Act, 1951. The appellant's period of stay in Japan could not be so long because he has no possibility to stay legally with the special permission. Therefore, it is not irrational to consider that his possible period of work would be 3 years. And it is reasonable to judge that he will get income in his home country after 3 years. The amount of his income shall be calculated as equal to that earned in Pakistan before he came to Japan.

2. Deduction of the amount of special supplement under the workmen's Accident Compensation Insurance Act from damages under the Civil Code

An employer is exempted from damages within the limit of the amount of compensation to be paid under the Workmen's Accident Compensation Insurance Act; the Government may provide labour welfare services in order to promote the welfare of workers. As the labour welfare service, special supplement allowances are paid in addition to the non-duty and physical handicap compensation benefit. For this purpose a Ministerial Ordinance was made concerning the payment of special supplement allowances. These special supplement allowances are not paid in order to compensate for pecuniary loss. So 353,787 yen paid as the amount of special supplement allowances cannot be deducted from damages. This Court considers the judgements of Tokyo High Court and District Court in error in the interpretation of Article 23 of the Workmen's Accident Compensation Insurance Act. The amount of compensation benefit except special supplement allowances was 1,423,910 yen under the Workmen's Accident Compensation Insurance Act. But pecuniary loss was counted as 1,640,135 yen. Therefore, the appellees shall have the obligation to pay 216,225 yen as damages for pecuniary loss. 1,750,000 yen shall be paid as damages for non-pecuniary loss and 200,000 yen as attorney's fee. In total the appellees shall pay 2,166,225 yen to the appellant with 5% interest

[*Source*: Case No. (0) 2132 of 1993, decided on 28 February 1997; Dodohanrei 708-23]

ANNOTATION

1. Applicable law had to be decided because this case is concerned with transnational litigation. In the case the labour contract was concluded in Japan. And the place of work was Tokyo in Japan. The appellees liable for damages in tort were located in Japan though

the appellant was a Pakistani. Therefore, it had to be considered under Article 7, Section 1 of the Act concerning the Application of Laws whether the appellees failed to perform their obligation of the labour contract to care for the employee's safety and health. And under Article 11, Section 1 of this Act the responsibility in tort under the Civil Code had to be judged. This choice of law is proper.

2. More than 300,000 illegal foreigners are working in Japan. Whether legal or illegal, foreign workers must be treated equally under the same conditions with Japanese employees, because under Article 3 of the Labour Standards Act an employer must not engage in discriminatory treatment with respect to wages, working hours or other working conditions by reason of nationality. Even though the appellant was an illegal foreign worker, his work was not contrary to public order and morals. So it was judged that the Labour Standards Act should protect his work. Thus the appellant could receive workmen's accident compensation and also damages for pecuniary and non-pecuniary losses suffered from the employer. On the contrary, it is evident that he would not be protected by the labour Standards Act if his work were contrary to public order like a smuggler.

3. The most important problem was how the amount of damages for loss suffered by after-effect of the injury should be calculated in case of an illegal foreign worker. This case is the first judgement of the Supreme Court on this problem. There are three opinions on this problem.

(1) The first is that the amount should be calculated by reference to his real earnings in Japan because he was working in Japan. This idea is based on the premise that he will work for a long time till his mandatory retirement age, namely, 60 years. But a foreign worker, in general, comes to Japan in the hope of several years' work. So this premise is different from the actual condition of the foreign worker. The appellant would be very glad to receive the amount of

damages under the first opinion because average earnings in Japan are far better than in Pakistan. Returning back to his mother country, he may be very comfortably off even if he did not work in Pakistan. This leads to a fear in Japan that more and more foreigners will come to work in Japan.

(2) The second opinion is that the amount should be calculated by reference to the level of earnings in Pakistan. This opinion ignores that the appellant was working in Japan for about 2 years, even though he was an illegal worker under the Immigration Control and Refugee Recognition Act.

(3) The third opinion is that of the judgement of the Supreme Court. The amount should be calculated by reference to the standard of real incomes during his possible period of work in Japan. And after that period it should be calculated by reference to the standard of income in his mother country. This opinion is a compromise between the first and the second opinion. In principle, the amount of damages suffered from the after-effect of the injury must be decided on the basis of earnings in the future. Tokyo District Court found it proper that he could work for a certain number of years after he was injured even if he was an illegal foreigner. The Supreme Court admitted that this certain period of work be deemed to be 3 years, because the appellant without proper status was compulsorily subject to deportation. This solution is thought to be tactful.

4. An employee is entitled to receive compensation benefit under the Workmen's Accident Compensation Insurance Act when he suffers an injury resulting from employment. On the other hand, he may litigate the liability for damages of the employer under the Civil Code. So it becomes a problem how to adjust workers' accident insurance compensation benefit with damages under the Civil Code.

The employer shall deduct the amount of workers' accident compensation, which has been already paid, from the amount of damages payable. This is provided under Article 84, Section 2 of the Labour Standards Act, to the effect that in the event an employer has paid compensation under this Act, the employer shall be exempt, up to the amount of such payments, form responsibility for damages under the Civil Code based on the same grounds. The workers' accident compensation insurance is a system making up for compensation for workers' accidents under the Labour Standards Act. So this provision is interpreted to extend to the relationship between the workers' accident compensation insurance and the employer's civil liability for damages.

But there are two exceptions. The purpose of the payment of workmen's accident compensation insurance is to compensate only for pecuniary losses, not for pain and suffering. Therefore, the amount of consolation money cannot be covered by the payment of workmen's accident compensation insurance. Another exception is the special supplement allowances payment discussed in this judgement of the Supreme Court.

Under Article 23 of the Workmen's Accident Compensation Insurance Act, the Government may provide labour welfare services in order to promote the welfare of workers. This provision is not intended to compensate for pecuniary losses. As a result, the amount of special supplement allowances cannot be deducted from the amount of damages under the Civil Code.

Supreme Court (Third Petty Bench)

(ii) Noriko Suzuki
v.
Yokohama City

Employment injury—compensation for pain resulting from excessive strain

HEADNOTES

Facts

The appellant was a governess at a Yokohama municipal nursery school since April 1968. She took care of children from one to five years old. From September 1970 she began to feel pain in her right shoulder and elbow.

She gave birth to her third child in June 1971. After maternity leave, she had to take care of the three children, aged seven, five and the newborn baby, this after she finished work each day at the nursery school. From October 1971 she received obstetric and gynaecology treatment for muscular pain in the waist and femoral regions resulting from childbirth. From April 1972 the pain became stronger along with pain in her right arm and elbow in addition to a stubborn stiffness in her shoulders.

In June 1972 the appellant was transferred to a newly established nursery school. The head of the new school had no experience in child welfare; three other governesses were also newly employed. She was thus obliged to act as a senior veteran in the preparatory work involved in opening the new school in that month. Thereafter she had the responsibility of caring for six children of one and two years of age. During her work she felt more pain in her shoulder and arms. At a hospital, in September 1972 she was diagnosed as having neck, shoulder and arm pain caused by work involving excessive strain on her upper limbs. Although she was under medical care, she was obliged to continue work as a senior employee because her colleague was absent for six months. She was not able to take sufficient rest and paid holidays and thus her pain became increasingly severe. In general, a nursery governess must move more strenuously to properly take care of small children because they are so active. She had no time for rest and was obliged to make frequent use of her upper arms to hold babies and small children. She also had to take care of children using an unnatural posture because of the children's small size.

She sued Yokohama City for 10 million yen for damages on the ground that the city violated its duty under her employment contract to exercise sufficient care to ensure her safety and health. In the Tokyo district court, Yokohama City was ordered to pay two million yen because it breached its duty to prevent the onset of her health problems, and to take care not to worsen the condition of the appellant. Yokohama City appealed to the Tokyo High Court. The appellant also appealed as she considered the amount of recovery insufficient. The High Court ruled for Yokohama City, holding that there was no reasonable relationship between the syndrome and her work as a senior nursery governess. The appellant appealed to the Supreme Court.

Decision

The Supreme Court quashed the judgement and sent the case back to the Tokyo High Court.

Law Applied

Civil Code, Article 415

If a contractor [employer] fails to act in accordance with its obligations and duties, the contractee [employee] is entitled to compensation for damages; the same shall apply in cases where performance becomes impossible for any reason imputable to the contractor [employer]

JUDGEMENT

1. Proof of a causal sequence in a lawsuit is not the same as proof in the context of the natural sciences, the latter entertaining no doubt at all. It is enough to prove that there is a high probability that

certain facts bring about certain results on the basis of evidence as verified by experiential knowledge. That is, it is necessary for the court to be convinced to the degree where a normal person would have no doubt.

2. A nursery school governess is compelled neither to repeat the same movements nor to maintain the same posture for an extended period. But such work does involve mental strain and physical fatigue because she must constantly care for children while exercising caution. And, also, the use of muscular strength around the arms and shoulders is required since she must hold children while in an unnatural position. The strain to her arm and shoulder is found to be not so light, although her work is not substantially heavier than other nursery governesses. The appellant began to fee pain in the shoulder and back regions as a preliminary symptom before she gave birth to her last child in 1971. This symptom became aggravated ten months later after the birth of the child. She was obliged to do preparatory work to open a newly established nursery school as a senior governess. And she was obliged to care for, by herself, six children from one to two years of age. Furthermore, she had to take charge of cooking for 12 children for seven days in August 1972 because a cook took summer leave. This work made the mental and physical burden too heavy for her. During the period in question she could not take sufficient rest to lighten her pain. From the above-mentioned facts, the Court finds that there is a high degree of probability to point to a causal sequence between the syndrome and her work as a nursery school governess. It is reasonable to recognize the causal sequence from experiential knowledge.

3. The Court considers the judgement of the court below inappropriate and unreasonable in the light of all the evidence. And there is error in the conclusion since that judgement had mistakenly interpreted the causal sequence. Accordingly, the appeal must be dismissed and the case remanded to the High Court for further investigation regarding the breach of duties of the part

of Yokohama City, and on the existence of fault on its part.

[*Source*: Case No. (gyou tsu) 85 of 1993, decided on 28 November 1997; Rodohanrei No. 727:14]

ANNOTATION

1. This is the first judgement of the Supreme Court as to the syndrome of arm and shoulder pain suffered by a nursery governess. In the past, this syndrome could be found in respect of a limited number of occupations, such as typists. However, recently the courts have recognized liability for such pain suffered by a nurse, a nurse-teacher and a nurse governess. Thus, the case law increasingly recognizes this syndrome as a work accident under the Workers Accident Compensation Insurance Act. But this was an action for damages brought under the Civil Code, Art. 415.

2. In Japan there is co-existence of workers accident compensation and damages against an employer under the Civil Code. If benefits are paid under the Workers Accident Compensation Insurance Act to workers or their survivors, the employer is exempt, but only up to the amount of such benefits, from liability for damages under the Civil Code. On the other hand, the employer is not immune from the obligation to pay damages that exceed the amount of insurance benefits. In this case there was no question of insurance benefits under the Act. The appellant worker brought the action for damages caused by a "work accident" only under the Civil Code.

3. There are two legal grounds to sue for damages arising out of a work accident. One is tort liability under the Civil Code, Article 709; the other relates to liability for non-performance of an obligation of the employment contract under Article 415 of the Code. There are three important differences between the two approaches. The first is the statute of limitations. In a tort suit the period is three years from the time when

the injured party became aware of the damages, while the period is ten years in a suit on a contract. The second difference is the possibility of "consolation" money for survivors which is available in a tort suit, but not for non-performance of an employment contract. The third difference is the starting point for reckoning a delayed loss. In a tort suit it is from the day after the occurrence of the work injury, while in the case of non-performance of an employment contract, it is the day after the claim for damages arises. The latter legal ground was selected in this case. An employer has a duty to guarantee the worker's safety and health under an employment contract. It is recognized as non-performance of the contract on the part employer when it is demonstrated by the workers or their survivors that, in the context of the substance of the contract, there was a breach of the employers' duty in the case of the work accident.

4. The crucial point is whether there is a causal connection between the work and the syndrome so as to show non-performance of the employment contract. The District Court and the Supreme Court answered in the affirmative, but the High Court in the negative. The District Court and the Supreme Court found a high degree of probability that the syndrome was a result of the work as a nursery governess, while the High Court did not. This is a most significant point in the Supreme Court judgement.

In 1975, the Labour Ministry issued an administrative notification on the standard to decide whether the syndrome of arm and shoulder pain are work-related conditions that happen in the course of, and arising out of, employment under the Workers Accident Compensation Insurance Act. It set out five points for the syndrome to qualify as work-related. The first is whether the complaining party used the upper arums repeatedly or consistently assumed the same posture. The second is whether the worker worded very long hours. The third is whether the work was heavier than other workers doing work of the same type. The fourth is that the condition did not occur from non-work-related causes. The fifth is whether the symptoms worsened during the worker's continuing his or her work. Until now, most judgements had been influenced by the administrative notification. The Supreme Court, however, neither mentioned this notification not did it adopt the standards set out in the notification. In particular, the first and third points were not invoked to rule on the causal sequence between her work and her condition. The Supreme Court found the causal relationship although she was neither compelled to repeat the same movements nor maintain the same posture for an extended time, nor work more strenuously than the other nursery governesses.

In sum, the Supreme Court established an original standard to judge whether claims for damages were admissible in the case of syndromes of arm and shoulder pain caused by work involving excessive strain on the upper limbs. Of course, the administrative notification was issued for deciding on work-related injury under the Works Accident Compensation Insurance Act. But the Supreme Court judged a claim for damages regarding these syndromes on the ground of the violation of a duty on the part of the employer under the contract of employment, thus establishing different standards between the two.

(11) DISMISSAL

Mitsuru Asano
v.
Kobe Koryo Gakuen School

Supreme Court (Third Petty Bench)

Mitsuru Asano
v.
Kobe Koryo Gakuen School

Legal nature of period of contract to determine suitability as a teacher

HEADNOTES

Facts

The appellant was engaged as a teacher in social studies as of 1 April 1984 by the appellee private high school. At the interview for the post, the director of the high school explained that the appellant's status would be that of a full-time lecturer and that the term of employment was one year; after one year the director would judge whether he should be re-employed on the basis of his record of service. The director made an offer of employment and the appellant agreed it on 5 March 1984. Both parties signed the written employment contract in the middle of May; it indicated that the appellant was employed as a full-time lecturer for one year till 31 March 1985 and that the employment would terminate without notice of termination or dismissal when the period expired.

Nevertheless the director gave notice that the employment would be terminated from the end of March 1985. The appellant then sought a judicial declaration affirming his status as a full-time lecturer. Kobe District Court and Osaka High Court judged that his contract of employment was terminated when the period of one year expired, because the contract was found to be for a definite period of one year. Before the High Court the appellant contended that the period of the contract was meant to be a probationary period to confirm whether he was suited to be a teacher, but the High Court denied his contention. The appellant appealed to the Supreme Court.

Decision

The appeal was rejected; the case was sent back to the High Court.

JUDGEMENT

1. When the period of an employment contract is fixed so as to confirm a worker's suitability, it is a reasonable interpretation that the period does not determine the existence of the contract, but is a probationary period, except in the extraordinary case in which an employment contract is agreed to end definitely when the period expires. In order to judge the legal nature of a probationary employment contract, it is necessary to look at the company's practice with regard to the treatment of a probationary employee and to granting him definitive employment. When a probationary employee is engaged on the same job as a permanent employee, and the employer treats both equally, but a new contract on definitive employment does not follow after the period of probation has expired, the probationary employment contract is interpreted as reserving the employer's right to terminate employment at the end of probationary period.

2. An employer is permitted to exercise his reserved right of termination only when the termination would be regarded as reasonable by society at large and when there is an objective, rational basis for the termination consistent with the recognized purpose of the reserved right. Though an employer is permitted

more freedom of dismissal on the basis of the reserved right to termination than in the case of ordinary dismissals from permanent posts, reasonable grounds are necessary to end a probationary employment contract when the probationary period expires.

3. In this case there remains a question whether it was expressly agreed to end the employment when one year had expired, according to the contend to the statement of the school director. The Court considers that the written labour contract does not appropriately express the agreed contend and purpose of the probationary employment contract on the following grounds: (1) The written contract was delivered to the appellant on 7 April and signed in the middle of May. This date is different from that of the mutual agreement. (2) The high school was opened in April 1983 and the number of students was expected to increase when the contract was terminated. So it was not necessary to employ a teacher for definite period. (3) The appellant was employed just after he graduated from a correspondence course of the Faculty of Sociology, Bukkyo (Buddhist) University. In general, a new graduate likes to work as a permanent employee in Japan.

Accordingly the judgement of the High Court put a wrong interpretation on the legal nature of the period of the employment contract. Therefore, it must be rejected. But it is necessary to make a thorough investigation of whether the contract is one with a probationary period reserving the employer's right to terminate the employment, and whether the termination could be regarded as reasonable. So the case must be sent back to the High Court for final decision.

[*Source*: Case No. (0) 854 of 1989, decided on June 5, 1990, reported at Rodohanrei No. 564:7].

ANNOTATION

1. In Japan a probationary period is generally provide for. Works rules or collective agreements

usually contain a provision on the subject. In most cases regarding probationary period, the main problem to be discussed has been whether refusal to employ the probationer as a permanent employee was effective or not under the provisions of the works rule or the collective agreement. But in the case here reported there was no works rule or collective agreement because the high school had just been founded and a labour union had not been organized. In this respect it is an unusual case. And it is natural that the content of the labour contract should have been contested.

2. The Supreme Court stated a general theory on the probationary period on the basis of Japanese custom at the work place. Though it mentioned that the probationary period should be interpreted by reference to the practice of each establishment, it considered the relevant contract to be an employment contract with a reserved right of rescission. This means that an employment contract was concluded from the beginning of employment and that a reserved right to rescission was attached to the employment contract. This legal framework denies the existence of a contract for probationary employment distinct from the contract for regular employment. Therefore, the employer's refusal of final employment must be considered as a dismissal of the employee, i.e., the refusal to grant him regular employment must be seen as an exercise of the right to dismiss after employment and not as an ordinary refusal to hire. This is a reflex of the customary probationary employment system in Japan. The content of work during a probationary period is not usually changed on final employment, and working conditions are not amended. Moreover, there are generally no particular contractual procedures when a probationary employee is promoted to regular employment; the employer merely issues a notice describing the name, job and assigned position of the employee.

The Supreme Court admits that there may be an exceptional case, in which, even though the contractual period is designed to confirm an employee's suitability, there is an express agreement that the expiry of the period shall end the contract. But in the present case the Supreme Court had doubts as to the existence of such an exceptional circumstance. As the Supreme Court sent this problem back to the High Court, the High Court must again judge whether an exceptional case can be found to exist.

3. If an exceptional circumstance cannot be found, the contract is considered to have a reservation permitting termination of regular employment during the period of probation. To terminate regular employment, there must be reasonable grounds for the termination. In other words, the company may exercise its right of termination only when it finds that an employee is not fit for regular employment, either as a result of investigation after he was employed or through observation of work performed during the probation period. This framework of judgement on the termination is deemed to be reasonable by academic theories and judicial precedents. The Supreme Court also sent this problem back to the High Court.

(12) WORK RULES

(i) **Omagari Agricultural Cooperative Association**
v.
Risuke Miura *et al.*

(ii) **Shigeru Sato**
v.
The Fourth Bank Ltd.

(iii) **Ugo Bank**
v.
Akio Abo and others

Supreme Court (Third Petty Bench)

(i) Omagari Agricultural Cooperative Association *v.* Risuke Miura et al.

Unilateral and disadvantageous changes of work rules by employer—Applicability to objecting employees—Criteria of reasonableness

HEADNOTES

Facts

Seven agricultural cooperative associations were amalgamated as the appellant association on August 1973. Hanadate agricultural cooperative association employed the three appellees, which was one of the seven associations. At the time of amalgamation the three appellees continued to be employed at the appellant association. Appellee 1 retired on May 1975. Appellee 2 retired on October 1980. Appellee 3 retired on January 1981. They were paid retirement allowances. But they had a dispute with the association regarding the amount of retirement allowances.

At the time of amalgamation, the appellant altered the rules of employment relating to the calculation of retirement allowances. Retirement allowances were calculated under the formula of "basic wages at the time of retirement multiplied by the rate of payment". The rate of payment was decided in proportion to the years of service. The longer the years of service, the higher the rate of payment. This formula had the role of promoting long-time employment.

Before the amalgamation, the seven agricultural cooperative associations had different provisions on the calculation of retirement allowances. But under the guidance of Akita prefecture agricultural cooperative association, a uniform retirement allowances rule was adopted at six agricultural cooperative associations, except at Hanadate association. At Hanadate association the uniform rule could not be adopted because of objections of the trade union. The appellant association tried to adjust the difference, but it failed. So the appellant association was oblige to adopt the new rule on retirement allowances unilaterally. Under the new rule the rate of payment lowered, in the case of the appellee 1 from 64 points to 55.55, in the case of the appellee 2 from 55 to 45.945, in the case of the appellee 3 from 61 to 53.75.

The three appellees argued that the new provisions could not be applied to them since the provisions were disadvantageous to them. Therefore, they claimed the difference between the allowances, which they could earn under the regulation of Hanadate association, and those of the new rule.

In the first instance the District Court did not uphold the appellees' claim, declaring the disadvantageous change reasonable. But on appeal, the High Court reversed because it judged the change as unreasonable. Then the appellees appealed to the Supreme Court, which finally rejected their claim.

JUDGEMENT

As has already been stated in the judgement of this Court of 25 December 1968 (*Yoshikawa* v. *Shukoku Bus Co.*, 22 MINSHU 3459), an employer, in general, may not deprive workers of their vested rights or force unfavourable working conditions on them by introducing or amending the work rules. At the same time, since work rules set for the generally applicable working conditions, so long as the rule in general has a reasonable basis, an individual cannot avoid the application of work rules to him by refusing to agree to the rules. This court does not find it necessary to change this dictum. Therefore, even though the revised provision of work rules is disadvantageous for the appellees, they ought not to be allowed to refuse its enforcement on the ground that they have not consented to the new provision, in so far as a reasonable change work rules was introduced.

The reasonableness of the change of work rules should be determined not only from the contents of the change but also in terms of the necessity of the change. And the change of work rules should be reasonable enough to be approved as the normative statement, taking into consideration the extent of the disadvantages of the said change for the employees. Especially when the provisions on important working conditions such as wages and retirement allowances have been changed unfavourable for the workers, they come into force if the changes have had so reasonable a content that the disadvantages for employees could be allowed by reason of a high degree of necessity.

This court would apply the above-mentioned principle to this case. (1) The rate of payment itself has been lowered. But the basic wages were raised at the time of amalgamation. So the amount of retirement allowances was not so much lower as the appellees argued. In other words, the extent of disadvantage was smaller than the amount claimed by the appellees. (2) The necessity of a change of work rules was high in order to unify the working conditions. The working conditions had to be standardized at the amalgamated association. Because the reality of enterprises employing number of workers is that working conditions are established by the employer and employees must accept uniform working conditions. (3) At Hanadate association uniform work rules on retirement allowances could not be made under the guidance of Akita Prefecture agricultural cooperative association with which Hanadate association was affiliated. So they directed their efforts to amending this situation. But their efforts could not produce an outcome. (4) After the amalgamation the age of retirement has been raised. And the employees could enjoy more advantageous treatment on holidays, rest time, traveling expenses and other allowances than that before the amalgamation. The rate of payment has declined but the other working conditions have been improved.

From the four points this court holds that the change of work rules on retirement allowances was reasonable. Therefore, the new work rules were binding on objecting employees.

[*Source*: Case No. (0) 104 of 1985, decided 16 February 1988].

ANNOTATION

1. About twenty years have passed since the Supreme Court ruled on the dispute regarding the legal effect of unilateral and disadvantageous modification of work rules in the Shukoku Bus Co. Case. (*Yoshikawa* v. *Shukoku Bus Co.*, 22 MINSHU 3459) After this judgement, this problem has been discussed and a number of court decisions have been accumulated. The second Supreme Court decision was given in the Takeda System Co, case (*Takeda System Co.* v. *Kaneda*, 4 International Labour Law Reports 132). The third case was *Okuni Taxi Co.* v. *Shigeru Mitsueda*, 425 RODOHANREI 75). The present case is the fourth judgement of Supreme Court. Established case law derives from the four judgements. Namely, judge-made law has been formulated as to the modification of work rules.

2. In Japan the role of the individual contract is very limited. In general, the employment contract has

only the provisions on the status of employees. It usually does not contain the provisions on working conditions. Japanese collective agreements, also, have a limited role in the industrial relations system. Collective agreements are almost always made on an enterprise basis. So only about 25 percent of all employed persons (95 percent of organized workers) are covered by collective agreements. Therefore, work rule (rules of employment) play a big role in regulating working conditions. Under the Labour Standards Act employers who have more than 10 employees continuously at work are obliged to make work rules in writing. Employers are required to ask the opinion of a majority union or a person representing the majority of employees but this does not mean that the consent of the union or person is necessary to make or alter the work rules. Accordingly employers can unilaterally make or change the work rules. And employers must submit them to the local labour inspection office, which is granted the authority to oversee work rules and to give direction to employers concerning work rules. The Labour Standards Act gives legal effect to work rules. The Act provides that a labour contract, which stipulates conditions inferior to those, set forth in the work rules in invalid insofar as any such conditions are concerned, and that such invalid working conditions shall be replaced by the standards fixed in the work rules (Art. 93). In spite of the above-mentioned provisions, there have been controversies on the legal status of the work rules and in particular on the effect of unfavourable alternation upon an employee who has not agreed to the change.

3. In the Shukoku Bus Co. case, the Supreme Court held that since work rules are recognized as the legal framework of the particular work place, the work rules apply to each employee, whether or not the employee has actual knowledge of the content or existence of the rules, and whether or not the employee has specifically agreed to accept the work rules, and that, therefore, the employer is clearly permitted to introduce work rules and to alter those rules

unilaterally but is not allowed to do so to the detriment of employees without their consent. However, the Supreme Court concluded that an employee couldn't avoid the application of work rules to him by refusing to agree to the rules, so long as the rule is reasonable. In Takeda System Co. case the Supreme Court confirmed its earlier decision regarding the legal nature and effect of work rules to objecting employees. Especially, the Supreme Court formulated the criteria to judge whether or not the altered work rules are reasonable. Namely, the Supreme Court held that the reasonableness of the change but also in terms of the necessity of such a change. In this Omagari City Agricultural Cooperative Association case, the Supreme Court set out the criteria in detail.

4. In this judgement there are four criteria. The first one is the content and extent of the disadvantages. The second one is the necessity of the change of work rules. The third one is whether or not the other working conditions are improved to relieve the disadvantages. The fourth one is the progress of negotiations with the trade union or groups of objecting employees. Supreme Court formed the judgement synthetically from the four points.

In the Okuni Taxi Co. case, the company had a provision on retirement allowances, which was calculated under the formula of "Basic wages at the time of retirement multiplied by the length of service". But the company unilaterally repealed the provisions on retirement allowances from 31 July 1978. Hence the length of service after the date of appeal could not be included to calculate the retirement allowances. The Supreme Court denied the legal effect of the disadvantageous provision because the company did not provide working conditions good enough to relieve the disadvantages and there was no special reason to approve the disadvantages. The Supreme Court in effect based its judgement on the above-mentioned third point. In the Omagari case the Supreme Court gave a different decision.

5. It is important that the Supreme Court found reasonable a disadvantageous change of a fundamental working condition such as retirement allowances. In Japan the ageing of population is increasing. There are some policies to solve this situation. One of them is to prolong the retirement age from 55 to 60 or even to 65 years. Since the retirement allowance is related to length of service, employees want to stay in companies for as long as they are allowed. Therefore, the employers expect to increase the commitment of employees to the companies by rising the retirement age. But this policy places a big burden on employers economically. So the employers prefer to reduce the amount of retirement allowances. From this judgement, this policy may have the possibility to be recognized as a reasonable change of working conditions.

Supreme Court (Second Petty Bench)

(ii) Shigeru Sato
v.
The Fourth Bank Ltd.

Legal effect of disadvantageous changes of work rules by employer

HEADNOTES

Facts

Work rules at the For the Bank located at Niigata prefecture stipulated that mandatory retirement age was 55 years, provided that an employee could work till 58 years when the bank considered it necessary at his or her request. They also provided that an employee might get retirement allowances calculated on basic salary at 55 years, and that special allowances could be paid for his or her continuous work after 55 years. But from the 1980's the Labour Ministry advocated the extension of the mandatory retirement age to 60 years under the

Law for Employment Promotion of Older Persons. Under this administrative guidance, a labour union organizing more than 90% of its employees proposed to the Fourth Bank that it bargain collectively on the extension of the mandatory retirement age. As a result, a new collective agreement was concluded on 30 March 1983; under it mandatory retirement was prolonged till 60 years and an employee from 55 to 60 years could get only basic salary as at 54 years. Thereafter the bank amended the provisions on mandatory retirement age, retirement allowances and salaries in the work rules whose contents were the same as those of the collective agreement. They entered into force on 1 April 1983.

The appellant became 55 years on November 1984 and retired mandatorily on 4 November 1989 under the amended work rules. He was not a union member at retirement age because he was an assistant department manager. He asserted that under the amended work rules his salary was less than under the old work rules. 1. As basic salary, 58,100 yen was reduced under the amended work rules. 2. 50,000 yen was reduced as allowances for a responsible position because his post was changed from assistant department manager to another post, which was newly established at the time of amending the work rules. 3. Annual increase of salary was abolished since he was 55 years old. 4. Bonuses were reduced because of reduction of basic salary. The amount of annual salary paid after 55 years was 63% or 67% of that paid at 54 years old. So he asserted that he would be paid 28,709,785 yen under the old work rules, but that he had received 30,787,278 yen under the amended work rules. This meant that the amount of salary paid to the appellant working from 55 to 60 years under the new work rules was almost the same as that paid to him working from 55 to 58 years under the old work rules. Therefore, he concluded that he was obliged to word free of salary for two years. 5. He was paid 12,299,000 yen as retirement allowances under the new work rules. But under the old work rules he would have been 12,057,300 yen. On this point he was treated rather favourable under the new work rules.

The labour welfare system, including employment accident compensation benefits and family benefit, was extended to employees between 55 to 60 years. And the bank established a new loan system for employees above 55 years and relieved them of the burden of repaying house loans.

Looking at other banks which extended mandatory retirement age from 55 to 60 years, the Court found that 70 or 80% of annual salary paid to employees at 54 years was paid to them from 55 to 60 years, and that sometimes only 50% was paid to them. It was common those annual bonuses were equivalent to three months' salary and that retirement allowances were calculated by reference to the salary paid at 55 years. The salary level at this bank was higher than that paid at some ten local banks to employees whose mandatory retirement was extended. According to national means tests, the salary level at this bank was higher than the average monthly consumer's expenditure. And also it was higher than the average monthly salary paid to employees from 50 to 60 years living in Niigata Prefecture. It could be found, in general, at many banks that employees after extension of the retirement age were placed in a new position (for example, professional post) because managerial posts were limited.

The appellant insisted that the amendment of the work rules was invalid in relation to him because the bank had made a disadvantageous change of working conditions, which infringed his existing rights under the old work rules. So he claimed the difference in salary and delinquent charges till he became 60 years old. Alternatively, he claimed them till he was 58 years old.

At Niigata District Court the amendment of the work rules was judged to be invalid, because the total amounts of salary and retirement allowances were reduced and furthermore the disadvantageous change in relation to the employees was not reasonable. But the change could be applied validly by the amendment of the collective agreement extending the retirement age to 60 years under Article 17 of the Labour Unions Act.

The labour union in this bank organized more than 90% of the employees. The Court found that the appellant was the same kind of employee in this bank as those covered by the collective agreement though he was not a union member. So his claim was dismissed.

Tokyo High Court judged that the change of retirement age and salary under the amended work rules had legal effect validly because it was reasonable, though it had a counterbalancing disadvantage in reduction of salary. So the claim was dismissed.

Decision

The appeal was dismissed.

Law Applied

Labour Standards Act:

Art. 93: Labour contracts, which stipulate working conditions inferior to the standards established by the work rules hall, be invalid with respect to such portions. In such a case the portions, which have become invalid shall be governed by the standards established by the work rules.

Art. 94: The work rules shall not infringe any laws and ordinances or any collective agreement applicable to the workplace concerned.

2. The administrative office may order the revision of work rules which conflict with laws and ordinances or with any collective agreement.

JUDGEMENT

1. In principle, an employer may not deprive workers of their vested rights or force unfavourable working conditions on them by introducing or amending work rules. But since work rules aim to set forth uniform working conditions, an individual worker cannot avoid the application of work rules to him by

refusing to agree to the work rules, so long as the rules have a reasonable basis. The reasonableness of the change or work rules should be decided not only is reference to the contents of the change but also in terms of the necessity of the change. And the change or work rules should be reasonable enough to be approved as the normative statement, taking into consideration the extent of the disadvantages of the change for the employees. Especially when the provisions on important working conditions such as wages and retirement allowances have been changed unfavourable for the workers by the work rules, they may be in force if the changes have had so reasonable a content that the disadvantages for employees could be allowed by reason of a high degree of necessity. Reasonableness could be judged synthetically from the following six points: (1) What is the degree of the disadvantages resulting from the change of work rules? (2) What is the degree and contend of need for the change of work rules? (3) Is the changed contend to the work rules adequate? (4) Are the other working conditions improved to set-off the disadvantages? (5) Does the labour union or group of employees negotiate with the employer? (6) What is the general tendency in our country in dealing with this problem?

2. The amount of annual salary paid to employees above 55 years was 63 or 67% of that paid to them at the age of 54 years. The amount of retirement allowances was not reduced by the change of work rules, but two years more were necessary to receive retirement allowances because the mandatory retirement age was extended from 58 to 60 years. So these disadvantages were thought to be very large for the appellant. But Japan was confronted with the problems of an ageing society from the 1980's. It was a national public policy and a social standard to extend the mandatory retirement age to 60. The Bank was required to endeavor to extend the mandatory retirement age as soon as possible by the Labour Minister and Prefecture Governor. Also, the labour union made the same

proposal to meet the social standard. Therefore, there was a high degree of need to extend the mandatory retirement age. But this policy would place big labour costs on employers because older employees received more salary under a seniority-based rate related to age and length of service. And it was likely to bring a shortage of posts for employees of middle or advanced age. So it was highly necessary for this Bank to cut labour costs and stop personnel stagnation. Especially in this Bank where the rate of middle and advanced age employees was higher than the average rate at local banks in Japan, it was thought to be inevitable to amend the salary level paid to employees above 55 years old.

It was found that the salary level paid to employees above 55 years was rather higher than the average level at the local banks. The contents of working conditions were almost the same as those of the other local banks, which had extended mandatory retirement age to 60. Extension of retirement age brought better working conditions to female employees and male handicapped employees. Also, it was deemed to be very profitable to secure employment till 60 years for employees in bodily good health. To relieve the disadvantages the Bank extended the labour welfare system and introduced a new house loan system.

Above all, the work ruled were changed under the collective agreement concluded between the Band and the labour union organizing more than 90% of employees and more than 50% of employees above 50 years old. It could be presumed that the contents of the change were reasonable because they were consented to after adjustment of conflicting interests. But the appellant was not a union member because he was an assistant department manager. It could be thought that the change of work rules brought severe disadvantages not only to non-union members but also to union members.

From the above-mentioned points, the Supreme Court found that there were reasonable grounds to extend the mandatory retirement age. Therefore, the amended work rules were validly binding on the appellant.

(Dissenting Opinion)

One Justice issued a dissenting opinion for the following reasons. He concluded that the change of work rules in this case was not reasonable. Reduction of salary and bonuses was so large that compensation measures could not relieve the appellant from the disadvantages. In this case an interim measure should have been taken to relieve the appellant from the disadvantages, unless there were a special situation in which it would be very difficult to adopt an interim measure. He found that there was no such special situation.

[*Source*: Case No. (0) 2122 of 1992, decided on 28 February 1997, reported at Rodohanrei No. 710:12].

ANNOTATION

1. This judgement of the Supreme Court is the sixth one in the dispute regarding the legal effect of unilateral and disadvantageous changes of work rules. There is no provision on this problem in the Labour Standards Act. So judge-made law has been formulated by six judgements of the Supreme Court. Among these, three cases have been reported in the International labour Law Reports (*Takaeda System Co.* v. *Kaneda*, 4 ILLR 132, *Omagari City Agricultural Cooperative Association* v. *Risuke Miura et al.*, 8 ILLR 134, *Asahi Fire and Marine Insurance Co.* v. *Jiro Takada*, 16 ILLR 455). The present judgement of the Supreme Court adopted almost the same framework as that in the *Omagari City Agricultural Cooperative Association's* case. This case had a feature in the facts that the employer changed the work rules after the collective agreement because the collective agreement is almost always concluded at the level of the enterprise.

2. The conclusion of the District Court and the High Court was mutually contradictory, though they had

the same standard for making a decision on this problem. So attention was paid to how the Supreme Court would decide on the legal effect of the disadvantageous change of work rules.

It was evident that the Supreme Court adopted the same standard as that which has been derived from judge-made law. Namely, the change of work rules comes into effect so long as it has a reasonable basis though it changes working conditions unfavourably to the employees.

Reasonableness should be decided by reference to the following points: (1) the degree of the disadvantages resulting from the change of work rules, (2) the degree and content of need for the change of work rules, (3) adequacy of the changed content of the work rules, (4) improvement of other working conditions to set-off the disadvantages, (5) process of negotiations with the labour union or group of employees. Among these points, there are problems on the fourth and fifth points.

On the fourth point it had to be discussed whether compensation measures could be seen to relieve the disadvantages in this case. The District Court denied this, but the High Court and the Supreme Court agreed the existence of compensation measures.

On the fifth point negotiation is necessary between the labour union and the Bank on the disadvantageous change of salary and bonus in return for extension of the mandatory retirement age. Under Art. 89 of the Labour Standards Act work ruled may be made or changed unilaterally by the employer. In changing work rules the employer shall ask the opinion on a labour union organized by a majority of the workers at the workplace concerned, where such a labour union exists, or of a person representing a majority of the workers, where no such labour union exists. This means that it is not necessary to get the consent of a majority union or a majority representative. But in this case, the change of the work rules was made with the consent of a majority union under collective bargaining. This involved adjustment of conflicting interests between the majority union and the Bank. Reasonableness of the change of work rules could be easily found from the consent of a majority union and the Bank. But it is doubtful whether the appellant's interest was fairly reflected in the collective bargaining because he was not a union member. The Supreme Court found that non-union members' interests were considered during the collective bargaining. The labour union organized more than 60% of the older employees above 50 years old. During the process of collective bargaining the labour union referred this problem to meetings at the shop level. At the meetings there were severe opposing opinions against the executive members of the labour union. So the labour union necessarily decided to conclude the agreement with due regard to several circumstance. The Supreme Court found that non-union members' interests were expressed through the older employees' opinions. But there was a dissenting opinion on this point. According to this opinion, an interim measure should have been taken to relieve the appellant from the disadvantages. On the other side, the majority opinion of the Supreme Court found that an interim measure was not proposed in the process of the shop-level meetings and collective bargaining. This led to the conclusion that reasonable ground could be found for the amendment of the work rules.

Supreme Court (Third Petty Bench)

(iii) Ugo Bank

v.

Akio Abo and Others

Work rules—unilateral change—legal effect

HEADNOTES

Facts

The appellant bank employed about one thousand employees. There were two labour unions in the bank: Ugo bank labour union (majority union) having 730 members, and Ugo employees' union (minority union) having about 30 members.

The appellant bank introduced the five-day working week system from March 1989 under the Ministerial Order effective from 1 February 1989 which provided for banks to be closed on Saturday and Sunday. Reacting to criticism by foreign countries, especially North American and Western European, the government introduced the five-day week into banking and public offices.

Before introducing the five day week, Ugo bank proposed to both labour unions a change in working hours in the work rules. The majority union agreed with the proposal, but the minority did not. The bank nevertheless applied the amendment of the work rules to members of both labour unions.

According to the amendment of the work rules, normal working hours are shortened per year, but were increased per day for certain days. The members of the minority labour union claimed the differential amount of wages for overtime work between the amount now to be paid and the amount, which should be paid under the old work rules.

The District Court denied the appellees' claim. The prolonged working hours per day were a disadvantageous change of working conditions to them, but this change was found to be reasonable owing to business necessity and the degree of disadvantageous change was not so great. The total working hours per year were shortened by the introduction of five-day week system without a wage cut.

The High Court reversed the judgement of the District Court finding the amendment of the work rules to be unreasonable. In particular, prolonged working hours by one hour imposed a substantial burden on members of the minority union, i.e. a decline of wages for overtime work (on average 18,000 yen per month) and an increase of hard work. And business necessity could not be found sufficient enough to admit prolonged working hours because there were no evidences that the five-day week would change the operations of the bank for the worse. Therefore, the High Court judged that the disadvantageous amendment of the work rules should not apply to the members of the minority labour union, which did not agree with it during collective bargaining. The High Court ordered the bank to pay the differential amount of wages for overtime work.

Decision

The Supreme Court quashed the judgement of the High Court.

Law Applied

Labour Standards Act Art. 89: An employee who continuously employs ten or more employees shall draw up work rules on the following items and shall submit the work rules to the administrative office. In the event the employer alters them . . . the same shall apply:

. . .

Art. 90: In drawing up or changing the work rules, the employer shall ask the opinion of either a trade union organized by a majority of the workers at the workplace concerned where such a trade union exists or a person representing a majority of the workers where there is no such trade union.

JUDGEMENT

1. Under the amendment of the work rules, working hours per day were prolonged by one hour

from 25th to the end of every month and on the first day of each month. And on the other days working hours were lengthened by ten minutes. Therefore, this amendment brought disadvantageous working conditions to the members of the minority labour union. Hence, it should be judged whether there was a reasonable ground for the amendment of the work rules.

2. At first this Court should consider whether substantial disadvantageousness was substantial or not for them. This Court finds that the level of disadvantageousness is not substantial for the following reasons. Working hours per year was shortened by 42 hours and 10 minutes although 1 hour or 10 minutes prolonged daily working hours by the introduction of the five-day week system. And the number of holidays was increased. Wages for overtime work would be reduced, but the employer had discretionary power to order overtime work under the Labour Standards Act. So overtime work for the same number of hours could not be expected because the bank would try to rationalize the business management. Therefore, this Court rules that the substantial disadvantageousness is not so substantial even though the amount of overtime work allowances would be reduced.

3. The next problem was the existence of a business necessity for the five-day week system. The government had a policy to introduce the system in the banking industry as a model case. So the appellant bank could not opt out of the system. The five-day week would reduce services of the bank and business activities. So it would be natural that working hours should be prolonged to avoid lowering earnings. There was a substantial business necessity to lengthen working hours on weekdays, especially at this bank where average working hours were shorter than other banks.

. . . From the above, this Court finds that there was a substantial business necessity to change the regulations of the work rules on working hours in order to maintain the competitive position of the bank.

4. Under the amendment of the work rules, working hours per week were no longer than other banks. Therefore, there could be found reasonable grounds for the amendment of the work rules. So the amendment of the work rules should be effective as regards the members of the minority labour union even though they objected its application.

[*Source*: Case No. (0) 1710 of 1997 decided on 12 September 2000: reported at Rodohanrei No. 788: 23].

ANNOTATION

1. There are in total 10 judgements of the Supreme Court on the effect of disadvantageous working conditions changed under the work. In 2000 there were 3 judgements of the Supreme Court on this question regarding banks. The other two cases were the Michinoku Bank case; wages, bonuses and allowances after 55 years of age were cut down in place of mandatory retirement at age 60, in the Hakodate Cooperative Bank case, the effect of the work rules on extended working hours (by 25 minutes per week day) was disputed at the time of the introduction of the five-day week system. So this was a similar case to the Ugo Bank case.

2. In Japan the work rules play an important role in regulating working conditions. Under the Labour Standards Act an employer employing more than 10 employees is obliged to promulgate work rules in writing. An employer is required to ask the opinion of a majority labour union or a person representing the majority of employees. But the consent of the labour union is not necessary to make or change work rules. Therefore, an employer can unilaterally make or change work rules. Advantageous change of the work rules would be welcome for the employees, but it has been disputed whether a disadvantageous change of the work rules should have legal effect since the employees would not consent to it. At first this problem was judged in the Shukoku Co. case [Supreme Court (All

Bench 1968] which has provided a framework for judgement as follows.

In principle, an employer may not deprive employees of their vested rights or force unfavourable working conditions on them by introducing or amending the work rules. But since the work rules aim to set forth uniform working conditions at the workplace, an employee cannot avoid the application of the work rules to him or her by refusing to agree to the work rules, so long as the work rules have a reasonable basis. This reasonableness should be decided not only by reference to the contents of the change but also in terms of the business necessity of the change. In other words, the change of the work rules should be reasonable enough to be approved as a normative statement, taking into consideration the extent of the disadvantages of the said change for the employees. And when the provisions on important working conditions such as wages and working hours have been changed unfavourably for the workers, they come into force if the changes have had so reasonable a content that the disadvantages for employers could be allowed by reason of a high degree of business necessity.

This framework of judgement has been adopted at all the judgements of the Supreme Court. It was also concretely applied to the Ugo Bank case.

3. The decision was different as between the High Court and the Supreme Court, although the same principle of judgement was adopted at both. What is the cause?

The first point is the different estimation on the degree of disadvantageousness of the changed work rules. The High Court decided that prolonged work hours by one hour from 25th to the end of every month imposed a heavy burden on the employees as shortened yearly working hours do not compensate the disadvantageousness taking into account the reduction for overtime work. But the Supreme Court judged that this unfavourableness was not substantially so significant since yearly working hours became shorter by 42 hours 10 minutes.

The second point is the different estimation on business necessity. The High Court found that extending working hours by one hour from 25th to the end of every month was not necessary to maintain earnings of the bank because the increased cost brought about by the five day week system was not so great. On the other hand, the Supreme Court judged that there was high level of business necessity to increase working hours on some weekdays in order to avoid lowering earnings and business activities and also to maintain the competitive position of the bank.

The third point relates to the strategy of the other banks to cope with the five-day week system. Many banks prolonged working hours on weekdays to introduce the system. The High Court judged that it was not a fair ground for this bank to adopt the same strategy as other banks since there were some banks, which introduced five-day week without prolonging working hours. But the Supreme Court found that there was reasonable ground to conform to the same policy as other banks because working hours at the appellant bank had been shorter than the other banks.

The fourth point is the judgement on the process of negotiations with labour unions. There were two labour unions at the appellant bank. The majority labour union agreed with the amendment of the work rules, but the minority labour union did not consent to the proposal of the bank. The High Court thought that the interests of the minority should be guaranteed although working conditions should be governed uniformly by the work rules. But the Supreme Court found that there was a need for uniform working hours although the minority union did not agree with the amendment of the work rules in the process of collective bargaining.

The Courts made opposite judgements on the basis of the important four points. This reveals that it is very difficult to judge the reasonableness in the amendment of the work rules. But the Supreme Court has a function to make decisive judgement. So this makes a good case for the employer.

CHAPTER

11

Collective Labour Relations

(1) COLLECTIVE AGREEMENT

(i) Japan Schering
v.
Eiko Ozaki *et al.*

(ii) Mitsui Warehouse and Harbour Works Ltd.
v.
Hiromi Miura and Masami Fukui

(iii) Japan Nippon Railway Liquidation Corporation
v.
Japan National Railway Worker's Union

(iv) Asahi Fire and Maritime Insurance Co.
v.
Jiro Takeda

Supreme Court (First Petty Bench)

(i) Japan Schering
v.
Eiko Ozaki et al.

Effect of an agreement denying wage increases to an employee attending on fewer than 80 percent of workdays

HEADNOTES

Facts

The appellant company imported and sold medical and pharmaceutical products. There were three labour unions in the company. During collective bargaining in the spring of 1976 the company proposed the following conditions to the three labour unions, in order to raise the rate of attendance: (1) An employee with an attendance rate of less than 80 percent shall be excluded from the annual wage increase. Attendance rate shall mean the proportion of actual working hours to scheduled working hours during the preceding year. Actual working hours shall exclude all time not worked, whether by reason of late arrival or leaving work early, paid annual leave, menstruation leave, leaves for congratulations and condolences, maternity leave, special childcare time for women with infants, employment accidents, strikes or union activities. (2) The new agreement on wages shall be effective as from the month when a settlement can be reached.

The "A" labour union, which was one of three labour unions to which the appellees belonged, objected to proposal (1). But the company insisted on the proposal as a condition for increasing wages. So the "A" labour union decided to agree with the proposals, in order to get increased wages, on 6 August 1976. In 1977, 1978, and 1979 also the union concluded an agreement including the 80 percent clause.

The appellees could not get increased wages, bonuses, and retirement allowances because their rate of attendance was less than 80 percent. They insisted that the 80 percent clause violated public policy and was null and void because that clause would substantially restrain the exercise of rights under the Labour Standards Act and the Labour Unions Act.

Osaka District Court and Osaka High Court judged that the 80 percent clause was totally in conflict with public policy and was null and void. The company appealed to the Supreme Court.

Decision

The appeal was partially rejected; the case was sent back to the High Court.

JUDGEMENT

It is reasonable to apply economic sanctions to an employee whose rate of attendance is low, in order to reduce absenteeism. Therefore, it is not unlawful to calculate the rate of attendance on the basis of time not worked otherwise than by virtue of rights under the Labour Standards Act and the Labour Unions Act. But the clause of the collective agreement would be null and void as a violation of public policy if it infringed the rights and substantially destroyed the purpose of guaranteeing the rights under these Acts, by enabling the company to calculate the rate of attendance on the basis, *inter alia*, of time not worked by virtue of the rights of these Acts.

In this case it is evident that the 80 percent clause covers not only time not worked for reasons for which an employee is responsible, but also time not worked by virtue of the rights under the Labour Standards Act and the Labour Unions Act. There are also some other problems with respect to the 80 percent clause. (1) If the employee did not get increased wages under the 80 percent clause, he would suffer considerable economic disadvantages. As in Japan wage increases are based upon the wages of the previous year, these disadvantages would continue until retirement and influence the amount of retirement allowance. (2) More than 20 percent of scheduled hours not worked can easily be arrived at then the employee is absent for a comparatively long time owing to maternity leave or employment injuries in addition to some annual paid leave. By reference to the above-mentioned problems, the Court finds that the 80 percent clause calculating time not worked on the basis of the rights under the Labour Standards Act and the Labour Unions Act has greatly restrained the exercise of these rights. Therefore, the 80 percent clause effective only insofar as the attendance rate is calculated on the base of time not worked for reasons for which an employee is responsible. It is null and void insofar as time not worked on the basis of the rights under the Labour Standards Act and the Labour Unions Act is included in the calculation of the attendance rate. The judgement of the High Court erroneously interprets the relevant law because it decides that the 80 percent clause is totally ineffective as being in violation of public policy.

[*Source*: Case No (0) 1542 of 1983, decided on 14 December 1989, reported at Rodo hanrei No. 553:16].

ANNOTATION

1. The Labour Standards Act guarantees various kinds of rights. For example, there are two kinds of rights regarding wages during absence from work. Wages must be paid during annual leave but are not due during maternity leave, menstruation leave, special childcare time and time for the exercise of civil rights under the labour Standards Act, unless otherwise specifically agreed between the employer and the employee. One problem at issue is whether it is permissible to reduce other benefits of an employee who exercises the right to take annual leave or menstruation leave.

For example, in the N.B.C. Industry Co. case, the company introduced a system of attendance and diligence benefits in order to improve the employees' attendance rate. Under this system menstruation leave was counted as days of absence. The Supreme Court judged as follows: "Although a compensation system based upon a labour agreement under which an employee is likely to lose an economic interest as a result of her taking menstruation leave may possibly in fact discourage her from exercising a right provided by the Law, we believe that such a system should not be regarded *per se* as a violation of Section 67 of the Labour Standards Law unless under the aim and operation of such a system, where heavy economic loss and other disadvantages result from taking menstruation leave, it is virtually impossible for an employee to take menstruation leave, so that the statutory purpose of the menstruation leave system is jeopardized." (5 ILLR 190) From this judgement we can understand that the system would be illegal if it became substantially impossible to take menstruation leave because considerable economic loss and disadvantages would result from taking it. The Supreme Court used the same legal framework of judgement in the Japan Schering Co. case hire reported. Namely, the Supreme Court considered the question whether the 80 percent clause would restrain an employee from the exercise of the rights under the Labour Standards Act and the Labour Unions Act. As a result, it held that the 80 percent clause was null and void only insofar as time off work on the basis of the rights under these Acts was treated as absence.

Article 134 of the supplementary provisions of the Labour Standards Act stipulates that an employer shall not reduce wages and treat disadvantageously an employee who takes annual leave. This clause was added during the amendment of the Labour Standards Act in 1987, in order to affirm that disadvantageous treatment for taking annual leave is null and void or enables an employee to claim damages. It is natural that the Supreme Court derived its judgement from the purpose of this clause though the facts of the present case occurred before the amendment of the Labour Standards Act in 1987.

Leave for congratulations or condolences are not provided for by the Labour Standards Act but by collective agreements. But such leave is not an absence for which the employee is responsible. So it is judged to be illegal to treat such leave as absence in calculating the attendance rate.

2. The High Court held that the 80 percent clause was totally null and void. But the Supreme Court disagreed with this judgement. The Supreme Court decided that the partial invalidity of the 80 percent clause did not. mean that it ceased to be valid in its entirely in relation to the wage increase agreement. The reasons were the following: (1) it was not contrary to the intention of both parties that the remaining part be valid in spite of the partial invalidity of the 80 percent clause. (2) Partial invalidity did not affect the wage increase clause itself, because the invalid part was stipulated only to exclude some employees from the wage increase. In other words, the invalid part was not a prerequisite of the increase in wages. The judgement may be considered to be reasonable on this point.

Supreme Court (First Petty Bench)

(ii) Mitsui Warehouse and Harbour Works Ltd.

v.

Hiromi Miura and Masami Fukui

Effect of dismissal under a union shop agreement

HEADNOTES

Facts

There were two labour unions in the appellant company. "A" labour union concluded a union shop agreement with the company to the effect that all drivers of container trailers had to be members of "A" labour union unless they were permitted not join it by negotiation between the parties, and that the company would dismiss drivers who did not become members of the labour union or who were expelled from membership. The two appellees were drivers of trailers. They withdrew from "A" labour union at 8:30 a.m. on 21 February 1983 because they did not agree with the policies of the union. Immediately thereafter they joined "B" labour union and notified the company of this at 9 a.m. "A" labour union asked the company to dismiss them under the union shop agreement. The company dismissed them at 6 p.m. on the same day. The two drivers asserted that dismissals were invalid. Osaka District Court and Osaka High Court ruled in favour of the drivers.

Decision

The Supreme Court rejected a further appeal.

JUDGEMENT

The purpose of a union shop agreement is to strengthen the solidarity of the labour union with the help of the employer who is required to terminate the employment of a worker who does not become a member of or withdraws from the union. But in case of multiple labour unionism a worker is free to choose his union. Therefore, the union shop agreement cannot force him to join one union rather than another. Also, each labour union's right of association must be respected, whether it has union shop agreement or not, because the union shop agreement must not be allowed to operate so as to impair another union's right of association in accordance with Art. 28 of the Constitution. Accordingly, the clause obliging the employer to dismiss a union member who joins another labour union or establishes a new union after losing his membership is invalid by virtue of Art. 90 of the Civil Code. (Violation of Art. 28 of the Constitution is interpreted to be an infringement of public policy in the meaning of Art. 90 of the Civil Code.) For the above-mentioned reasons the dismissal of such a union member must be held to be invalid as being without justifiable ground.

In this case, the two appellees joined the other labour union just after they withdrew from the union [party to the agreement]. So the appellant company was not obliged to dismiss them under the union shop agreement. In other words, the union shop agreement could not provide a reasonable ground for dismissing them. Hence the dismissals must be held to be invalid, because they amounted to an abuse of the employer's power of dismissal.

[*Source*: Case No. (0) 386 of 1985, decided on December 4, 1989.]

ANNOTATION

1. Union shop agreements are common in Japan. According to an investigation by the Central Labour Relations Commission in 1979, 88.6 percent of collective agreements covering companies with more than 1000 workers have union shop clauses. There are three types of union shop agreements in Japan. One is called a complete union shop agreement because an employer must immediately dismiss all union members who lose their union membership. The second is called an incomplete union shop agreement because it only empowers an employer to dismiss union members for example, such an agreement may provide that the employer can dismiss after joint consultation with the labour union. In this type of agreement, dismissal by the employer has no direct connection with the union member's withdrawal or expulsion from the labour union. The third type is called declaratory union shop agreement: in it the employer's duty of dismissal is not dealt with. It only provides that the workers must be

members of the labour union. In Japan the second type is often found in collective agreements. But in the case here reported the first type had been used.

2. There are many problems regarding union shop agreements. Art 28 of the Constitution guarantees the right of employees to organize labour unions, to bargaining collectively and to engage in concerted activities. According to the majority view, the employees' right to organize does not include the right not to organize. In other words, only the positive right to organize a union is guaranteed by the Constitution. The employees may be compelled under Art. 28 of the Constitution to organize or to join a labour union. Therefore, the union shop agreement is considered to be constitutional. In pursuance of Art. 28 of the Constitution, Art. 7, Sec. 1, proviso of the Labour Unions Act stipulates that an employer shall not be prevented from concluding a collective agreement with a labour union which requires, as a condition of employment, that the workers be members of the union, if that union represents a majority of the workers in the plant or workplace. Therefore, a union shop agreement is legal if the labour union represents a majority of the workers in the establishment covered.

But what is the effect of a union shop agreement when there are multiple labour unions in the establishment? In the case here reported "A" labour union had a union shop agreement, but "B" labour union did not. The union shop agreement compelled the employees to join "A" labour union; they could not join "B" labour union. This was not permitted by the Constitution. Art. 28 of the Constitution offer protection to both unions equally. And the Labour Unions Act also prohibits discriminatory treatment of the two unions. Compulsion to join "A" labour union does not amount to equal treatment of both unions. And such compulsion also limits the employee's right to choose a labour union. Freedom to choose a union is guaranteed by the Constitution. By reference both to the equal treatment of the two labour unions and the employees' freedom to choose a union, the effect of the union shop agreement must be limited in case of multiple labour unions. This reasoning can be found in the judgements of the lower courts as well as in that of the Supreme Court.

The judgement of the Supreme Court has two notable aspects in its reasoning. One is that expulsion from the labour union treated equally with withdrawal from it. The case deals with withdrawal, but the judgement refers not only to withdrawal, but also to expulsion. This shows that the Supreme Court regards expulsion and withdrawal as equally unwelcome to the labour union. Another aspect is that the Supreme Court finds an illegal part of the union shop agreement to be invalid under Art. 90 of the Civil Code. Hitherto the Court has based itself on a theory that the union shop agreement ceased to be applicable to union members once they had withdrawn from it and joined another labour union or established a new, separate labour union. Either reasoning leads to the same conclusion. Dismissal is effective only when union members neither join another labour union nor establish a new labour union after they withdraw from the labour union with a union shop agreement. It may be concluded that the effectiveness of a union shop agreement is so limited in case of multiple labour unions in as establishment.

Supreme Court (Third Petty Bench)

(iii) Japan Nippon Railway Liquidation Corporation
v.
Japan National Railway Worker's Union

Bargaining Issues under article 8 of Public Corporation Labour Relations Act—civil action to confirm position to call for collective bargaining

HEADNOTES

Facts

The appellee labour union is an enterprise union composed of employees of the Japan National Railway Liquidation Corporation. The appellant corporation was founded in April 1987 by the Japan National Railway Reform Act to reconstruct railway undertakings. Previously there was a public corporation called the Japan National Railway Corporation (JNR). Under a policy of division and privatization, JNR was divided into seven companies, which re-employed the railway workers in April 1987. Workers who were not hired by the new railway companies changed jobs or were transferred to the Japan National Railway Liquidation Corporation.

The employee of JNR had been given free passenger tickets under a Regulation on Free Railway Passenger Tickets. The second Committee on Public Administration Reform recommended the abolition of the free passenger ticket system in July 1982, because the railway corporation had a huge deficit. JNR thereafter gave consideration to changes in the system and issued notice of its abolition. Prior to the notice the appellee labour union had on several occasions called for collective bargaining on the system, but the corporation refused on the ground that the subject related to the management and operation of the public corporation and as such was excluded from collective bargaining by article 8 of the Public Corporation Labour Relations Act. The union sued in Tokyo District Court for (1) confirmation that the corporation was under an obligation to bargain about the system of free passenger tickets; and (2) 5 million yen damages with as from October 1983.

Tokyo District Court allowed the first claim, but not the second. Tokyo High Court came to the same conclusion. The reasoning was as follows: (1) Article 7 of the Labour Unions Act imposes on an employer an obligation in public law not to refuse collective bargaining without good reason. The Act gives the Labour Relations Commission the power to issue remedial orders to prevent any refusal to bargain. Article 7 also has an effect in private law: the labour union has the right to ask the court to confirm that the employer is under an obligation to engage in collective bargaining. (2) The problem of free passenger tickets is a matter affecting working conditions in the meaning of article 8 of the Public Corporation Labour Relations Act. Article 7 of the Labour Unions Act applies to a public corporation. Accordingly, it must be confirmed that the railway corporation has an obligation to bargain collectively on the free passenger tickets issue. (3) Damages could not be awarded for the unlawful refusal to engage in collective bargaining because of the limited degree of unlawfulness, the nature of the damage suffered etc.

Decision

The appeal was dismissed.

Law Applied

Public Corporation Labour Relations Act

Article 9: In addition to the matters provided for in article 11 and article 12, section 2, the following matters regarding employees may be subject to collective bargaining and may be dealt with in collective agreements: Provided that matters affecting the management and operation of the public corporation shall be excluded from collective bargaining:

(1) Matters concerning wages and other earnings, working hours, rest periods, holidays and vacations;
(2) Matters concerning the standards of promotion, demotion, transfer, discharge, suspension from office, seniority and discipline;

(3) Matters concerning safety, hygiene and employment injury compensation; and
(4) Matters concerning working conditions other than those provided for in the preceding items.

Labour Union Act

Article 7: The employer may not engage in the following practices:

(1) . . .
(2) refuse without good reason to bargain collectively with the representatives of his employees; . . .

JUDGEMENT

1. This Court finds that there is merit in the action for an affirmation that the labour union is in the legal position to claim that the corporation shall engage in collective bargaining. Japan National Railway Liquidation Corporation was established in April 1987 and does not manage railway business. However, the appellee labour union wanted to get free passenger tickets from the Corporation in the same manner as previously from JNR. Therefore, collective bargaining with the Japan national Railway Liquidation Corporation did not lose significance for the appellee union.

2. The problem of free passenger tickets is a matter affecting working conditions in the meaning of article 8, section 4 of the Public Corporation Labour Relations Act. It is thus a subject for collective bargaining.

[*Source*: Case No. (0) 659 of 1987, decided on 23 April 1991. Reported at Rodohanrei No. 589:6].

ANNOTATION

1. In this case the Supreme Court provides a solution for the problem whether the right to call on an employer to engage in collective bargaining is protected by civil action. Under article 7, section 2 of the Labour Unions Act; it is the function of the Labour relations Commission to provide a remedy for refusal to bargain collectively. This is called administrative relief.

In Japan civil actions may be used to remedy some kinds of unfair labour practices. For instance, when an employee is dismissed because he performed proper union acts; the dismissal is null and void. The employee can sue directly in the civil court for remedies for the dismissal, which is an unfair labour practice, and the civil court can affirm that the dismissal is null and void, or order compensation for damage arising from unfair dismissal. The Japanese unfair labour practices system follows that of the USA, but the possibility of recourse to civil courts in respect of certain unfair labour practices constitutes on difference between them.

2. Until now it was not certain whether article 7, section 2 of the Labour Unions Act gives employees a private law right to demand collective bargaining. It is of course recognized by the courts that a labour union or an employee can sue for damages arising from a tortuous refusal to bargain collectively. But opinion has been divided on whether a union or an employee can claim that the employer respond to a call for collective bargaining, or sue for an order of provisional disposition requiring the employer to respond to collective bargaining pending the final judgement. Recently the prevalent view has been negative, because it is difficult to specify in a concrete manner the content of the right of the employee to demand collective bargaining or of the obligation of the employer to engage faithfully in collective bargaining.

A new legal doctrine now asserts, by reference to article 7, section 2 of the Labour Unions Act, which a union can be in the legal position to claim that an employer shall engage in collective bargaining, although it cannot have a legal right in private law to make such a claim (Kazuo Sugeno, *Rodoho,* Kobundo Publishers, 2nd ed., p. 443). This doctrine thus distinguishes between the legal position and the legal right. The legal position is an aggregate of the rights and obligations of both parties. Given the difficulty of giving concrete content to specific rights and obligations, it is best to refer to the legal position. The Supreme Court now allows the action for an affirmation that the union is in the legal position to claim that the employer shall engage in collective bargaining.

3. The Supreme Court denies the corporation's assertion that the free tickets system is a matter affecting the management and operation of the corporation. The corporation argued that free tickets are given for public purposes and business needs, and that it has the power to decide whether they shall be issued, to amen the system or to abolish it. However, it was found that free tickets for employees were a benefit for the staff of the corporation, which had considerable value. Even if the system was one with respect to which the employer had a power of decision, it was subject to collective bargaining insofar as it affected an employee benefit.

4. The restructuring of JNR (see above, under Facts) was subsequent to the judgement of Tokyo High Court. It was thus natural that Japan National Railway Liquidation Corporation should become the appellant and the party to collective bargaining.

Supreme Court (Third Petty Bench)

(iv) Asahi Fire and Marine Insurance Co.
v.
Jiro Takada

Amended provisions of collective agreement disadvantageous to workers—effect—unorganized workers—retroactivity

HEADNOTES

Facts

The appellee was formerly employed in the railway insurance department of a non-life-insurance company. When that department was taken over by the appellant company, he became its employee on 1 February 1965. At that time he entered into an employment contract with the appellant company, which recognized that the collective agreement and work rules applicable at the railway insurance department would have effect until a new agreement was concluded. This meant that his mandatory retirement age was 63, although the retirement age of other employees of the appellant company was 55 under a collective agreement between that company and the enterprise union.

The company subsequently negotiated with the labour union with a view to unifying working conditions. On 11 July 1983 they conclude an agreement unifying the mandatory retirement ages and amending the provision regarding the calculation of retirement allowances. On the same day the work rules were also amended, to correspond to the provisions of the new agreement.

The new agreement and work rule had the following provisions:

(1) The mandatory retirement age would be 57. Retirement allowance would be paid at that age. After that, a union member could be re-employed as a special employee for a period of one year, renewable up to the age of 60. The period of re-employment could, as an interim measure, be prolonged up to the age of 62 if the employee was more than 57 years old at the time of the conclusion of the new agreement. The salary payable would be 60% of that paid at the time of mandatory retirement.

(2) An employee with 30 years' service would receive an amount equivalent to 51 months' salary as retirement allowance. As an interim measure, in 1983

only, an amount equivalent to 60 months' salary might be paid. (Prior to the amendment of the agreement, the amount payable to a union member was the equivalent of 71 months' salary.)

(3) 120,000 yen would be paid to each employee in compensation for the unified working conditions disadvantageous to employees. Each employee formerly working in the railway insurance department and more than 50 years old on 1 April 1983 would receive 420,000 yen.

(4) The new agreement would be effective as from 1 April 1983.

The appellee was over 57 years old when the new agreement became effective. He was accordingly paid a retirement allowance equivalent to 60 months' salary and, from May 1983 on, paid 60% of salary as a special employee. He asserted that he should be paid full salary because his mandatory retirement age was 65; the former agreement between the railway insurance department and the union provided that the mandatory retirement age was 63, but as a custom it was prolonged to 65; he was thus a regular employee until the age of 65 and should be paid accordingly.

He retired on 10 December 1988, when the period of re-employment expired. At the time of his mandatory retirement, he was a managerial officer and accordingly not a member of the union under the collective agreement. But more than three-fourths of the employees at the branch where he worked were union members.

Kokura branch of Fukuoka District Court held that the new collective agreement could be applied to the appellee under article 17 of the Trade Unions Act, and that the amendment of the works rules had binding effect even though it introduced less favourable working conditions for the employees. However, the new agreement, which was concluded on 11 July 1983 but was made retroactively applicable by its terms as from 1 April, could only be applied to the appellee from 11 July because he was not a union member and was thus subject to the agreement only by virtue of its extensive effect under article 17 of the Trade Unions Act. He thus had to be paid salary and bonus as a regular employee from April to July 1983 and the company was ordered to pay the difference between the salary he was paid as a special employee during that period and that to which he was entitled—1,325,228 yen—plus 5% interest per year.

Fukuoka High Court affirmed the judgement of the District Court. In addition, it dealt with a claim by the appellee that he should be paid the difference between the retirement allowance he would have received under the old agreement and the allowance paid to him under the new. The High Court held that the new agreement had no effect in relation to him, as there was no reasonable ground for amending the amount of the retirement allowance. The company was ordered to pay the difference, with interest. The company appealed to the Supreme Court.

Decision

The appeal was rejected.

Law Applied

Trade Unions Act

Article 17: When three-fourths or more of a particular category of workers normally employed in a factory or other work place are covered by a single collective agreement, the remaining workers of that category employed in that factory or work place shall *ipso facto* be bound by the same agreement.

JUDGEMENT

1. The new collective agreement was concluded on 11 July 1983. On the same day the works rules regarding mandatory retirement age and retirement

allowances were amended to correspond to the contents of the agreement. The new agreement provided that it had retroactive effect as from 1 April 1983. However, the appellee had already worked as a normal employee and was thus entitled to claim full salary from 1 April to 11 July 1983. The new agreement and the amended works rules could not retroactively deprive him of his right after it had come into existence. The company thus had to pay him full salary for the period 1 April to 11 July 1983.

2. It cannot be held that a provision in a collective agreement should not be applied to unorganized workers under article 17 of the Trade Unions Act because it introduces a working condition, which is less favourable than one, currently applicable to them. This is so because: (a) the article does not limit the scope of the extending effect on workers of the same category; and (b) the aim of the article is to standardize working conditions and to maintain fair labour standards in a particular work place.

At the same time, the view can be taken that the article should not be applied to unorganized workers in special circumstances in which such application is judged to be unreasonable in light of the degree of disadvantage and of details regarding the conclusion of the agreement providing for worse working conditions. Unorganized workers cannot participate in the decision-making of the trade union and, conversely, the union is not entitled to affect their working conditions.

In the present case, it was reasonable to amend the agreement because the company was in financial difficulties. However, if the amended agreement were extended to the appellee, he would be treated as retired and paid reduced retirement allowance because he was 57 years old when the agreement was concluded. His right to receive retirement allowance would be changed by the trade union after that right had come into existence. Also, the amount of the reduced allowance would be very disadvantageous for him. It would thus be highly unreasonable to submit him to a provision for a retirement allowance less than the amount due under the former agreement. Therefore, the effect of the amended agreement did not extend to him.

3. Even though the revised provision of the work rules was disadvantageous for the appellee, it should be effective insofar as it is judged to be reasonable after being considered not only with regard to the content of the change but also in terms of the need for the change.

In this case, it could be affirmed that there was a great need for a reduction in the standard for calculating retirement allowances, because the management of the company was in a worse position than before. However, it cannot be judged to be reasonable to reduce the amount to less than the 20,078.800-yen calculated under the former work rules. Therefore, the amended work rules on retirement allowance had no effect within the limits set by the amount calculated under the former work rules.

[*Source*: Case (0) of 1993, decided 26 March 1996, reported at Rodohanrei No. 691:16.]

ANNOTATION

1. The reported case was concerned with the question of how the working conditions of unorganized workers should be treated when the conditions of organized workers become worse than theirs as a result of the amendment of the collective agreement and the consequential amendment of the work rules. Three points fell to be discussed. The first was whether the amended provision of the agreement and of the work rules could be applied retroactively to unorganized workers. The second was whether the amended agreement extended to unorganized workers under article 17 of the Trade Unions Act, seeing that three-fourths of the employees at the work place were members of the union. The third was whether the unfavourable amendment of the work rules was applicable.

2. It is possible in some cases to admit that an amended collective agreement may have retroactive effect. However, a right that has already come into existence cannot be change retroactively by the agreement. This affirmation can be found in the judgement of the Supreme Court in the case of *Masami Arai* v. *The Hong Kong and Shanghai Banking Corporation* (9 ILLR 516).

3. It has been affirmed that provisions of a collective agreement, which advantage unorganized workers, shall apply to them. The issue under discussion was whether provisions disadvantageous to them shall also apply. There are two conflicting interpretations on this point.

One is that the extension of the agreement to unorganized workers applies even though their working conditions are worsened thereby. Provisions in a collective agreement regarding working conditions have normative effect, whether they advantage the workers or not.

The other is that the extension does not apply to unorganized workers when their conditions would be worsened thereby. This view emphasizes that they have no vote to decide on such worsening. The collective agreement is then seen as having normative effect only when it provides advantages.

The courts have sought a compromise between these two approaches. For instance, in *Y. Tsujimura* v. *Tokyo Research on Commerce and Industry Co.* (13 September 1984, Rodohanrei 439:30), the Tokyo District Court, while affirming the extending effect on unorganized workers under article 17 of the Trade Unions Act in order to standardize conditions of work, held that there might be exceptions in special situations where the application of a collective agreement to them would lead to unfair or unreasonable results. The Supreme Court took the same position.

However, it proved difficult under the former judgements to find a special situation. It is remarkable that the Supreme Court in this case held that there was such a situation. It considered it to be strikingly unreasonable to reduce the amount of retirement allowance after the right to receive a certain amount came into existence.

4. The work rules were amended by reference to the amended collective agreement and working conditions provided for therein revised unfavourably for the workers. According to precedent, an employee cannot avoid the application of amended work rules insofar as the amendment has a reasonable basis (*Yoshikawa* v. *Shukoku Bus Co.*, 22 MINSHU 3459, *Omagari City Cooperative Association* v. *Tisuke Miura et al.*, 42 MINSHU 60, 8 ILLR 134). Following the precedent, the present judgement denied the existence of a reasonable basis. This was done by reference to the same standard as that applied to a special situation (see under 3)

In Japan a collective agreement deals with working conditions of union members at a factory or work place because it is concluded at the factory or work place. Work rules also lay down working conditions at a factory or work place. Since collective agreements and work rules thus have the same role, it is not surprising that reasonableness should be decided by reference to the same standard.

(2) UNION ACTIVITIES

(i) **Hiroshi Yamamoto**
v.
Chugoku Electric Powers Co.
(ii) **Kagawa Prefecture Labour Relations Commission**
v.
Kurata Gakuen, Educational Foundation

Supreme Court (Third Petty Bench)

(i) Hiroshi Yamamoto et al.
v.
Chugoku Electric Powers Co.

Discharge for distribution, outside working hours and outside working premises, of union handbills criticizing atomic power generation

HEADNOTES

Facts

The five appellants were employees of the Chugoku Electric Power Co. and union officers of Yamaguchi Prefecture branch of the Japan Electric Power Industrial Union (Denson Roso). To oppose atomic power generation, they distributed union handbills, outside working hours, to inhabitants of the town, in which it was planned to build an atomic power station. The following statements were to be found on the bills: "Many employees of Chugoku Electric Co. are opposed to atomic power generation"; "Radio-activity will always be spread by an atomic power station"; "There is no guarantee that there will not be accidents"; "The fishing zone will be completely destroyed". The company ordered the appellants to stop distributing the bills, but they did not obey the order. The company then imposed disciplinary sanctions on them on the ground that their conduct gave cause for disciplinary action under the working rules in that the contents of the bills were false and malicious, and so brought dishonour on the company and obstructed the normal operation of its business.

The appellant sought a declaration that the disciplinary actions were null and void as well as payment the amount by which their wages had been reduced and damages. They argued (1) that the bills were distributed outside working hours and outside the workplace, and that their action was thus not within the scope of the working rules or subject to disciplinary action; and (2) the disciplinary action infringed the freedom of expression and thought provided for under articles 19 and 21 of the Constitution.

Both Yamaguchi District Court and Hiroshima High Court reasoned as follows: (1) when an employee enters into an employment contact, he is under a duty to work for the employer and adhere to workplace order. The employer, with a view to maintaining workplace order and operating his business smoothly, has a power to impose disciplinary penalties on anyone who has disturbed that order. He may impose such penalties even for conduct outside working hours, outside the workplace and unrelated to the job. (2) In this case, much of the content of the handbills was false and wrongfully abused the company. The employees thus, by intent or negligence, caused disadvantage to the company and had, accordingly, disturbed workplace order.

Decision

The appeal was dismissed.

Law Applied

Constitution of Japan

Article 19: Freedom of thought and conscience shall not be violated.

Article 21: Freedom of assembly and association as well as freedom of speech, press and all other forms of expression is guaranteed. There shall be no censorship and the secrecy of any means of communication shall not be violated.

JUDGEMENT

1. From the facts found by the High Court, it is reasonable to conclude that the distribution of handbills at issue amounts to illegal union activity, and that the disciplinary action does not fall within the category of an unfair labour practice.

2. An employer is empowered to impose disciplinary sanctions on an employee so as to maintain workplace order, if the contents of handbills distributed by the employee are untrue or an exaggeration or distortion of facts regarding the management policy and business of the company and the distribution threatens to obstruct the smooth operation of the business, even though the bills, the contents of which were related to the employee's job, were distributed outside working hours and outside the workplace (*Shiro Takama v. Kansai Electric Power Co.*, decided on 8 September 1983, reported at Rodohanrei, No. 415, p. 29). Considering the present case in light of that opinion, the Supreme Court approves the judgement of the High Court. The conduct of the appellants falls within the grounds for disciplinary action defined as follows under the working rules: "when an employee spoils the company's reputation"; and "when an employee, by intent or serious negligence, acts against the company's interests".

3. The disciplinary action does not wrongfully infringe freedom of expression and does not regulate the beliefs of the appellant, which are guaranteed under articles 19 and 21 of the Constitution. It accordingly does not violate public order and morals.

[*Source*: Case No. (0) 156 of 1990 decided on 3 March 1992; reported at Rodohanrei No. 609:10].

ANNOTATION

1. In principle, a company cannot control an employee's activities outside working hours and outside the workplace, because the relationship between employer and employee under the employment contract is carried on at the workplace during working hour. But the problem arises whether an employee's conduct outside working hours and outside the workplace can nevertheless be the object of disciplinary sanctions.

The Supreme Court has considered two types of cases raising this issue. One concerns actions by the employee, which are not directly related to his job. For example, some employees who participated in demonstrations against the extension of the U.S. air base in Tachikawa were arrested and prosecuted under the Special Criminal Code based on the U.S-Japan agreement. The employing company dismissed them, as a disciplinary penalty, because their conduct "was dishonourable and seriously affected the company's reputation" and so fell within one of the grounds for disciplinary sanctions under the work rules and the applicable collective agreement. The actions of the employees were not directly related to their jobs. The Supreme Court held that a company was empowered to regulate conduct of an employee which might seriously affect its prestige, even if the employee's action was taken in the course of his private life and was not directly related to his job, because it was necessary for the operation of the business of the company that it should maintain social prestige and a good reputation (*Shigeru Sakata et al.* v. *Nippon Kokan Co.*, decided on 15 March 1974, reported at 733 Hanrei Jiho 23).

The other type of case concerns actions by the employee, which are directly related to his job, although taken outside working hours and outside the workplace. The case here reported belongs to this latter category. Generally speaking, an action directly related to the job is more likely to provide a basis for disciplinary penalties than one not so related. In the reported case, there were two grounds for disciplinary action. One was that the actions of the appellants damaged the reputation of the company. The other was that they threatened to obstruct the smooth operation of the business. This does not go so far as to allege that the smooth operation of the business was in fact obstructed. But it is the latter reason, which shows the difference between the two types of cases.

2. Some reference should be made to the contents of the handbills. The bills criticized management policy on atomic power generation. In general, an employee is free to express his own opinion when he disagrees with the company's policy. Articles 19 and 21 of the Constitution guarantee this freedom. But criticism must be kept within proper limits and made in a proper manner. In this case the Supreme Court found that the contents of the bills were untrue and exaggerated or distorted the facts. By reference to this finding, the decision is thought to be reasonable. The question remains—although the expressions used in the bills are no doubt improper—whether it is clearly said that there is no danger in atomic power generation.

Supreme Court (Third Petty Bench)

(ii) Kagawa Prefecture Labour Relations Commission
v.
Kurata Gakuen Educational Foundation

Interference with union activities—disciplinary action for distribution of handbills without the employer's permission—discriminatory treatment of union members

HEADNOTES

Facts

The respondent, an Educational Foundation, managed two senior and junior high schools. At one senior and junior high school some teachers organized a labour union in October 1976. That union filed unfair labour practice charges with the Kagawa Prefectural Labour Relations Commission on the following grounds.

(1) Article 14, Section 12 of the Work Rule of the Foundation provided that an employee should not post notes and distribute documents, except for business purposes, without written permission. The president of the labour union placed union bills on the desks of teachers, without permission, during the five or ten minutes preceding school hours on 8, 9 and 16 May 1978. A newsletter was so folded as to conceal the printed side; in it there was news of collective bargaining at the Foundation and of wage increases at other private high schools, as well as a commentary on the unfair labour practices system. There was no trouble with the respondent during the distribution of the newsletter; however, the principal of the senior and junior high school thereafter gave the union officer a warning on the ground of violation of the Work Rule.

The union argued that the disciplinary action was discriminatory treatment contrary to article 7, section 1 of the Labour Unions Act and control or interference with union activities contrary to article 7, section 3 of the Act.

(2) At the time of collective bargaining in October 1977 and March 1978, the union proposed the establishment of a notice board at a place not passed by students. The principal refused the proposal on the grounds that there was no place in the school building where students could not come and that he could not check in advance the contents of documents posted on the notice board. As a result, the collective bargaining could not proceed.

The union complained that the employer without proper reasons refused collective bargaining.

(3) A member of the executive committee of the union was a teacher of mathematics. He was in charge of the first year class of the senior high school in 1974, the second year class in 1975 and the third year class

in 1976; he thus remained in charge of the same students for three consecutive years. In 1977 he was put in charge of the class of second year students of the junior high school, but in 1978 he was not appointed as teacher of the third year class. In the school it was customary for a teacher in charge of a first or second year class to remain in charge of the same students for the following year.

The union asserted that he was not appointed as teacher of the third year class because of his union activity and that this was discriminatory treatment in the meaning of article 7, section 1 of the Labour Unions Act.

(4) A union member employed as a teacher of social studies wished to publish an essay criticizing the educational policy of the Foundation in the newsletter of the first year class of the high school. The chairwoman of the Foundation ordered him to amend it, and he complied with the order. In class, he criticized the fact that the Foundation had bought a lot of land while paying low salaries to the teachers the chairwoman thereupon indirectly encouraged him to undertake to retire voluntarily from the school. In the newsletter of the union, he alleged that his father had died because he had been encouraged to retire voluntarily. The chairwoman condemned him, but he did not acknowledge any fault. Therefore, she directly encouraged him to retire voluntarily instead of being dismissed on the ground that he was not competent to be a teacher. Subsequently, following a letter of apology by him, the proposal for voluntary retirement was withdrawn.

The union asserted that the encouragement of voluntary retirement constituted control of or interference with union activities in the meaning of article 7, section 3 of the labour Unions Act.

Kagawa Prefectural Labour Relations Commission allowed all the claims of the union. It ordered the Foundation to withdraw disciplinary action, to negotiate regarding the union notice board, to follow the normal pattern of assignment of teachers and to stop controlling union activity by the encouragement of voluntary retirement of a union member. The Foundation initiated an action to revoke that order.

Takamatsu District Court approved the decision of the Labour Relations Commission, but Takamatsu High Court judged that the four points at issue did not fall within the concept of unfair labour practices. The Labour Relations Commission now appealed to the Supreme Court.

Decision

The appeal succeeded as regards the first three points; the fourth was sent back to the High Court.

Law Applied

Labour Unions Act [called Trade Union Law in *Jap. 3—Ed.*]

Article 7: The employer shall not engage in the following practices:

(1) discharge or apply discriminatory treatment to a worker by reason of his membership of a labour union, his attempt to join or to organize a labour union, or his performance of proper acts of a labour union;
(2) refuse, without fair and appropriate reasons, to bargain collectively with the representative of the workers employed by him; and
(3) control or interfere with the formation or management of a labour union by workers or give financial support thereto by defraying the union's operational expenditure. . . .

JUDGEMENT

1. Formally, the distribution of union bills violated article 14, section 12 of the Work Rule, which prohibited the distribution of documents on the premises of the school without written permission. However, even when there is a formal violation, it is still possible to find the person concerned not guilty, in a particular situation in which the distribution could not disturb the order of the school or lack educational consideration for the students. A particular situation may be found to exist by reference to various circumstances, such as the content of the bills, the manner of distribution etc. (*Ishihara v. Nippon Telegraph and Telephone Public Corporation*, Supreme Court, Third Petty Bench, 13 December 1977, 31 Minshu 974).

In the present case, the content of the bills was concerned with union activities. They did not instigate or stimulate illegal acts. The bills were distributed before school hours and placed folded on the desks of teachers. Therefore, it could not be found that the order of the school would be disturbed.

Another aspect to be examined is that of educational consideration for the students. It could be thought that the students must be isolated from disputes between the school and teachers. However, in this case bills were distributed during between the school and teachers. However, in this case bills were distributed during hours when students would rarely go to the teachers' room, so there was no doubt that the union took sufficient account of the students. Therefore, it is an appropriate to find that the distribution in question was made in a particular situation. As a result, the disciplinary punishment was null and void because the distribution did not violate article 14, section 12 of the Work Rule.

Moreover, from the above-mentioned facts it could be found that the Educational Foundation assumed a stance of hatred I relation to the labour union and intended to deny the exercise of all union activities on the premises of the school. Hence, the disciplinary punishment constituted discriminatory treatment in the meaning of article 7, section 1 of the Labour Union Act as well as control and interference with the management of the union in the meaning of article 7, section 3 of the Act.

2. The Supreme Court could not hold to be reasonable the appellants assertion that a notice board should not be provided on the premises of the school at all, by reference to the educational consideration to be given to the students. It was natural that the two parties should negotiate, at the collective bargaining table, the conditions for putting up a notice board. In the past, the content of a document posted on the notice board was disputed because the principal of the school had not been able to check it in advance. However, this was not an appropriate reason for refusing to bargain.

3. The Court considers that the person concerned was not appointed as a teacher in charge of the third year class of the junior high school because he was an active member of the union. In 1977 and 1978, only union members were not appointed as teachers in charge of such classes, although it was usual for teachers to remain in charge of the same class for the following year. This action constituted discriminatory treatment in the meaning of article 7, section 1 of the Labour Unions Act.

4. Takamatsu High Court held that it was not an unfair labour practice to encourage a union member to retire voluntarily from the school. However, the respondent based its conclusion on a different type of encouragement from that alleged. Therefore, this Court considers the judgement of the High Court to be irrational and inappropriate in the light of the evidence on the fourth point. The matter is sent back to the High Court.

[*Source*: Case (gyou tyu) 155 of 1991, decided on 20 December 1994, reported in Rodohanrei 669:13].

ANNOTATION

1. It took about 17 years until the Supreme Court decided this case. Even then the case was not finally resolved, since the fourth point was sent back to the High Court. 17 years are a very long time. It is thought that during that time the courts tried to get the parties to reach a compromise - unsuccessfully because neither party was prepared to yield. In Japan it is often said that it takes a long time to resolve a dispute in which teachers, doctors or priests are involved, because they have a tendency to hold unshakable beliefs and to refuse to compromise.

2. There have been three types of disputes concerting the distribution of handbills. The first related to the disciplinary punishment of an individual employee who distributed political bills without the employer's permission. The second related to disciplinary punishment for the distribution of bills, without the employer's permission, in pursuance of a union resolution. The third posed the question whether it was control and interference with the management of the labour union for the employer to issue a warning regarding or to obstruct distribution of bills without his permission. The special feature of the present case was that it was disputed whether disciplinary punishment for the distribution of bills without the employer's permission fell within article 7, section 3 of the Labour Unions Act.

3. Why did the Supreme Court arrive at a different conclusion than the High Court? On the first point, the framework of the Supreme Court decision was different from that of the High Court.

The Supreme Court's judgement followed the decision in the *Nippon telegraph and Telephone Public Corporation* case, which provided a precedent regarding the legal effect of the distribution of bills without the employer's permission. The High Court, on the other hand, followed the different precedent of *National Railways Corporation* v. *Ikeoka et al.*, decided on 30

October 1979 (33 Minshu 647), which dealt with the legal problem of the use by a union member, for union activities, of the facilities of the enterprise.

The difference in approach resulted from the method of bills distribution. Generally bills were delivered by hand to union members. However, in the present case union newsletters were put on the desks of the teachers buy union members without the employer's permission. The High Court accordingly looked at the matter from the point of view of the degree of encroachment was on the employer's right of property, since the distribution used school facilities. The Supreme Court, on the other hand, considered that the degree of encroachment was less than in other union activities using school facilities and followed the *Nippon Telegraph* precedent.

In the *National Railways Corporation* case, it was decided that the use of facilities without permission was not a proper union activity, as it violated the employer's right to use and control the facilities so as to maintain a proper work environment and carry on business in an orderly manner, unless special circumstances rendered the employer's refusal to allow the union to use enterprise facilities an abusive exercise of the right of the employer. In general, it is very difficult to find that there has been an abusive exercise of the right of the employer. So the sphere of proper union activity became narrow.

On the other hand, it was held in the *Nippon Telegraph and Telephone Public Corporation* case that, even if distribution of bills without permission formally violated the Work Rule, it was possible to find the union member not guilty in a particular situation in which the distribution of bills would not disturb the order and discipline of the enterprise. In general, it is easier to find that there is a particular situation than to find that there has been an abusive exercise of the right of the employer.

4. In the *Nippon Telegraph* case, political bills were distributed. In the present case the bills were concerned with union activities and were distributed as a union activity. It is thus of interest that the Supreme

Court applied the precedent of the *Nippon Telegraph* case to the distribution of bills concerned with union activities.

As a second feature, a particular situation was found to exist from the viewpoint of educational consideration for the students. There was a premise that the union of school teachers should not involve the students in a labour dispute at the school, but newsletters were distributed before school hours and only in the teachers' room. Therefore, the Supreme Court found that the labour union gave enough consideration to the students.

5. The following point came into question: why did the Supreme Court decide that the disciplinary punishment was null and void? The Supreme Court judged the legal effect of the disciplinary action ordered by the employer. However, its decision was unnecessary because the issue was whether the action was an unfair labour practice in the meaning of article 7, sections 1 and 3 of the Labour Unions Act. The Supreme Court should have decided that the disciplinary punishment was applied in respect of proper acts of the labour union and constituted control or interference with the management of the union. This problem revealed that the Supreme Court judged an unfair labour practice case differently from the Labour Relations Commission.

6. As regards the refusal to bargain collectively on the problem of the union board, the Supreme Court judged that the respondent violated the duty to bargain in good faith. The respondent had a duty not only to listen to the union's contentions, but also to respond to them and to discuss with the union's representative with a view to trying to achieve agreement by a good faith response. However, it was found that the respondent did not try to explain its reasons sufficiently to constitute a counter-argument to the contentions of the union and, as a result, which the respondent had no intention from the beginning to enter into a collective agreement on the subject of a union notice board. This was a typical case of a refusal to negotiate in good faith with the labour union.

(3) RIGHT TO STRIKE

(i) **Fukuoka Local Labour Relations Commission**
v.
Kitakyushu City

(ii) **Mikuni Taxi Limited Liability Company**
v.
Genkichi Noguchi

(iii) **Yutaka Nakamura and Others**
v.
Mitsubishi Heavy Industries Co.

Supreme Court (First Petty Bench)

(i) Fukuoka Local Labour Relations Commission *v.* Kitakyushu City

Constitutionality of prohibition of strike for employees in local public service—Refusal of overtime work ordered by labour union and strike

HEADNOTES

Facts

Kitakyushu City (the appellee) made a plan to rebuild the local transportation system under the amendment of the Local Public Enterprise Act of 1966. The City and the labour union of the transportation section discussed the plan under an agreement on workers' consultation. Before a conclusion was reached, the City made an amended plan and presented it to the municipal assembly. To protest against it, the labour union organized a concerted refusal of overtime work and of work violating labour safety and sanitation rules. The labour union also ordered half of its members to take annual holidays, as a concerted activity. The City suspended union leaders from office duties and gave warnings to some of them, on the ground that they violated Article 11, Section 1 of the Local Public Enterprise Labour relations Act. The labour union filed an unfair labour practice complaint with Fukuoka Local Labour ,Relations Commission. The Commission issued a remedial order to rescind the disciplinary measures. Fukuoka District Court upheld the order, but Fukuoka High Court rescinded it. The reasoning of the High Court was as follows: Article 11, Section 1 of the Local Public Enterprise Labour Act was constitutional; concerted activities violating that Article were not protected by Article 7, Section 1 of the Labour Unions Act, which prohibits discriminatory treatment of an employee by reason of proper labour union activity, etc. Then Fukuoka Local Labour Relations Commission appealed to the Supreme Court.

Decision

The appeal was dismissed.

Law Applied

Constitution

Article 28: The right of workers to organize and bargain and act collectively is guaranteed.

Local Public Enterprise Labour Relations Act

Article 11, Section 1: The employees and the labour union shall not, against the local public enterprise, resort to a strike, slowdown and any other acts of dispute hampering the normal operations, not shall any employees or union members and officials of the union conspire regarding, instigate or incite to such prohibited acts.

Article 12: The local public enterprise may dismiss employees who have acted in violation of the provisions of the preceding Article.

JUDGEMENT

1. It is an established precedent of the Supreme Court that Article 17, Section 1 of the Public Corporation and National Enterprise Labour Relations Act does not violate Article 28 of the Constitution. The Court finds that the same conclusion applies to Article 11, Section 1 of the Local Public Enterprise Labour Relations Act for the following reasons.

(1) Employees of local public enterprise have the same legal status as local public personnel regarding the determination of working conditions. Their working conditions are settled by decision of the municipal assembly in compliance with the principles of financial democracy declared in Articles 41 and 83 of the Constitution. Therefore, they cannot be decided by collective bargaining alone as in the case of private companies. Article 7 of the Local Public Enterprise Labour Relations Act provides that a part of working conditions may be the object of collective bargaining and an agreement may be concluded in relation to them. When the agreement is in conflict with a by-law of the local public body, the chief of the local public body shall, within ten days after its conclusion, present a bill on the necessary revision or abrogation of the by-law to the assembly of the local public body, in order that the agreement may case to conflict with the regulations and other rules (Article 9). These provisions create a space within which collective bargaining may function. But law, by-law and the regulations and budget of the local public body control working conditions.

(2) The absence of restraint in labour relations by the market mechanism can be seen in local public enterprise. Then the right to strike would not help the employees to obtain proper working conditions.

(3) The purpose of the Act is to establish peaceful labour-management relations to secure the normal operation of local public enterprise at maximum efficiency and thereby to contribute to the promotion of the welfare of the people. The employees of local public

enterprise have, in substance, a duty of work to the peoples of the city as a whole. Industrial action of the employees would impede the common interests of the local people and in turn have a bad influence upon those of the nation as a whole.

(4) Proper measures should be taken to compensate for the limitation of the right to strike. The employees of local public enterprise are provided vicarious compensation measures by law. Wages are to be determined in balance with the cost of living and wages of national and local public personnel. Labour Relations Commissions have jurisdiction to conciliate, mediate and arbitrate labour disputes in local public enterprises. And also a compulsory mediation and compulsory arbitration system is introduced in local public enterprise which is not institutionalized at private companies.

2. The labour union refused to conclude an agreement on overtime work and refused to renew the agreement as a weapon to compel the public enterprise to abandon the plan.

At the transportation section, overtime work was usual under the agreement between the labour union and the local public enterprise. Refusal of overwork thus amounted to obstructive operation of normal transportation. Therefore, this refusal of overtime work amounts to the strike prohibited by Article 11, Section 1 of the Local Public Enterprise Labour Relations Act.

[*Source*: Case No. (Gyo-Tsu) 37 of 1981 decided on 8 December 1988: reported at Rodohanrei No. 530:6].

ANNOTATION

1. This is the first judgement in which the Supreme Court decided on the constitutionality of Article 11, Section 1 of the Local Public Enterprise Labour Relations Act. The judgement is based on the line of thinking in the Nagoya Central Post Office Case decided on 4 May 1977 (3 I.L.L.R. 299). In that case, the issue was whether the prohibition of strikes for the

employees of a Public Corporation and National Enterprise violated Article 28 of the Constitution. The Supreme Court admitted the constitutionality of Article 17, Section 1 of the Public Corporation and National Enterprise Labour Relations Act on the following grounds: (a) the principle that the working conditions of the employees in a question were decided by law approved in the Diet; (b) lack of restraint by the market mechanism in determining working conditions; (c) the bad effect of industrial actions on the common interests of the nation; (d) preparation of vicarious compensation measures. These grounds are applied to this case. By this judgement, the Supreme Court has established the constitutionality of Article 11, Section 1 of the Local Public Enterprise Labour Relations Act. (Three public corporations are now private companies. Therefore, the Public Corporation and the National Enterprise Labour Relations Act is changed into the National Enterprise Labour Relation Act.)

"Local public enterprise" as used in the Local Public Enterprise Labour Relations Act includes any enterprise which undertakes the following services and which is operated by the local public body: (a) local railway services, (b) tramway service, (c) automobile transportation, (d) electricity service, (e) gas service, (f) water supply service for industrial service, as well as (h) any enterprise to which the provisions of Chapter 4 of the Local Public Enterprise Act are applicable. So the scope of local public enterprise is not established and is different in each local public body. A private company in another city may manage a local public enterprise, which is operated by the local public body at one city. And the local public body and a private company may manage one service competitively. Therefore, this judgement raises the problem whether it is constitutional that the employees of all local public enterprises are prohibited uniformly from striking merely because they are in a local public enterprise.

2. Another problem is the legal status of a refusal to do overtime work. In this case the labour union

ordered its members to refuse overtime, by refusing to conclude or to renew an agreement on overtime work. Overtime work is allowed fewer than two conditions by the Labour Standards Act. One is the conclusion of an agreement with the majority union or with the representatives of the majority of the employees in the absence of a majority union. The other is the submission of the agreement to the Labour Standards Inspection Office. An employer cannot order the employees to do overtime work without an agreement. And the majority union has the freedom to conclude an agreement or not. It is not compelled to conclude the agreement. So it may refuse to conclude or to renew the agreement on overtime work. But the Supreme Court found that overtime work was usual, under the precondition of an agreement, and that refusal of overtime work would obstruct the normal operation of services. Refusal of overtime work was not used for the purpose of abolishing overtime work itself, but as a weapon to put pressure on the employer to end the plan. From the two points of view, the Supreme Court decided that the refusal of overtime work ordered by the labour union came under the "strike" prohibited by the Act.' But some academic groups object to this judgement for the following reasons. (a) It is strange that a labour union should be compelled to conclude an agreement, according to the interpretation of the Supreme Court. (b) In this case there was no agreement. But the members of the labour union had to do overtime work without an agreement in order to avoid punishment. This means that they were forced to do illegal overtime work by disciplinary punishment.

Supreme Court (Second Petty Bench)

(ii) Mikuni Taxi Limited Liability Company
v.
Genkichi Noguchi and Others

Illegality of sit-down strike—compensation for damage

Facts

The appellant was a limited liability company operating 42 taxis. It had 115 employees. The six appellees worked for the company as taxi drivers and were also union officers at the Kouchi Regional Branch of the National Taxi Drivers Labour Union.

Since 1976 the employees had been employed on a percentage basis. Every year the union submitted a demand for the guarantee of a fixed income plus piece-rated wages. The company always rejected that demand. During the spring offensive of 1982 the union and the company bargained collectively on this issue but reached no agreement. The union then decided to call a 48-hour strike from 9 to 11 July and so notified the company. The company requested the union not to obstruct the work of persons holding administrative positions because the company was entitled to operate its business even during a strike.

The tactic of the union during the strike was to obstruct the operation of only six taxis scheduled to be driven by union members. One of these taxis was at Obita car shed and the other five at Hyakokichou car shed. The six appellees sat around these taxis with other union members. A managing director of the company handed the following warning paper to a Kouchi branch officer of the National Taxi Drivers' Union: "1. [the strikers] shall leave the two car sheds as soon as possible, 2. They will be punished if they do not obey the order, 3. The company will sue for damages". The union members did not comply with the order. They continued to sit and lie on mats around the six taxis until at 10 p.m. on 10 July; they left the sheds because of heavy rain. The strike thus lasted 42 hours.

The company claimed 482.112 yen as damages from the appellees on the ground that they illegally obstructed its operation. Kouchi District Council allowed the claim; it found that the union occupied six taxis exclusively for two days without regard for the warning and held that this was an infringement of the employer's property right and an illegal obstruction of the company's freedom to operate its business. Takamatsu High Court reversed. It held that the six appellees should be exempted from civil liability because, in its view, the strike did not infringe the company's property right and did not obstruct its freedom to operate normally.

The company appealed to the Supreme Court.

Decision

A strike means the suspension of work, which an employee is required to perform under the employment contract. The strike is proper if it takes the form of a collective withdrawal of work. It is not proper when it illegally constrains the free will of the employer or infringes the latter's property right, because even during the strike the employer may take the measures necessary to continue the operation of its business. Therefore, in the taxis industry a labour union may not exclusively occupy taxis and thus obstruct their use by non-union members during the strike.

Law Applied

Trade Unions Act

Sectoin 8: No employer shall claim an indemnity from a labour union or its members in respect of damages suffered as a result of a strike or other dispute acts, which are proper acts.

JUDGEMENT

1. A strike is, in essence, a measure such as the withholding of labour which an employee is required to perform under the contract of employment; it follows that the strike may obstruct the normal operation of the company. Thus the strike is intended to prevent the company, through united action, from using the manpower of union members. However, the labour union is not permitted to constraint the free will of the employer or to infringe the latter's property right.

An employer need not stop the operation of his business during a strike; he may take measures to make continued operation possible. Of course the union may use persuasion in relation to non-union members and persons holding managerial positions, so as to obstruct the company's operation. But the union is not permitted to occupy taxis exclusively, so as to prevent their use by non-union members.

2. The propriety of a strike depends upon its purpose and the means used to attain the purpose. In this case, the aim of the strike was to improve working conditions. There was thus no problem as regards its purpose. The union only stopped the operation of six taxis which union members were scheduled to drive and did not prevent access to engine keys or automobile inspection cards. There were no violent or destructive acts during the strike. It can also be found that the union sought to prevent trouble. However, union members sat around six taxis for two days and did not obey the company's order. As a result, the company was unable to take these six taxis out from the car sheds. From this it may be found that the union exclusively occupied six taxis and prevented the company, with a certain degree of coercion, from taking them out. For these reasons the strike can be judged to have been improper.

The case must be referred back to the High Court, for investigation of the amount of damages.

[*Source*: Case No. (0) 676 of 1989, decided on 2 October 1992, Rodohanrei No. 619:8].

ANNOTATION

1. The first point to be mentioned is that the Supreme Court clearly sets fourth the standard for deciding the propriety of a strike from the point of view of the means used. In Japan civil and criminal liability does not arise from proper industrial action, including strike action.

Under section 8 of the Trade Unions Act a labour union or its members are not liable to pay a compensation for damage caused by proper industrial action. According to section 7(1) of the Act an employer may not discriminate against employees because of their participation I proper union activities, including proper strikes; such discrimination is regarded as an unfair labour practice. Therefore, the Labour Relations Commission or the courts remedy any discriminatory treatment due to a proper strike. Section 1(2) of the Trade Unions Act states that "the provisions of article 35 of the Penal Code shall apply to collective bargaining and other proper acts of a labour union". Article 35 of the Penal Code provides that acts performed with the authorization of the law or as a legitimate business activity shall be deemed lawful, even though these acts might otherwise constitute a certain type of offence. The proper acts of a labour union are thus regarded as legally authorized acts. Legal protection is, as indicated above, given to proper industrial action, including strikes. The manner of determining the propriety of a strike thus becomes important.

In general, the propriety of strikes is examined from four points of view, namely (a) their parties, (b) their objectives, (c) their procedure, and (d) their means. The judgement here reported considered the matter essentially forms the last point of view. The Supreme Court affirmed that a strike would be deemed improper if it consisted of positive actions which constrained the free will of the employer and infringed the latter's property right.

2. The second point to be noted is that the Supreme Court confirmed the employer's right to operate the business even during a strike. The employer can do so by using non-union labour and manages. The Supreme Court made it clear that this conclusion was applicable to the taxi industry, in which it is easy to negate the effects of a strike by using non-union labour to drive the taxis. It followed that the union was precluded from occupying taxis, if the employer's right to operate the business was to be safeguarded. On the other hand, it was necessary for the union to obstruct the employer's access to taxis, because the use of non-labour to drive them could easily made the strike ineffective. To reconcile these opposing considerations, the Supreme Court held that the union could not occupy the taxis *exclusively*. It was open to the union to persuade non-union workers not to drive the taxis.

3. What was the nature of the action of the labour union? It could be regarded as a sit-down strike or as a form of picketing. In Japan a sit-down strike is deemed to be proper as long as it does not exclude the employer's right of occupancy or obstruct the operation of the business (Kazuo Sugeno translated by Leo Kanowitz, Japanese Labour Law, University of Washington Press, 1982, p. 559). The propriety of picketing is judged in civil cases by reference to three standards: (a) persuasion by speech; (b) persuasion by speech coupled with group demonstrations; and (c) passive use of coercion. Most judgement opts for persuasion by speech.

From the judgement here reported it is evident that the Supreme Court had in mind the standards for deciding the propriety both of sit-down strikes and of picketing.

Supreme Court (Second Petty Bench)

(iii) Yutaka Nakamura and Others

v.

Mitsubishi Heavy Industries Co.

Impropriety of political strike—disciplinary suspension—legality

HEADNOTES

Facts

The three appellants worked at the Nagasaki shipbuilding section of the appellee company and were also leaders of the Nagasaki shipbuilding branch of the Mitsubishi Heavy Industries local union of the All Japan Shipbuilding and Mechanical Labour Union.

On the instruction of the Nagasaki Prefectural Labour Unions Committee, the Nagasaki shipbuilding branch on 5 October 1978 decided by ballot to strike, to protest against the entry of an atomic submarine named "Mutsu" into Sasebo port. The strike took place on 16 October, from 16:30 to 17:00; 243 union members stayed away from their posts for some 30 minutes. The union branch gave notice of the strike only ten minutes before it started.

Just before the strike, the company called on the union not to proceed with it, seeing that the company could not deal with the political problem about which the union was concerned. The union nevertheless called the strike. The company thereupon disciplined the three appellants—after the facts had been considered by a disciplinary committee—in reliance on article 72 of the work rules, which provided that the company could discipline an employee who did not obey an order or instruction of his superior without just cause. It found that the appellants had obstructed the production process and the good order of the workplace. One of the appellants was suspended from work for five days the other two for three days. The first retired from the company after the disciplinary punishment. The others sought to have the suspension annulled as contrary to section 7(3) of the trade Unions Act and article 90 of the Civil Code, and claimed wages for the period of suspension.

Nagasaki District Court rejected the claims, for the following reasons: (1) the political problem could not be dealt with by the employer in collective bargaining. Strikes were a necessary measure to obtain an advantageous response from an employer in collective bargaining. Accordingly, the political strike did not fall under the guarantee of article 28 of the Constitution, and was improper. (2) the appellants had argued that the work rules were premised on individual labour relations in ordinary circumstances and did not apply to industrial action. However, employees could not be excluded from these rules even during industrial action. The appellants had induced union members, in an improper strike, to leave their posts and obstruct the company's operation; they themselves had also left their posts. These actions constituted an infringement of the order of the workplace, which was prohibited by the work rules. (3) The appellants were not punished only because of their position as union leaders; they were disciplined because of their actions during an improper political strike. Therefore, the disciplinary punishment did not fall under section 7(3) of the Trade Unions Act or Article 90 of the Civil Code.

Fukuoka High Court upheld the judgement of the District Court, for the following reasons: (1) The purpose of the strike was to protest against the entry of the atomic submarine into Sasebo port and the policy of the Government, Nagasaki Prefecture and Sasebo City to enforce that entry. The appellants could not bargain collectively with the company, because this problem was not related to working conditions. (2) Notice of the strike was only given to the company ten minutes before it took place. It was thus possible to find that the operation of the business had been considerably obstructed by the strike, because the company had had no time to devise a counter plan. (3) Union members enjoyed immunity from liability only when dispute acts were entirely proper. They were individually liable for improper acts. Union leaders thus could be disciplined under the work rules because they led union members in an improper political strike and themselves walked off their jobs. (4) The Court could not find that it was the company's intention to weaken the Nagasaki shipbuilding branch of the union by means of the disciplinary punishment. That punishment accordingly did not constitute an unfair labour practice.

The appellants appealed to the Supreme Court.

Decision

The appeal was dismissed.

Law Applied

Constitution

Article 28: Workers have the right to organize and to bargain and act collectively.

Civil Code

Article 90: A legal act the object of which is contrary to public order or *bonos mores* is null and void.

Trade Unions Act

Section 7(3): The employer may not control or interfere with the establishment or management of a labour union by workers or give financial support thereto by defraying the union's operational expenditure.

JUDGEMENT

This Court considers the findings and the judgement of the High Court rational and appropriate in the light of all the evidence. There is no error in its conclusion. Accordingly the appeal must be dismissed.

[*Source*: Case (0) of 1310 of 1992, decided on 25 September 1992. Rodohanrei No. 618:14].

ANNOTATION

1. The judgement here reported is the first in which the Supreme Court deals with disciplinary punishment on the ground of a political strike. There had been some previous decisions on criminal penalties for such strikes (*Public Prosecutor* v. *Shigeru Sakane et al.*, Full Bench, decided on 2 April 1969, Kei-Shu, Vol. 23, No. 5, p. 685; *Public Prosecutor* v. *Tetsuo Turuzono et al.*, Full Bench, decided on 25 April 1973, *ibid.*, Vol. 27, No. 4, p. 547; *Public Prosecutor* v. *Shouji Sakata and Tatsuo Hirayama*, Third Petty Bench, decided on 28 February 1978, *Hanrei Times,* No. 361, p. 227). The present judgement adopted the same reasoning as those, which dealt with criminal penalties.

The strike in this case had the political purpose of protesting against the entry of an atomic submarine into a local port and the policy of the central and local government in this respect. It was thus natural that it should be found to have been a purely political strike.

There are three views on the propriety of political strikes:

(a) Industrial action is a means for making collective bargaining function. Therefore, political strikes are improper because they cannot be dealt with through collective bargaining.

(b) Political strikes may be divided into "economic political strikes" and "purely political strikes". The former are defined as related to policies and legislation with a bearing on working conditions in which workers have an economic interest. A "purely political strike" had no direct relationship with workers' economic interests. Therefore, the former is guaranteed by article 28 of the Constitution, as related to working conditions, whereas the latter only falls under article 21 of the Constitution, protecting freedom of speech and expression.

(c) All political strikes fall under article 28 of the Constitution because they are a necessary means to protest against the support given to employers by national and local government.

It is evident that the judgement here reported adopted the first view.

2. The appellants claimed that work rules did not apply to the acts of workers during a strike because they are premised on industrial relations in normal times. It followed, according to them, that union members could not be punished under the disciplinary provisions of work rules even if industrial action was improper. The Supreme Court clearly negative this assertion.

According to the judgement, any departure from the discipline of the workplace is permissible only during proper industrial action. Union leaders and members cannot be disciplined if they leave their work during proper industrial action. On the other hand, they may be punished under the disciplinary provisions of work rules if the industrial action was improper.

In this case, the provision of the work rules on which the disciplinary punishment was based specified that employees might not refuse the instruction of a superior without just cause or obstruct the order of the workplace. Union leaders are not liable for improper industrial acts solely by virtue of their position. The Court accordingly examined in what respect they infringed the order of the work place and disobeyed the instruction of a superior. If found that the appellants induced union members to walk off their jobs in an improper political strike and themselves left their work during such a strike. These actions were tantamount to an infringement of the provisions of the work rules. The disciplinary punishment was thus valid.

(4) UNFAIR LABOUR PRACTICES

(i) **Central Labour Relations Commission**
v.
Japan Ciba-Geigy Co.

(ii) **Saiseikai Social Welfare Corporate**
v.
Central Labour Relations Commission

(iii) **Seiwa Electric Industrial Co.**
v.
Central Labour Relations Commission

(iv) **Kinki System Management Co.**
v.
Osaka Prefecture Labour Relations Commission

(v) **Japanese Government**
v.
Yokohama Branch of National Customhouse Trade Union ***et al.***

Supreme Court (First Petty Bench)

(i) Central Labour Relations Commission *v.* Japan Ciba-Geigy Co.

Interference with trade union activity—manager's freedom of speech—use of company facilities for union meeting, distribution of union handbills on company premises and provision of union bulletin boards—unfair labour practices

HEADNOTES

Facts

The appellee is a subsidiary company of Ciba-Geigy Co., the headquarters of which are in Basel, Switzerland. There were two labour unions at this chemical company. Labour union "A" was set-up on 4 April 1974 and was affiliated to the *Kagaku Domei* (Chemical Labour Unions Federation) of *Sohyo* (General Council of Trade Unions). It had only 17 members. Labour union "B" had about 1000 members and was set-up on 15 April 1974. Labour union "A" filed an unfair labour practice complaint with Osaka Local Labour Relations Commission on the following five grounds.

(1) A factory manager made a speech on labour union "A" at a morning meeting at which about 230 employees of the factory attended. He said that labour unions affiliated to *Sohyo* were not good because it was radical, and that the members of labour union "A" should withdraw with courage from the union.

(2) On 9 April 1974, labour union "A" asked the company for use of the dining room, to have a union meeting from 5 p.m. for workers of the factory, but at 5:45 p.m. for the staff the management section. The company authorized the union to use the dining room from 6 p.m., so as not to obstruct normal operations. But labour union "A" held the meeting in the dining room from 5 p.m., without the permission of the company. The company asked the union to stop the meeting, but the union continued the meeting till 7 p.m.

(3) The rules of employment prohibited distribution of handbills without the permission of the company. On 27 May 1974 the members of labour union "A" distributed bills on company premises without permission. A manager asked the members to distribute the bills outside the premises, but they did not obey the order because they thought that a labour union could distribute bills freely even within the company premises. The company gave a warning that the members of labour union "A" would be subjected to disciplinary punishment if they were to continue to distribute bills on the company premises without permission of the company.

(4) On 13 May 13, 1974, labour union "A" demanded 4 times the monthly basic wage as the

summer bonus. Instead of answering the demand, the employer proposed the following conditions: (a) The union would not conduct union activity and company premises without permission of the employer, (b) The company would consider whether a check-off system should be introduced after the union presented a list of its members to the company. (c) The company would not provide a union office. (d) The company would not meet the demand to shorten working hours. (e) The company would pay 3 times the monthly basic wage as the summer bonus. (f) The company would lend the union a bulletin board, but the content of bulletins should be limited to matters permitted by the company and the bulletins should be submitted previously to the company. Finally, the union should not carry out political activities on the company premises at all.

The company made the same proposal to labour union "B". On 7 June, after collective bargaining, the company agreed with labour union "B" accepted. The company and labour union "A" bargained collectively on summer bonus and the conditions. They concluded on 11 June that the company should pay the amount of three months' basic wages; for the rest they agreed only on conditions (a) and (b). As a result the members of labour union "A" were paid summer bonus four days' labour than those of labour union "B".

(5) On 3 July 1974, labour union "A" asked the company for the loan of a union bulletin board. The company rejected the demand because it had not been solved by collective bargaining. Again, on 24 July the union proposed that there is bargaining on a union bulletin board. But the company gave the same answer and said that it would lend the board only if the union accepted the relevant conditions. Labour union "A" could not borrow the board because it did not accept the conditions.

Osaka Local Labour Relations Commission allowed the complaint filed by labour union "A" on the following grounds. (1) It was found that the factory manager slandered the union and induced members to withdraw from it. This was an unfair labour practice under Art. 7, Sec. 3 of the Labour Unions Act. (2) The company intended to restriction activity and to make it difficult for the union to hold a meeting by refusing use of the dining room. This refusal was found not be excusable on the ground of operational obstruction. Therefore, it was an unfair labour practice. (3) It was an abuse of right for the company to request the union to exhibit the content of handbills in advance though the union had given notice that it would distribute bills. Distribution took place around the time-recorder located near the gate, because it was difficult to distribute the bills outside the gate. It did not obstruct the attendance of employees. In these circumstances, the warning of disciplinary punishment was found to restrict union activity on the pretext that the labour union violated rules of employment. (4) The proposals by the company were different in character from summer bonus. It was not rational for the company to insist that labour union "A" should accept all the proposals. As a result, the company paid summer bonus to the members of labour union "A" later than to those of labour union "B". This treatment was found to be discriminatory enough to weaken the power of the union. (5) The conditions for lending a union bulletin board were found to restrict considerable union organizational activities on company remises. And the company lent a union board only to labour union "B" and refused to lend one to labour union "A" owing to the failure to arrive at an agreement. These were unfair labour practices.

The Central Labour Relations Commission gave the same decision as Osaka Local Labour Relations Commission. So the company filed an administrative lawsuit with Tokyo District Court for the cancellation of the remedial order. The Court set aside the order on items (2), (4) and (5) on April 25, 1985 but confirmed that these were unfair labour practices in respect of items (2), (4) and (5) the Court held as follows.

(2) The company has a right to own and manage material facilities to maintain a proper and healthy work

environment and to secure the disciplined carrying-out of business employees are not allowed, in general, to use those facilities except in fulfilment of their duties. And labour unions are guaranteed no special right to use enterprise premises. But labour unions and their members are entitled to use the facilities with the employer's consent. It is natural that enterprise unions find it very convenient to use enterprise facilities for union activities. But mere convenience or necessity neither gives a union the legal right to use those facilities, not does it create a duty for the employer to endure union use of them. Accordingly, it is no illegal for the employer not to give his consent, unless special circumstances render the employer's rejection of union use of those facilities an abusive exercise of his right. In this case, the company should not be deemed to have arbitrarily or abusively declined union use of those facilities. The company rather permitted the union to use the dining room from 6 p.m., therefore, it was not an unfair labour practice for the employer to refuse union use of the dining room from 5 p.m.

(4) The conditions proposed by the employer were not found to be irrational. Indeed, the employer and labour union "A" agreed on some of the proposals. The date of payment of summer bonus was only four days later [than for members of union "B"]. Therefore, it was not found that the employer had an intention to postpone payment by refusing collective bargaining and to weaken labour union "A"; the employer's behaviour was not an unfair labour practice prohibited by Art. 7, Sections 1 and 3 of the Labour Unions Act.

(5) It was evident that the employer had no obligation to lend a union board to a labour union. And it was not unfair for the employer to make the loan subject to some conditions. In this case, a majority labour union accepted the conditions and borrowed a union board, but a minority union refused to accept the conditions. Different treatment resulted from the voluntary decision of the two labour unions; they had a free choice as to whether to accept the conditions or

not. An unfair labour practice did not come into existence. But if an employer were to propose conditions with the intention of weakening a minority union, the employer's proposal would be an unfair labour practice, by discriminating against the minority union. The employer's intention would be found from the content of the conditions and the circumstances, which led to the proposals. In this case, the conditions were found to be rational. And it was found from the circumstances at the time that the employer did not present the conditions in order to weaken labour union "A". In conclusion, it was not an unfair labour practice on the part of the company not to lend the union a board on enterprise premises.

Tokyo High Court confirmed the judgement of Tokyo District Court on 24 December 1985. The company made a final appeal to the Supreme Court on items (1) and (3). On the other hand, the Central Labour Relations Commission appealed to the Supreme Court on items (2), (4) and (5).

Decision

Both appeals were dismissed.

JUDGEMENT

This court finds the finding and the judgement of the court below rational and appropriate in the light of all the evidence in this case. There is no error in its conclusions. The appeal of both sides is accordingly dismissed.

[*Source*: Case No. (Gyou-Tsu) 56 and 57 of 1986, decided on 19 January 1989: reported at Rodohanrei No. 533:7]

ANNOTATION

1. Employers are prohibited by Art. 7, Sec. 3 of the Labour Unions Act from controlling or interfering

with the formation or management of a labour union by workers. Control or interference may include a variety of acts. One of the problems, which arise concerns speeches and statements made by an employer. An employer has freedom of speech under the Constitution. The question is how much this freedom should be limited to protect the workers' right to organize and manage labour unions. The Labour Relations Commission applies a rule similar to the one applied in the U.S.A. It holds that a speech by the employer involving threats of unfavourable treatment for employees engaging in union activity, or of reprisals against union members, constitutes control of or interference in the formation or management of labour unions. In the case reported here the factory manager induced union members to withdraw from the union. Form this speech he was presumed to have the intent to control and interfere with union management.

2. Almost all Japanese labour unions are enterprise-wide unions. So they conduct union activity in facilities of the enterprise. This gives rise to the problem whether or not union activity using enterprise facilities encroaches on the property right of the employer. On the other hand, the activity of labour unions is guaranteed by the unfair labour practices system: it is an unfair labour practice for an employer to control or interfere with union activity. Then the problem at issue is how the union's right to conduct its activity and the employer's right to won the company facilities should be harmonized. There was a Supreme Court precedent of this problem (*National Railways Corporation* v. *Ikeoka et al.* decided on 30 October 1979, 33 Minshu 647). In the present case the same judgement was adopted.

An employer has the right to own or manage company facilities, and unions are not entitled to use these facilities without the permission of the employer or an agreement between the union and the employer. Therefore, the use of facilities without permission is not a proper union activity, as it violates the employer's right to use and control the facilities so as to maintain a good and proper work environment and carry on business in an orderly way, unless special circumstances render the employer's refusal to allow the union to use enterprise facilities an abusive exercise of the right of the employer. Such an abusive exercise of the employer's right constitutes an unfair labour practice under Art. 7, Sec. 3 of the Labour Unions Act. In judging whether the employer's right is exercised abusively, the Court gives consideration to many facts, for example, the reason for the refusal, the union's purpose in using the facilities, the time and manner of using the premises, the degree of obstruction to normal operations resulting from the union's use, and the degree of the employer's effort to reach an agreement on using facilities.

On the other hand, the Labour Relations Commission issues remedial orders to employers in order to ensure the effectiveness of the prohibitory provisions of Art. 7 of the Labour Unions Act. The Commission tries expeditiously to restore and maintain the normal order of labour-management relations. So the Commission does not lay emphasis on the rights or obligations, which form the basis of the judgement of the Court. The Commission is given broad discretionary powers to establish good labour-management relations. From this point of view, the Commission considers whether the employer's refusal of the use of facilities constitutes an unfair labour practice. The Commission is composed of workers, employers and public members. They are not always lawyers. And it is the opinion of the Commission that the aim of the unfair labour practice system is to restore and maintain the normal order of labour management relations. Therefore, the framework of the Commission's decision is different from that of the Court. This is a major reason why the Commission reached a different conclusion from the Court in this case. But if the Court were to judge the abusive exercise of an employer's right flexibly, the conclusion would be similar to that of the Commission.

The Court did not do that in judging whether the employer's refusal to lend the dining room was an unfair labour practice.

3. The Court adopted the same standard in judging whether it was an unfair labour practice for the employer to refuse to lend a union bulletin board. But there was another problem on this point: there was different treatment of two unions. This made it necessary to consider the justification of different treatment. When there were two unions in a company, the employer had to maintain a neutral stance in relation to them. Therefore, he should not treat the two unions discriminatorily in lending the union board. If he refused to lend it to labour union "A" while he agreed to lend it to labour union "B", he committed an unfair labour practice, unless he had any reasonable ground for different treatment. The Court admitted some reasonable causes for the discrimination in this case.

4. As to distribution of handbills, the Court agreed with the Commission. When members of a labour union distribute bills on the company premises, the problem at issue is whether they encroach on the employer's right of property. But in general the degree of encroachment is less than in the case of the union board or of a union meeting in company facilities. In the judgement of the District Court, it was held that rules of employment on distribution of bills were valid and reasonable. The purpose of prohibiting distribution of handbills was to check the dissemination of unreasonable statements so as to keep a good and proper work environment. The employer could give a warning that distribution of bills without permission would be punished, unless special circumstances rendered the employer's warning an abusive exercise of the right. In this case the Court held that there had been abusive exercise of the employer's right. It was found that the contents of the bills did not create disturbance at the work place, and did not obstruct the normal operation of work. Bills were distributed early in the morning before the commencement of work. Though

this was done on company premises, it was not found that there was a reasonable ground for a warning. In general an abusive exercise of the employer's right may be found more readily in regard to union bills, because their distribution involves relatively little disturbance of normal operations.

5. In relation to summer bonus there was the same problem as with regard to the union bulletin board. The employer submitted the same conditions for accepting the union's proposal to both unions. One union refused to accept the conditions and the other union accepted them. As a result the working conditions applying to the members of the two unions became different. Did Labour Union Act prohibit this discriminatory treatment? This problem was discussed in the *Japan Mail Order* case (4 International Labour Law Reports 278), which was the first judgement on the subject of the Supreme Court.

In the present case the conditions of the employer were found to be rational. And the employer did not insist on all the conditions. The employer and labour union "A" were able to conclude an agreement on some of the conditions. The different treatment only consisted in the date of payment of the summer bonus; it was paid four days later. From these facts it was found that the employer did not have an intention to discriminate between the unions and to weaken labour union "A".

Supreme Court (Second Petty Bench)

(ii) Saiseikai Social Welfare Corporate

v.

Central Labour Relations Commission

Refusal of check-off and unfair labour practice

HEADNOTES

Facts

Saiseikai Social Welfare Corporate managed Saiseikai Central Hospital in Tokyo. In the hospital there was a Central Hospital branch of the All Saiseikai Labour Union. Though no check-off agreement had been concluded between Saiseikai Central Hospital and the labour union branch, the hospital deducted union fees from the wages of employees who were union members and transferred amounts deducted in a single sum to the labour union branch. This custom continued for 15 years. But in 1975 another labour union was organized and some members seceded from the labour union branch. They asked the hospital to stop the check-off. The hospital accordingly refused to make the deductions from the wages of union branch members. Subsequently the hospital proposed the conclusion of a check-off agreement, but the union branch did not agree with the proposal. The union branch then proposed the resumption of check-off, but the hospital refused because it was unable to confirm whether the list of union members was correct or not.

Tokyo Local Labour Relations Commission held that the hospital interfered in union administration by unilaterally stopping the check-off without reasonable ground. The Commission ordered the hospital to resume check-off from all members of the union branch when the branch proposed this to the hospital and provided a list of union members. Central Labour Relations Commission sustained the order. The hospital then sought judicial review before Tokyo District tuned down the claim and Tokyo High Court also dismissed the hospital's appeal. The hospital made a final appeal to the Supreme Court.

Decision

The appeal was allowed.

JUDGEMENT

Article 24, Section 1 of the Labour Standards Act stipulates that wages must be paid in full to the workers. The purpose is to maintain the workers' livelihood. But the proviso of Section 1 stipulates that partial deductions from wages may be permitted in cases provided for by law or order or in case of a written agreement with a trade union which is composed of a majority of the workers at the workplace or with a person representing a majority of the workers when there is no such a union. Check-off is a partial deduction form employees' wages by the employer. Therefore, check-off is impossible without a written agreement.

After another labour union was organized, more that 100 members seceded from the union branch. So it was doubtful that the union branch was composed of more than half the employees in the hospital. And the check-off had been operated for 15 years without a written agreement. Therefore, the purpose of stopping the check-off was to comply with Article 24, Section 1 of the Labour Standards Act. In addition, the hospital was unable to confirm who the union members to whom the check-off was to be applied were, although it had the intention to operate a check-off if the union membership could be confirmed. Furthermore the hospital proposed a written agreement on check-off to the labour union branch, but the agreement could not be concluded because of the union objections. From the above circumstances it may be found that the hospital did not have the intention to engage in unfair labour practices; the refusal to operate the check-off does not amount to an unfair labour practice.

A dissenting opinion is added to the judgement. According to this opinion, a check-off agreement under the Labour Standards Act is not necessary. Check-off is possible without such an agreement. And refusal of check-off was tantamount to control of union administration because it would weaken the financial basis of the union branch.

[*Source*: Case No. (Gyo Tsu) 57 of 1988, decided on December 11, 1989].

ANNOTATION

1. The check-off system is popular in Japan. This system is available to 91.8 percent of labour unions according to an investigation in 1988 by the Ministry of Labour. As union dues financially support union activities, it is an important task of labour unions to collect union uses. But this task is a charge on labour unions. So the check-off system is used to free labour unions from the burden of collecting dues. In other words, the check-off system is a convenience for labour unions. This gives rise to the problem whether the cheche-off system constitutes financial aid to labour unions, which is prohibited by Art. 2 and Art. 7, Sec. 3 of the Labour Unions Act. In Japan an employer regards as a guarantee of union activity rather than as financial assistance the check-off system. Therefore, it is not an unfair labour practice for an employer to conclude a check-off agreement with labour unions.

2. One issued in the case have reported is whether the proviso of Art. 24, Sec. 1 of the Labour Standards Act must be applied to check-off. The Supreme Court answered it in the affirmative, on the ground that check-off constitutes a partial deduction from wages in the meaning of the proviso of Art. 24, Sec. 1 of the Act. This judgement is different from that of the Labour Relations Commission. The Labour Relations Commission considers that a written agreement in pursuance of the proviso of Art. 24, Sec. 1 is not necessary for an employer to operate a check-off system for the following reasons.

One reason is that only union members are concerned by the check-off. The labour union does not conclude a written check-off agreement as representative of all the workers in the workplace. An agreement, say, on overtime work applies to all the workers in the workplace and the labour union concludes the agreement as representative of all the workers in the workplace. In this respect, the check-off agreement is different from that on overtime work. Hence the proviso of Art. 24, Sec. 1 does not cover the check-off agreement.

Another reason is that a minority labour union organizing less than half the workers in the workplace would not be able to conclude a check-off agreement if such an agreement were covered by the proviso of Art. 24, Sec. 1 of the Act. As a result, a formal guarantee of check-off could not be given to the minority labour union. This would give rise to discriminatory treatment of the majority union and the minority union.

The third reason is that there would be little scope for the employer to deduct union dues arbitrarily from wages, even though a check-off agreement could not be concluded. Union members would not suffer from an arbitrary wage deduction. Hence, there would be little problem, even if the proviso of Art. 24, Sec. 1 did not apply to the check-off system.

But the Supreme Court rejects the reasoning of the Labour Relations Commission. The Supreme Court does not permit customary check-off without an agreement, though the Labour Relations Commission does. The most important problem posed by the judgement of the Supreme Court is that a minority labour union organizing less than half of the workers cannot conclude a check-off agreement. The Supreme Court does not respond to this problem.

3. A further issued are whether unilateral refusal of check-off constitutes an unfair labour practice. In the orders of the Labour Relations Commission, unilateral refusal of check-off without reasonable grounds is considered to be control of or interference in labour union administration, because check-off is a means to guarantee the union's right to carry out union activities. In this case the Commission accepted customary check-off without an agreement under the proviso of Art. 24, Sec. 1 of the Labour Standards Act. And it found that the sudden refusal to pursue check-off, during the spring wage offensive, was intended to weaken the

financial base of the labour union. Hence, the Commission considered the refusal of check-off to be an unfair labour practice.

But the Supreme Court denied that there was an intention to engage in an unfair labour practice and overturned the order of the Commission. The crucial reason is that the refusal to operate check-off was found to correct an earlier violation of the Labour Standards Act. This means, however, that the Supreme Court overturned the standard of judgement on refusal of check-off, which had been established by the Labour Relations Commission for a long time.

Supreme Court (Third Petty Bench)

(iii) Seiwa Electric Industrial Co.
v.
Central Labour Relations Commission

Legality of bargaining in writing—remedy for unfair labour practice—written "oath" that practice would not be repeated

HEADNOTES

Facts

Seiwa labour union was organized on 11 January 1988, and proposed that the company bargain with it, with a view to the conclusion of a collective agreement. The company replied in writing on 18 January, indicating that it would respond to the substance of the union's proposal, also in writing, at later date. Thereafter the union on several occasions asked the company for a direct meeting, but the company did not comply with that request. On 8 February the company, in writing, refused to conclude the agreement proposed by the union, and asked for a reply by letter. Again, the union on several occasions asked for direct talks with the company, unsuccessfully.

Thereupon the union filed an unfair labour practice complaint with Fukushima Local Labour Relations Commission. The Commission decided that the company had refused to bargain collectively without good reason, thus violating section 7(2) of the Trade Unions Act. It ordered the company to bargain with the union as soon as possible and to report the result of the bargaining within 15 days of receipt of the order of the local Commission.

Before Fukushima District Court the company sought the annulment of the orders of the Central Labour Commission. It argued, firstly, that it had performed its duty to bargain in good faith, because it was legal to bargain exclusively by the use of documents. It argued, secondly, that the requirement that it hand a written oath to the union was a violation of article 19 of the Constitution guaranteeing freedom of thought and conscience. The District Court rejected the two arguments on the following grounds:

(1) In principle an employer and a labour union must meet directly for collective bargaining. Bargaining by means of written documents were not permissible unless, exceptionally, it was difficult to meet directly; in this case there was no such exceptional circumstance. Thus the company clearly did not fulfil its duty to bargain collectively, in good faith, with the union.

(2) The Commission ordered the company to hand a notice of oath to the union that it would not repeat such an unfair practice in the future. The term "oath" as used in this order was not related to freedom of thought and conscience; it was intended to be an expression of the company's intention to comply with its duty not to use unfair labour practices. It thus did not infringe the company's right to keep silent, in conformity with article 19 of the Constitution.

Tokyo High Court sustained the judgement of the District Court. It gave the following two reasons for its decision: (1) direct talks are necessary for the establishment of a better mutual understanding. The exchange of documents may be permissible as a supplementary means of bargaining, but it cannot be substituted for direct talks. Therefore, bargaining by means of documents does not constitute collective bargaining in the meaning of the Trade Unions Act. (2) The term "oath" was used in order to emphasize the company's promise that it would not repeat unfair labour practices. It was thus not related to the company's thought and conscience.

The company appealed to the Supreme Court.

Decision

The appeal was dismissed.

Law Applied

Trade Unions Act

Section 7: The employer shall not commit the following acts:

. . .

(2) Refuse to bargain collectively with the representatives of the workers employed by him without good reason.

Constitution

Article 19: Freedom of thought and conscience shall not be infringed.

JUDGEMENT

This Court considers the findings and judgement of the court below rational and appropriate in the light of all the evidence. There is no error in its conclusions. Accordingly, the appeal is dismissed.

[*Source*: Case No. (Gyou-Tsu) 57 of 1991, decided on 6th April 1993. Rodohanrei No. 632:20].

ANNOTATION

1. The Trade Unions Act only prohibits a refusal to bargain collectively. There is no definition of collective bargaining. In particular, there is in Japan no provision comparable to that of article 8(d) of the Labour Management Relations Act of the United States, which states that to bargain collectively consists in the performance of the mutual obligation of the employer and the representative of the employees to meet at reasonable time. This gives rise to the question whether bargaining by exchange of documents may be permissible under section 7(2) of the Trade Unions Act. In the case here reported the Supreme Court dealt with this question for the first time.

2. The Supreme Court did not completely rule out bargaining by exchange of documents. It admitted the possibility of using it as a supplementary means of bargaining when, exceptionally, it was difficult for the parties to meet. For example, the company might propose an exchange of documents instead of a direct meeting when there was apprehension that a direct meeting would have to be conducted in circumstances exceeding the bounds of social propriety, such as kangaroo courts and intimidation. And to make the issues of collective bargaining clear it might be desirable to exchange documents. But in the present case it was found that the company insisted on bargaining exclusively by means of exchange of documents although it could have met directly with the representatives of the union. Hence the Supreme Court held that the company did not comply with the duty to bargain in good faith with the labour union.

3. The second problem was whether the Labour Relation Commission's order requiring the company to hand a written notice of oath to the union was an infringement of the freedom of thought and conscience protected by article 19 of the constitution.

A similar case was that of *Oriental Motor Co.* v. *Chiba Local Labour Relations Commission* (11 ILLR 49).

In that case the employer was ordered to post a notice of apology on its front gate, expressing regret for committing an unfair labour practice and promising that such misconduct would not be repeated. The Supreme Court considered that the order did not go so far as to require the employer to apologies; in fact, rather, it was designed to inform those concerned that the employer had been found to have committed an unfair labour practice and thereby to prevent the latter form repeating such a practice. The order was, therefore, held not be in violation of article 19 of the Constitution.

The same reasoning was adopted in the case here reported. The term "oath" was used in the order of the Commission. However, the use of that term was found not to imply that the employer was put on oath. The Supreme Court found that it merely emphasized the employer's promise that it would not repeat the unfair labour practice.

In principle, the terms "apology" and "oath" are related to freedom of thought and conscience. Under article 19 of the Constitution an employer may not be compelled against his will to express an apology or to make a vow in relation to the union. Accordingly, the Supreme Court interpreted the orders at issue as merely being aimed at informing those concerned of the fact that the employer had been found to have committed an unfair labour practice and thereby to prevent its repetition. However, for the reasons mentioned, the Labour Relations Commission has recently tended to avoid using terms such as "apology" or "oath" in its orders.

Supreme Court (Third Petty Bench)

(iv) Kinki System Management Co.
v.
Osaka Prefecture Labour Relations Commission

Labour relations Commission—lawfulness of order—when to be determined—relevant considerations

HEADNOTES

Facts

1. The appellant company was responsible for the transport of the moneys and papers of the Amagasaki Credit Union and for managing and guarding the buildings of the various branches of the Union. Mr. Yasumura joined the company on 27 July 1983., At that time there was no labour union in the company. On 10 March 1984 the employees organized a union and Mr. Yasumura became its president. The labour union joined the Osaka branch of the National Union of General Workers in November 1988 and Mr. Yasumura became a vice-president of the branch.

The labour union and Osaka branch jointly proposed that the company negotiate on ten items at the spring offensive. The company refused because it did not wish to bargain with the union.

2. In 1979 the company had laid down a rule, which permitted an employee, after mandatory retirement, to be employed part-time for one year if the company and the employee were in agreement. Customarily, the company asked the retired employee whether he wished to be employed again or not, and if the reply was affirmative the employee was re-employed part-time unless there was some reason disqualifying him. Mr. Yasumura retired on 9 January 1989, but he was not re-employed as a part-time employee. The labour union negotiated on the matter with the company on 21 December 1988, but the problem was not resolved. Therefore, Mr. Yasumura, the labour union of the company and the Osaka branch of the National Union of General Workers filed a complaint with Osaka Prefecture Labour Relations Commission on the ground that the refusal to re-employ Mr. Yasumura as a part-time employee was an unfair labour practice in terms of article 7(1) and (3) of the Trade Unions Act.

The Labour Relations Commission (the appellee) issued a remedial order on 27 April 1990. The content of the order was the following:

(a) The company should treat Mr. Yasumura as a part-time employee from 10 January 1989 and pay the amount of wages and bonuses with 5% interest per year from that date to the date at which he started work.

(b) The company should hand a document to the complainants stating that it would not repeat the unfair labour practice, because its failure to treat Mr. Yasumura as a part-time employee from 10 January 1989 was found to amount to such a practice in terms of article 7(1) and (2) of the Trade Unions Act.

3. An appeal was filed by the company under the Administrative Procedures Act, with a view to cancellation of the remedial order. At Osaka District Court, the company argued that Mr. Yasumura was not suitable for re-employment because he had received a reprimand for bill padding transportation fees. Had the company's argument been found to be appropriate, the refusal to re-employ would not have constituted an unfair labour practice? However, the argument was advanced for the first time at court; it had not been asserted during the negotiation with the union. Therefore, the Court did not rely on the argument in deciding whether the order was lawful or not. Rather, it found that the company disliked Mr. Yasumura's trade union activities. As a result, the Commission's order was sustained by the District Court.

Osaka Prefecture Labour Commission requested the Osaka District Court to issue an emergency order under article 27(8) of the Trade Unions Act to require the employer to comply with the order of the Commission. The District Court issued such an order on 26 February 1993.

4. The company appealed to Osaka High Court, insisting that it had no intention of committing an unfair labour practice. It also argued that the remedial order was illegal because it required Mr. Yasumura's re-employment for more than one year, contrary to the

rule on the subject, given that the order was issued more than a year after his retirement.

Osaka High Court upheld the judgement of the District Court for the following reasons: (a) The company did not argue during the procedure at the labour relations Commission that there were work rules on re-employment after mandatory retirement and that the period of re-employment was only one year. The fact that the argument was only put forward in the District Court meant that it had to be regarded as being in bad faith. (b) A remedial order had to be decided not only with a view to providing relief for individual damage to the worker based on infringement of his right, but also by reference to the infringement of union organizing activities in general, so as to eliminate and correct such infringement and restore and maintain the normal order of labour-management relations envisaged by the law. From both points of view it was judged that the Commission did not exceed the limits of the reasonable exercise of its discretionary powers.

The company also argued that the order should be cancelled as circumstances had changed: Mr. Yasumura no longer desired to be re-employed as a part-time employee. Osaka High Court held that the argument was unfounded, because the lawfulness of the order had to be determined as of the time of the disposition, i.e. the time at which it was made. Even assuming that the lawfulness of the order could be determined as of the end of the hearing in judicial review, the Court could not accept the company's assertion. The labour union had asked the company to obey the order, but the company had replied that Mr. Yasumura would be re-employed for four days and paid wages for one year from 10 January 1989. This violated both the remedial order and the emergency order. Mr. Yasumura only declined to work on the basis of the company's contravention of the orders; otherwise he desired to be re-employed part-time after mandatory retirement.

For the preceding reasons, the High Court affirmed the judgement of the District Court. The Company appealed to the Supreme Court.

Decision

The appeal was dismissed.

Law Applied

Trade Unions Act

Article 27, Paragraph (6): In the event . . . the Central Labour Relations Commission has issued an order, the employer may, within 30 days from the service of the order concerned, file an appeal to cancel the order. The Period shall be unchangeable.

Paragraph (8): In the event the employer files an appeal with a court in accordance with the provisions of paragraph (6), the court with which the appeal is filed may, at the request of the Labour Relations Commission concerned, issue an order in the form of a decision to require the employer concerned to comply in full or in part with the order of said Labour Relations Commission pending final judgement by the courts, or it may cancel or modify the decision on application by the parties concerned or *ex officio.*

JUDGEMENT

According to the fact-finding of the High Court, the appellant argued during the procedure at the Commission that the company had a discretionary power to re-employ Mr. Yasumura. During that time it did not insist that the period of re-employment was only one year and that there was a works rule. Furthermore, it did not show the relevant evidence. The first time the argument was made was at the District Court. On the basis of the fats found by the High Court, this Court considers the judgement of the High Court rational and appropriate.

[*Source*: Decision of 21 December 1995, reported at Rodohanrei No. 694:22].

ANNOTATION

1. The Supreme Court affirmed the judgement of the High Court, but did not give its reasoning in detail in the judgement. This means that the Supreme Court shared the opinions of the High Court. Some points are discussed further here.

An employer may file an appeal to cancel an order of the Local Labour Relations Commission under the Administrative Procedures Act. The order is cancelled if it is judged to be illegal. The first point discussed is whether the lawfulness of an order must be determined as of the time it is made or as of the end of the hearing in judicial review. In general, the judgement refers to the time of the administrative disposition, because the purpose of an appeal is to conduct a hearing on the propriety of the administrative disposition. The Supreme Court has taken this view for a long time.

There may, however, be a need to consider a special circumstance, which renders it impossible to comply with the remedial order after its issuance and before the end of the judicial review by which the court determines the lawfulness of the order. When there is such a special situation, the court dismisses the appeal because the employer would gain nothing from the cancellation of the order. Was there a special circumstance in this case? Neither the High Court not the Supreme Court touched on this problem.

2. The appellant argued that the remedial order was illegal because it directed the company to re-employ Mr. Yasumura for more than one year—more than one year having elapsed since the mandatory retirement—although the period of re-employment was set at one year. However, the Supreme Court maintained that the system regarding unfair labour practices had two purposes. The first was to provide relief for individual damage caused by the infringement of the worker's rights and interests by unfair labour practices. The second was to restore and maintain the normal order of

collective labour-management relations envisaged by the law. Therefore, a remedial order had to be made with a view not only to remedying the individual harm but also to restoring and securing normalcy of the industrial relations system by removing and correcting any infringement of trade union activities. This had been so in the Daini Hato Taxi case (*Tokyo Labour Relations Commission and Tokyo Automobile Transport Workers' Union et al.* v. *Auzen Kogyou K.K.*, 4 ILLR 165). In the present case, the company's argument was based only on the first purpose of the unfair labour practices system. The High Court and the Supreme Court denied that argument by reference to the two purposes.

Supreme Court (First Petty Bench)

(v) Japanese Government
v.
Yokohama Branch of National Customhouse Trade Union *et al.*

Unfair labour practices—civil service trade union

Facts

1. The National Customhouse Trade Unions (X Union) was organized in 1947 among employees working at customhouses in Japan. The Yokohama branch (B union) became active to protect against the Peace Treaty between Japan and USA since the National Customhouse Trade Unions are affiliated to Sohyo (National Level Labour Unions Federation) in 1958. Though national public employees are prohibited from the right to strike under the National Civil Servants Act, B union adopted intense tactics involving protest marches in the office and workshop rallies during working hours. Critical voices became strong among B union members because the trade union could not protect union members' interests. As a result, a group opposing B union leaders organized another labour

union (C union) in May 1964. Many union members withdrew from B union and entered into C union. C union became a majority union at Yokohama Customhouse. Therefore, the number of B union members decreased to 196 in 1974 from 1300 in 1963.

Opposing groups organized another labour union not only at Yokohama, but also at Kobe, Nagasaki, Nagoya, Osaka, Hakodate, Tokyo and Moji. These 8 labour unions established a new Customhouse Labour Union (Y union) for common activities in 1965. About 5800 employees entered into Y union among a total of 7500 customhouse employees. So the number of X union members decreased to about 700. Thus X union became a minority union.

2. X union claimed damages against the Japanese Government because the Government interfered with and controlled the management of X union which amounted to an unfair labour practice under Article 1, Paragraph 1 of State Compensation Act, and 110 members of X union also claimed damages on the reason that they were treated discriminatorily with respect to promotions and salary increases because they were members of X union and held to a certain political creed.

3. The plaintiffs emphasized the following circumstances. According to the minutes of high-rank officers at Tokyo Customhouse made in 1967 and 1968, the leaders of Custom Bureau of the Ministry of Finance and Tokyo Customhouse preferred Y union to X union. And the document of Custom Bureau in 1986 at the Ministry of Finance showed that the authorities had intentions to distinguish the members of X union from those of Y union in the treatment of promotion and salary increases. And a memo of the manager of Yokohama Customhouse in 1972 had expressed the intention to induce the union members to withdraw from X union.

But Yokohama District Court did not admit the assertion of the plaintiffs on 24 December, 1992. The District Court found that Yokohama Customhouses wanted only to regulate illegal labour union activities in order to enforce properly the National Civil Servants Act and that the authority had decided to order the promotions and salary increases within its discretionary power. The plaintiffs were treated disadvantageously with respect to promotions and salary increases owing to their illegal activities. So the District Court judged that there could not be discriminatory treatment with respect to promotions and salary increases owing to a certain political creed and that the right to organize of X union was not violated by the Customhouses authority.

The Tokyo High Court reversed that judgement on 24 February, 1999. The High Court found that there was the intent of domination and interference with X union in the memo of the high-ranked officer at Yokohama Customhouse though there could not be found intentions from the documents made by Tokyo Customhouse and Custom Bureau. The High Court found that Yokohama Customhouse advised union members to resign from or non-union employees not to join X union and supported to organize B union and Y union. But the court judged that there could not be discriminatory treatment on promotions and salary increases because the personnel appraisals were worse with respect to the members of X union than those of Y union and non-union employees. They continued to do illegal protests and assemblies without permission. They often took leave on nominal reason of illness and many times they were late comers. So their service records were much worse than non-union members and Y union members at Yokohama Customhouse. Late promotion and worse salary increases could be proper results produced within the discretionary power of the authorities.

Both the plaintiffs and defendant appealed to the Supreme Court.

Decision

The Supreme Court affirmed the High Court's decision.

Law Applied

State Compensation Act

Article 1, Paragraph 1: When a public servant, in the course of his or her employment in an exercise of the public authority of the State or a public body, illegally causes harm to another person either intentionally or through negligence, then the State or public body is responsible for compensating the loss.

Civil Code

Article 709: A person who violates intentionally or negligently the right of another is bound to make compensation for damages arising therefrom.

JUDGEMENT

1. The Tokyo High Court found that there was domination and interference with respect to X union on the part of Yokohama Customhouse authorities because at Yokohama Customhouse the top leaders advised the senior officers and employees to persuade the union members to resign from X union. The senior officers and employees could persuade legally the union members not to play active roles in illegal activities, but in this case their conduct went beyond the limits. So the High Court judgement could be affirmed though it partly involved improper expressions. This Supreme Court found that the intention to dominate X union could not be presumed from the documents made by Toyo Customhouse and Custom Bureau at the Ministry of Finance but that there was in general an intention on the part of Yokohama Customhouse to dominate and

interfere as regards X union as witnessed by the memo written by senior officer at Yokohama Customhouse and also because the authorities of Yokohama Customhouse induced the union members to withdraw from X union. This amounted to illegal action harmful to X union under Article 1, Paragraph 1 of State Compensation Act.

2. The Tokyo High Court refused to award damages to individual union members because their work records were worse than the other non-union members and Y union members at Yokohama Customhouse. This judgement was found to be rational and appropriate in the light of all the evidences presented to the High Court. Therefore, there was no error in the judgement and the appeal was accordingly dismissed.

3. Justice Fukawaza mentioned that the defendant's intention of domination in respect of X union could be presumed from the documents made by Tokyo Customhouse and Custom Bureau. So this fact-finding should be amended, but the decision could be affirmed.

[*Source*: Case No. (0) 853, 854 of 1999, decided on 25 October, 2002: Rodohanrei 814-34].

ANNOTATION

1. In recent years minority unions in large or middle-sized enterprises where a majority union exists have brought cases before the Labour Relations Commission or courts. Multi-unionism has been on the rise, partly due to new unions splintering off from pre-existing ones during crises such as prolonged strikes or militant strategies, and partly because of the merger of companies which leaves the respective enterprise unions intact and unchanged especially if the original companies belonged to different national trade union bodies which are ideologically opposed. In this case, an opposing group formed another labour union against X union which was adopting militant strategies. Two labour unions existed side by side. Therefore, this case

is a typical one with multiple labour unions in one establishment.

2. The trade Unions Act has provisions for remedying violations constituting unfair labour practices through the Labour Relations Commission established as an expert administrative agency. But national public employees cannot have recourse for unfair labour practices before the Labour Relations Commission because they are not subject to the Trade Unions Act. National public employees involving officers at Customhouses have been guaranteed the right to organize under Article 28 of the Constitution. Under Article 108(7) of the National Civil Servants Act, they shall not be treated in a disadvantageous manner by reason of such employee's begin a member of a trade union, having tried to join or organize a trade union, or having performed proper acts of a trade union. A judicial remedy can be granted to such discriminatory treatment suffered by public employees' union members. Furthermore they can make a complaint on disadvantageous treatment to the National Personnel Authority under Article 89 of the national Civil Servants Act. They can also take a measure on working conditions to the National Personnel Authority or chief of the office attached under Article 86 of the same Act. The National Personnel Authority has a quasi-judicial function and its decisions are binding for the ministries and agencies.

In Japan judicial remedies are available also in private companies subject to the Trade Unions Act in case of unfair labour practices. This is a characteristic in the Japanese unfair labour practices system.

3. In this case national public employees and their trade union sought to get damages as a judicial remedy at the court. The Tokyo High Court and the Supreme Court found that the customhouse authority controlled and interfered in union affairs which amounted to unfair labour practices, but that the authority did not treat X union members disadvantageously with respect to promotions and salary increases.

Similar cases occurred at Kobe, Osaka and Toyo Customhouse. On 25 October 2002 the Supreme Court rejected unfair labour practice charges at Kobe and Osaka Customhouse, but the Court admitted control and interference regarding X union at Toyo Customhouse on 13 December 2002. Different judgement came from finding of facts on the documents issued by Tokyo Customhouse and Custom Bureau. And in this case the Supreme Court did not find the control of, or interference with, union affairs from the documents, but rather from the memo made by senior officers at Yokohama Customhouse.

In a minority opinion, Justice Fukuzawa found the dominance on X union from the documents made by Tokyo Customhouse and Custom Bureau because that time it was a big problem at all customhouses how to tackle with X union adopting militant strategies. This minority opinion showed that it was a crucial point how to estimate the documents.

4. In this case discriminatory treatment on promotion and salary increase was collectively found as between X union members and other employees at Yokohama Customhouse. But promotion and salary increase were individually decided on personnel evaluation. So the Court examined individual work records of the plaintiffs. As a result, their personnel appraisals were found to be worse than Y union members and non-union employees. This conclusion was affirmed unanimously by the District Court, High Court and Supreme Court. This showed that the court admitted the wide discretionary power on personnel evaluation of the Customhouse authorities.

5. In Japan a judicial remedy separate from administrative remedy by the Labour Relations Commission is available for unfair labour practices. There are several patterns on judicial remedies for unfair labour practices. One is that disadvantageous treatment such as dismissal as an unfair labour practices is null and void under civil law. As a second type, claims to prevent or remove the control on union

affairs can be possible. As the third pattern, damages can be awarded to trade unions which suffered from unfair labour practices as torts. This case belongs to the third pattern.

6. It is natural that unfair labour practices automatically do not constitute torts because elements of both torts and unfair labour practices are separate. This case dealing with public service employees was brought under the State Compensation Act based on torts under Article 709 of the Civil Code. There are four important factors constituting torts: violation of rights or illegality of damaging act, intentional or negligent act, occurrence of damages and causation. In this case the Supreme Court judged that there was a violation of the right to organize. To give a remedy, two million yen was awarded to X union as consolation. And 0.5 million yen was ordered as advocate's fee. These amounts are average ones decided within the discretionary power of the judge.

Index